HEAD START

HEAD START

How to Develop Your Child's Mind

Robert Fisher

Illustrated by Tom Fisher

SOUVENIR PRESS

Copyright © 1999 by Robert Fisher

The right of Robert Fisher to be identified as author
of this work has been asserted by him in accordance with
the Copyright, Designs and Patents Act 1988.

First published 1999 by
Souvenir Press Ltd,
43 Great Russell Street, London WC1B 3PA

All Rights Reserved. No part of this publication
may be reproduced, stored in a retrieval system,
or transmitted, in any form or by any means, electronic,
mechanical, photocopying, recording or otherwise,
without the prior permission of the Copyright owner.

ISBN 0 285 63493 3

Typeset by Rowland Phototypesetting Ltd,
Bury St Edmunds, Suffolk

Printed in Great Britain by
Creative Print and Design Group (Wales), Ebbw Vale

Contents

Acknowledgements   7
Author's Note   8
Introduction   9

1 **Brain Power:** developing your child's many
   intelligences   13
2 **A Way With Words:** developing linguistic
   intelligence   44
3 **Number Sense:** developing mathematical
   intelligence   86
4 **Finding Out:** developing scientific intelligence   125
5 **Seeing More:** developing visual and spatial
   intelligence   153
6 **Music in Mind:** developing musical intelligence   181
7 **Body Power:** developing physical intelligence   201
8 **Self-control:** developing personal intelligence   221
9 **Knowing Others:** developing social intelligence   244
10 **Your Philosophical Child:** developing
   philosophical intelligence   268

Appendices
A Helping a child learn to read   292
B Maths vocabulary   295
Further Reading   298
Index   300

Acknowledgements

I would like to express my thanks to the many people who have helped me to research and write this book. Firstly to my family, my wife Celia, and my two children Tom and Jake. Their insights and comments have been a constant source of creative inspiration as well as a challenge to my own thinking.

I am grateful to the many friends who have allowed me to share their stories of family life and the sayings of their children. Special thanks are due to colleagues and fellow researchrs who have commented on chapters in this book, in particular Juliet Edmonds, Sara Liptai, and Lizann O'Conor. Thanks are also due to the many teachers and children in schools who have helped me in my research into practical ways of teaching children to think.

My thanks go to the many researchers and experts in the field of cognitive psychology who have contributed to our growing understanding of how the mind works, in particular to Professor Howard Gardner of Harvard University for his pioneering work on the theory of multiple intelligences, and to Professor Matthew Lipman of Montclair University for developing the theory and practice of philosophical enquiry with children.

The four lines of verse on page 74, taken from 'The Elephant's Child' from *Just So Stories* by Rudyard Kipling, are reproduced by kind permission of A.P. Watt Ltd. on behalf of The National Trust for Places of Historic Interest or Natural Beauty.

Author's Note

The whole of this book applies equally to boys and girls. In order to avoid constant references to 'he or she', 'him or her' and so on, I have chosen to alternate between the two, so that sometimes the child under discussion is 'he' and at others 'she'. It should be clearly understood, however, that in either case the child could just as well be of the opposite sex.

Introduction

I think but I don't always know what I think. Dan, aged 7

I know I could do more for my child, but I don't know what. Parent, aged 43

Your child is amazing. Your child is a unique bundle of possibilities, with a mind and brain different from every other person who has ever lived. There is nothing in nature as complex or wonderful as your child's brain. It is his most valuable asset. This book aims to help you boost your child's brain power, build his confidence and improve his ways of thinking. It offers activities to expand your child's mind and add value to the quality of time you spend together. It is about teaching your child to think and to make the most of his mind. It aims to help you to raise a bright and happy child.

This is a book about all children, whatever their age and ability. It is about fulfilling the potential of your child, and improving the quality of his life. It is about who your child is, how he learns and achieves happiness through making the most of his mind. This book is not about preparing your child for a particular future: it is about developing all aspects of his mind, so that he is prepared for a future that cannot be known.

This book is about helping your child at home; it is not about current trends in education at school. As I write the curriculum offered in schools is becoming narrower, focusing more and more on the 3Rs of reading, writing and arithmetic. The narrower education becomes in school the more important it is that children have richness and diversity of experience at home. Looking at your child's school work will show you how much education has changed since you were at school. Ways of teaching change, but what is important for humans remains constant. Your child is multi-talented, not with a simple set of narrow skills and a fixed intelligence, but with many forms of intelligence, each with a potential for development that is unknown. Your child is a traveller in an unknown land and you are his guide.

The time you spend with your child is important not just for developing her thinking, but for catering for all her needs. The first of these is for love: the emotional bonds that develop between you and your child are more important than any teaching or coaching you do. A bright child is one who first and foremost feels loved. A bright child is one who is physically cared for, and brought up in a safe environment. A bright child is also a social child. In the early years a child depends on parents who will create a social network of friends and family. A bright child benefits from contact with and care from others, and the most significant 'others' in the early years are those with whom the child lives. This book is about caring for one important aspect of your child's development – her thinking mind.

This book is concerned with the first decade of life, covering the years of childhood roughly from birth to puberty. Its central belief is that any child can be a bright child. The reason for this is simple – no one knows the limits of a child's potential in any aspect of her intelligence. All children are at potential, as well as at risk. The risk is that a child will not realise, or be helped to realise, her full potential. Unless your child is brain-damaged the potential for developing the fluid elements of intelligence is always there. You have a bright child if you think your child is bright and if you work to help her reach her potential. Do not accept that your child cannot succeed, for *your* belief that your child can with effort succeed will help create the most important of *her* growing beliefs – her self-belief.

Every child is a bright child but no two children are bright in the same way. Similarly, no two parents will bring up a child in the same way. No child is perfect and no parent is perfect. All we can do as parents is work on ways of being more effective and do our best in caring for our children. One way to become more effective may be to benefit from what has worked for others, and the ideas presented here have worked for others in bringing up bright children.

The book is informed by the research of many people. Many of the ideas derive from my own years of research into teaching children to think, and from my experience as a teacher and a parent. The book has also drawn on the experience of a wide range of parents and teachers. I have quoted some of these, and I have also used the views of children to inform and illustrate key ideas. As Tom, a nine-year-old, said during one of our discussions, 'It's good to ask children about what we think. We don't know all the answers, but we do know some of the questions, and what works for us.'

The book is divided into the following chapters:

Chapter 1: Brain Power looks at how your child's brain works. It shows that your child has not just one but many different kinds of intelligence. This chapter shows how you can help your child develop brain power through putting these aspects of his mind to better use.

Chapter 2: A Way with Words explains the importance of language in developing your child's thinking and learning. It shows how to make the most of speaking to and listening to your child, how to enrich the experience of reading and of stories, and how to develop the skills of writing.

Chapter 3: Number Sense shows how to develop your child's mathematical thinking. It explains what mathematics your child needs and how to foster her growing confidence and ability in maths, through developing her understanding of numbers, shapes and measurement.

Chapter 4: Finding Out explores how to help your child find out more about the world through developing his scientific intelligence. It explains ways to build on your child's natural curiosity about the world, and how to harness his urge to explore and to value the environment.

Chapter 5: Seeing More explores ways to develop your child's visual intelligence to help improve her thinking and learning. It shows how to boost your child's visual powers, to help her see more in the world around her.

Chapter 6: Music in Mind shows how music can help develop your child's mind. Musical thinking is a special kind of intelligence that can be enhanced in all children. This chapter shows how you can help them get 'in tune'.

Chapter 7: Body Power looks at the links between the brain and body. This chapter explains what physical intelligence is, how it can be developed and used to accelerate your child's learning and give him confidence in his physical abilities.

Chapter 8: Self-control is about one of the keys to success and happiness in life. This chapter looks at how to help your child develop self-awareness and control over her emotions, so that she can be helped to make the most of who she is.

Chapter 9: Knowing Others is about social intelligence and how it can be developed, so that your child can gain social confidence, relate well to others and benefit from what others have to offer.

Chapter 10: Your Philosophical Child describes how to help your child discuss and solve problems. It shows how to make discussions with your child an adventure in ideas and how you can develop the philosophical intelligence of your child.

Let's begin by considering your child's most important organ – his amazing brain.

1 Brain Power

developing your child's many intelligences

If a child has been his mother's undisputed darling he retains throughout his life the triumphant feelings, the confidence in success, which not seldom brings actual success with it. Freud, from 'A Child-hood Recollection'

Everyone is clever at something. I wonder what I'll be clever at. Greg, aged 6

I was reading my children a famous story about a teddy called Edward Bear who belonged to Christopher Robin. The little boy used to trail him downstairs so that the back of his head bumped from step to step. It was the only way the bear knew of coming downstairs, although sometimes he felt that there must be another, if only the bumping would stop so he could think of it. But he wasn't really sure ... After the reading I asked them if they could help Edward Bear (alias Winnie-the-Pooh) think of other ways to go downstairs. After a slow start ideas began to flow:

'He could ask someone to carry him.' 'Why would they want to do that?' 'Well he could say to them, "If you carry me downstairs I'll tell you a funny joke".'

'He could slide down the banister, holding his arms out like this to keep his balance.'

'He could make a parachute out of a bedsheet and float down.'

'He could sit on a tray like a sledge, and if it was the right angle slide down.'

'They could fix a chair like a lift to the side of the stairs. He could sit in it and someone could pull him up and down.'

'They could build a trapdoor and he could slide down a rope.' 'If he did that mightn't he land on someone's head?' 'Not if the rope was tied to a bell, and every time he used it a bell rang.'

After we had finished thinking of ideas I asked how many different ways there were of coming down stairs and got the answer: 'As many ways as you can think of.' 'How many ways is that?' I asked. 'No one knows, because someone might always think of another idea.'

Every child is born with an amazing brain. There is nothing in nature that we know of as complex or as powerful; it is at the peak of nature's organising power. An average child is born with a hundred billion brain cells, called neurons. These neurons sprout thousands of connections, each of which stores information and links it to what we already know. It was these connections that enabled my young child, when he saw a hairy four-legged animal, to say it was a dog. Unfortunately at the time he was looking at a horse. The brain is wired to make connections, even if sometimes they are the wrong ones.

A brain learns by making new connections or pathways between items of knowledge, and this ability means the brain can keep you learning from birth until death. But the earliest years are the most vital for learning, for it is then that the main pathways are laid out in the different areas of the brain. Take language, for example. The accent you learn in the first five years will probably stay with you the rest of your life. It is very difficult to change later because it has been implanted in the main pathways of the brain that deal with language. So while you add new words as you grow older, the way you speak will be largely determined by the connections you make in your early years.

The power of the brain lies in the number and complexity of connections it can make, not only in language but in other kinds of intelligence that are part of the brain. The main highways and all the interconnecting pathways allow infor-

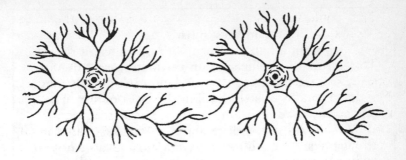

Brain power is built by making connections

mation stored in one part of the brain to be connected with information locked away in other areas. This ability of the brain to make connections is the source of human learning, of all our creativity and culture. It is also the reason why we laugh or joke or can solve a riddle. Here is a joke recently told to me by a child:

Child: Knock, knock.
Me: Who's there?
Child: Joe.
Me: Joe who?
Child: No Joe King!

You solve a riddle or see a joke by making a connection, or as the child then said: 'Get it?'

This book is about helping your child to build her brain power by using her different intelligences to make connections in the mind. Let's look at these in more detail.

WHAT ARE YOUR CHILD'S INTELLIGENCES?

Your child will use many different kinds of thinking to help her achieve success in life. There are at least nine kinds of intelligence that power her thinking mind (see diagram on p. 17). Each has a physical location in the brain, and provides a distinctive way of thinking. Each one enables us to solve different kinds of problem and achieve different kinds of success in the world.

Did you know . . . ?

The brain a baby is born with contains all the elements of intelligence. In the first year of life a baby's brain triples in size to ¾ of adult size. It takes the next 17 years to develop the last quarter. The fully grown adult brain weighs about three pounds, and is the most complex object so far discovered in the universe. We still only have a hazy idea of how it works, but we do know ways that help it work better, and that is what this book is about.

These different intelligences enable your child to engage in different kinds of learning. All humans, unless brain-damaged, have these different forms of intelligence. Some will be more developed than others, but your child has them all ready-wired into her brain.

Usually we think of ourselves as having one mind, but our minds are more like an orchestra in which different parts contribute. We are sometimes aware of the need to bring these different parts of the mind to bear on a problem. Gemma, aged nine, seemed to be aware of this when she said, trying to get to sleep, 'Sometimes I talk to myself, sometimes I sing to myself, and sometimes I count. Sometimes different parts of my mind just talk to each other.'

Your child's mind does not just have one voice and one set of thoughts, but different voices and different sorts of thinking. To make the most of her mind we need to be aware of these and of the abilities which derive from each kind of intelligence. Every child, male or female, from whatever background, has each of the following forms of intelligence:

- Linguistic intelligence: using language to learn, and being able to speak, read and write.
- Mathematical intelligence: understanding numbers and being logical in thinking.

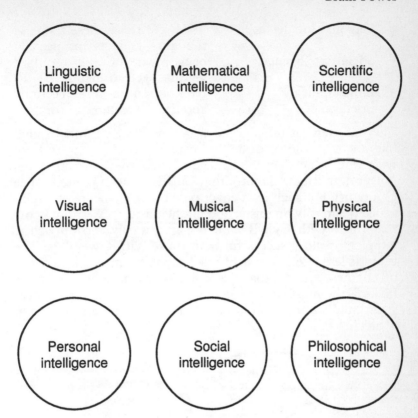

Nine intelligences that power your child's brain

- Scientific intelligence: learning about the world, and being curious to find out more.
- Visual intelligence: learning through seeing, and being aware of shapes and space.
- Musical intelligence: learning through listening, and being aware of sounds.
- Physical intelligence: learning through the body, and developing physical skills.

- Personal intelligence: being aware of oneself, one's thoughts, feelings and needs.
- Social intelligence: being aware of others, and relating well to them.
- Philosophical intelligence: thinking and asking questions about the meaning of life.

The old view of intelligence was that it was a fixed thing, like a sort of motor of a fixed capacity that you were born with and which never changed. When they measured the power of this mental motor they called it your IQ (Intelligence Quotient), but such tests cover only some elements of intelligence (primarily linguistic and mathematical). We now know that those with high IQs do not necessarily end up richer, happier or more successful than those with lower IQs. The brain is less like a motor of fixed capacity, more like a series of engines whose capacities are unknown. What counts is making the most of the engines (or intelligences) that power your child's mind, and home life plays an important role in achieving this.

DEVELOPING YOUR CHILD'S MANY INTELLIGENCES

None of us has a brain that is working at full capacity; we all have mental capacities that are underdeveloped. We do not know what we might have achieved with the right help, enough time and sufficient stimulus. We all need the stimulus of mental exercise to keep our minds in trim. Like a muscle, the human mind expands and develops with use and, like the body, is kept fit through regular activity. The aim of this book is to show how to exercise the different aspects of your child's intelligence, to help him expand the power of his mind. It is something that children also wish for themselves. Sophie, aged eight, said, 'I wish I had a bigger brain.' Sophie cannot change her brain but what she can do is make better use of it, if she is shown how. Like the story of the tortoise and the hare, it is not how quick or clever you are at the beginning that counts: in the long run what is important is the effort you make to overcome the problems you face. And every child will have problems to face.

If your child	What you can do	What your child can learn
Thinks he is stupid, cannot think or learn things	Show him how he can achieve success in learning something new	Sees that he can learn new things with help if he tries hard
Thinks she is good at learning some things and not others	Encourage her to practise what she is good at and help her in what she finds difficult	Learns that you can improve on what you are good at, and in what you find difficult
Thinks he is clever, and good at all kinds of thinking and learning	Give him new challenges, and praise or reward his effort	What is important in life is the effort you make, not how clever you are

Under the old view of intelligence, children were thought to be born either bright or dull and there was not much you could do about it. The view now is that every child is potentially bright in some aspects of his or her intelligence and less bright in others. We do not know which aspects will become

19

most highly developed. There are of course limits to your child's intelligence, but we do not know what these are. We should therefore educate our children in a spirit of optimism. This makes sense, for we know that people will tend to do better when they are confident and make the effort to succeed. If we are pessimistic about what our children can know and do, we limit them by our expectations. If we do not expect much of our children they will probably not expect much of themselves.

Children become very aware of what their parents think of them, and this affects what they think of themselves. A child who is regarded as bright and successful will tend to live up to this image. A child who is thought of as stupid will come to think of himself as a failure, especially when faced with problems. Sometimes children get confused by mixed messages and don't know what to think of themselves.

All children can be put at risk by people who try to diminish them, or who laugh at their efforts or scorn their lack of knowledge, or who revel in the fact that they are less good at doing something than they might be. Growing up means having to cope with people who put you down. It is doubly difficult for children if the people who are putting them down

Encouraging adult and inhibiting adult (see note, p. 43)

are the ones they live with every day of their young lives. Parents can inhibit and diminish a child's developing mind or can encourage their child to achieve his potential (see diagram above).

HOW DO INTELLIGENCES DEVELOP?

Good parents, like good schools, make their children more intelligent. But what is intelligence and how is it developed?

There are three aspects to each of your child's intelligences. First, there is the brain that he or she was born with. Her brain is similar to yours but differently wired. The physical hardware of her brain is fixed and cannot be changed (unless she has brain damage or surgery). What she is born with is what experts call our 'neural intelligence'. But the ways in which her brain is used and developed, what we might call

21

the software, provide the fluid elements of intelligence. Her brain is developed through use at home, at school and through the experiences of life.

The second aspect of intelligence is the way your child's brain is developed through everyday experience and culture, by others.

The third aspect is what she develops through her own thinking and doing. This is the part of her intelligence that she can expand for herself, when she does her own learning, for example when she sets her own goals and achieves her own targets.

Three dimensions of an intelligence

- Born-with intelligence—the brain we are born with, which stays with us for life.
- Developed intelligence—the brain developed by others: family, schools, friends, work, etc.
- Self-developed intelligence—the brain we develop through our own thinking and learning.

Children tend to develop one of two beliefs about intelligence: either that it is of a fixed nature and does not change, or that it can be improved through effort. Children who believe that intelligence can improve tend to be more successful learners than those who think that their intelligence is fixed. There are dangers in children thinking that they were born with a fixed intelligence, whether fixed to be stupid or average or very intelligent.

The trouble with telling children all the time that they are very clever is that it leaves them vulnerable to self-defeating worry if they fail. If children are persuaded they are not intelligent it can quickly become a self-fulfilling prophecy— every failure confirms it, so they stop trying. What children need to learn is that any aspect of their intelligence can be improved, either through their own efforts or with the help of others. Ben, aged nine, showed some understanding of this when he said, 'It doesn't help if people just keep telling you to try harder, what you have to do is tell yourself.' But if you need to do more than tell your child to try harder, how do you help your child to help herself?

The process of developing each form of intelligence involves input (you providing a stimulus that is challenging), and output (your child making an effort to succeed), which hopefully leads to self-control (your child learning how to succeed in what she does).

INPUT:	what you do	You stimulate your child's many intelligences and encourage her to believe that intelligence is not fixed but is improved through effort.
OUTPUT:	what your child does	Your child gains confidence in using many forms of intelligence and comes to see that her thinking can improve through effort.
SELF-CONTROL:	what your child learns	Your child is able to use her different forms of intelligence to improve her thinking and learning in school and throughout life.

Did you know . . . ?
The brain is a hungry organ, the hungriest in the human body. Although it makes up only 2 per cent of total body weight it consumes 20 per cent of the body's total oxygen intake. This oxygen is essential for brain functioning. After five to ten seconds without oxygen we lose consciousness, after 20 seconds we lose muscle control, after four minutes neurons in the brain become seriously damaged, and after ten minutes we are dead.

WHAT YOU CAN DO TO HELP

A teacher once brought a pack of marshmallows into her class of four- and five-year-old children and told them that she was going to give each of them marshmallows. Would they prefer one marshmallow or two? The children said they wanted two. She put one marshmallow in front of each child and said they could eat it, but if they left it there for five minutes they could have that one and another. The teacher went away to see what would happen. Unknown to the children this was an experiment to see what they would do— would they eat the marshmallow they had or wait five minutes for another?

Some of the children could not wait and ate the marshmallow at once. Others hesitated, looked at the marshmallow, looked away, squirmed in their seats, played with their fingers, looked to see what others were doing—then ate it. Some of them also did these things but waited the full five minutes without eating their marshmallow, and when the teacher returned were rewarded with another. Because this was an experiment the children's progress was tracked to see which group if any would be more successful at school and in life. The researchers found that one of the groups turned out to be more successful than the others in getting good grades at school and later had more successful careers. Which group was it?

The most successful turned out to be the group that waited. What might be the reasons for this? One reason seems to be that children who are impulsive, who have not learnt to be mindful, to stop and think, tend not to do so well in life as children who stop and think before they act, and make the effort to put off immediate gratification for the future reward of more marshmallows later. Or, in the words of one street-wise fourteen-year-old, 'You got to be cool, work out the options, do a bit of headwork first and it'll pay off later.'

So what will help your child become more mindful and less impulsive?

The following is an experiment to see how mindful someone is in listening. Ask the following questions in quick succession (and give the answer if the other person cannot):

Question: What do we call a tree that grows from acorns?
Answer: Oak.
Question: What do we call a funny story?
Answer: Joke.
Question: What do we call the sound made by a frog?
Answer: Croak.
Question: What do we call the white of an egg?
Answer: Yolk!

The white of an egg is called albumen. Why did you say yolk?

Children love these kinds of word trap, but they have a serious side for they show how easy it is for us to fall into the pitfalls of repetition in our lives. The rhythm of the familiar lulls us into mindlessness. One reason we like jokes so much is that the punchline makes an unexpected connection.

This ability to 'see' connections in jokes is just one of the aspects of an intelligence we all have—linguistic intelligence.

Linguistic intelligence: developing a way with words

What is your child's favourite joke? Here is the favourite joke of one five-year-old:

Question: What did one grape say to the other grape?
Answer: Nothing, you silly. Grapes can't talk.

We all have this capacity to play with words. Humour and wordplay are unique human characteristics. Where do we get this way with words from? How do we help a child develop his ability to use words? Nature gives us a head start, for we come into the world ready prepared for words, due to perhaps the most important kind of intelligence of all—linguistic intelligence.

All people need a well-developed linguistic intelligence to communicate successfully what they want and need. Some kinds of career require a highly developed linguistic intelligence to do well, such as an actor, author, lawyer, religious leader, sales person, teacher, TV/radio presenter or poet. A child who has well-developed linguistic intelligence will learn through speaking, listening, reading and writing, will enjoy the use of words, for example in writing or drama, and be good at communicating with others.

Chapter 2 explores ways to help develop the important aspects of your child's linguistic intelligence: speaking and listening, reading and writing, and thinking. Your child of course needs more than words, he needs also to learn about those other strange products of the human mind that cause both misery and joy—numbers.

Mathematical intelligence: developing a sense of number and logic

Number sense is an inborn capacity, and with enough practice any child can succeed at arithmetic. Although we are born with a sense of number, however, it is our experience of life that determines whether we make the most of our mathematical intelligence.

The amazing ability that some *idiots savants*, that is children often with very low IQs and few social skills, have with number, shows another interesting feature of mathematical intelligence. Many of these children have a gift for calendrology, that is the ability to compute what day of the week any given day was. Such skill is not innate but learnt through a pathological ability to concentrate on calendars at the expense of almost everything else, including other human beings. You would probably not wish such limited single-mindedness for your child, but it shows that success in arithmetic does not depend on any general intelligence, but on a particular innate sense of simple logic and number, just as other modules in the brain enable us to carry out tasks with language. Sarah, aged six, expresses a common experience when she says: 'I can do the sum, but I can't tell you how.'

Mathematics of course involves more than an ability with number. Your child needs language to help him make sense of mathematical problems, and to make connections with facts stored in the memory. Learning multiplication tables involves both memory and language, which is why some brain-damaged people whose memory of language is impaired find it hard to do multiplication sums although they are good at other kinds of arithmetic.

Knowledge of geometry, of shape and space, also requires the use of other kinds of intelligence, especially visual-spatial intelligence. So although we are born with a special kind of number sense which is the basis of logical-mathematical intelligence, your child needs to develop other elements of intelligence for all-round mathematical success.

Brain research shows that some areas of the brain play a more prominent part in mathematical calculation than others. But why some people are brilliant at maths is not yet properly understood. We do know, however, the kinds of activities that will strengthen your child's mathematical intelligence. As Janie, aged eight, says in a school report on maths which she wrote for herself, 'I'm not much good at maths. I know I could do better. But I need help.'

Did you know . . . ?
Girls are out-performing boys at tests of maths in England and Wales at the age of 14, but among the most gifted at maths there are many more boys than girls.

Chapter 3 looks at ways to help your child with maths at home and school. It shows how the logical nature of maths can help with other kinds of thinking, in particular scientific thinking. As Jeremy, aged 11, explains, 'Maths is a kind of foreign language you have to learn. It gives you a special way of describing and finding out more about the world.' This urge to find out about the world is another fascinating facet of the human mind."

* For more on the innate human sense of number see *The Number Sense: How the Mind Creates Mathematics* by Stanislas Dehaene, published by Routledge, 1998.

Scientific intelligence: finding out about the world

When the great scientist Sir Isaac Newton looked back on his life spent trying to find out more about the world, he said he seemed to have been like 'a boy playing on the seashore, and diverting myself now and then finding a smoother pebble or prettier shell than ordinary, whilst the great ocean of truth lay all undiscovered before me.'

Children are natural scientists. Like scientists they have a need to make sense of the world around them, to see if they can find out more about the things they can hear, see, touch and smell. From their youngest days they engage in simple kinds of scientific thinking as they investigate the objects they see around them, and experiment to discover what those objects can do. Once when a baby sent a plate crashing on to the floor from her high chair at a party her mother said, 'Oh, don't mind Jane, she's just experimenting with gravity!' Small babies know a lot about the properties of objects, but they are always surprised by gravity.

Young children develop many beliefs about the world as they try to make sense of their experience. James, aged five, has some odd beliefs about matter. He knows that a bag of rice weighs something, but says that a grain of rice weighs nothing. He says that when you keep cutting an apple in half, eventually you will get to a piece so small it will be nothing, take up no space and have no apple in it. 'How can you have a piece which is nothing?' I ask. 'It's so small it's not there,' he replies. James' idea is not silly because some objects are too small to detect with the human eye. But his idea is wrong since something cut in half is still a smaller something, until you can cut no further. Science is not only about what we can see, it is also about how we make *sense* of what we see.

Science is not just what we find in books or learn in school: it is a way of understanding the world. This way of knowing is a particular kind of human intelligence—scientific intelligence. Because we all have this intelligence it does not mean we automatically do well in science at school or want to read scientific books. It is an intelligence that helps us to find out about the world around us, about the plants in the garden and the shells on the beach, and the curiosity to find out more. Zoe, aged six, echoed the thoughts of many when she said, 'I'd quite like to see a volcano, but I don't want to read about it.'

Over thousands of years we have developed tools of scientific investigation that can be applied to problems in any area of study—for example, what happened in the past (history), in other places (geography) or in the physical world (physics, chemistry and biology). Not all societies have needed these tools. In the simple life-style of hunter gatherers only the simplest of scientific reasoning was needed to hunt animals or grow crops. Success in complex modern societies relies, however, on some understanding of science.

Did you know . . . ?

Societies, like people, vary in the value they put on scientific knowledge. Some traditional societies, such as the Hindu kingdoms of India, produced virtually no written history; instead of history they had myth, legend and religious texts, whereas others like the ancient Chinese kept extensive records of the past. Families vary too in the records they keep of the past.

In Chapter 4 we look more closely at what scientific intelligence is and how it can be developed. It is of course closely linked to other forms of intelligence—language to describe the world, maths to measure the world and visual intelligence to observe the world.

Visual intelligence: learning to see

'I'll know what it is when I see it,' said Amy, aged four, when something was pointed out which she could not at first see. Every second of the waking day your child is doing remarkable things. She senses the world, she recognises faces instantly, she can distinguish millions of shades of colour and thousands of smells. She feels the slightest touch of a feather and hears distant birdsong. She does these things, it seems, without effort. A normal child needs no help to see, smell, touch, taste or feel. So is your child just a passive receiver of colours and sounds, like a camera or a tape-recorder, or something more?

Your child's brain is more than a camera or tape-recorder. A camera or tape machine records, but makes no sense of what it records. It has no visual intelligence.

Your child's senses have different control centres in the brain which, like tiny scientists, help her to make sense of what she sees, hears, smells, touches and tastes. She may call upon memories of past experience to help her understand new experience. When she is not sure, these sensory centres in the brain make educated guesses—for example, 'It looks like a kind of . . .' or 'It sounds like a sort of . . .'

When my baby son first saw a picture of a lion he said, 'Dog'. It was a dog-like creature. He was reasoning by analogy. Later when he saw a statue in Trafalgar Square he recognised it as a lion. The eye needs the mind, needs visual intelligence, to tell us what we see.

We are all born with visual intelligence, but it needs to be developed. The trouble with the mind is that it wants an easy life, and slips into unthinking habits. We don't look carefully if the mind says there is no need to, if we can see (and can label something) at a glance, why bother to study it further? Children easily slip into the habit of not paying attention, of being content with the quick look, of being visually lazy. But we can develop a more intelligent eye at any age. When Grandma Moses began her successful painting career at the age of ninety she was using a visual intelligence that had always been there, from childhood, but just not developed or fully stretched by her experience.

The senses of a normal child are wonderfully acute. He can see the smallest specks of colour, and if he really listens he can hear a pin drop. But paradoxically what he does not see and hear is as important as what he takes in. Every species senses and interprets the world in a different way. We can only imagine the range of smells and sounds a dog can experience, or what some animals can see through high-performance eyes. The visual receptors in the eyes of an eagle are more highly developed than in a human eye. The eagle can spot a rabbit five kilometres (three miles) away; a human can only see a rabbit up to one kilometre (about 1,000 yards) away. Only a fraction of the information that is available arrives in the brain to be interpreted and processed. We know that the child's brain breaks down the information it receives into manageable bits to make sense of it, but how does he put the bits back together? How does he make sense of this flood of information, and how can we help him to do it better?

Did you know ... ?
The retina of the eye is only as thick as this page, yet it enables us to distinguish up to eight million shades of colour. But we only recognise variations of colour if we look with conscious attention. Try this experiment: choose a colour and look around you. How many different shades of that colour can you (or your child) see?

We see through our eyes but it is the brain that makes sense of what we see. Without connections to a thinking brain our eyes become useless. Brain research can tell us much about how our brain makes sense of what we see. We now know that the visual area of the brain, which is at the back of the head, takes up 30 per cent of the cortex, touch takes up 8 per cent and hearing 3 per cent. Your child learns through all these senses. In Chapter 5 we explore visual thinking, and then consider that other form of sensory intelligence, hearing, and why learning to listen is as important as learning to see.

Musical intelligence: learning to listen

> Music alone with sudden charms can bind
> The wand'ring sense, and calm the troubled mind.
> William Congreve, *Hymn to Harmony*

A young child was making an awful banging sound with a spoon on tins in the kitchen. 'What's that noise?' I shouted.

'It's only Tom,' replied my wife, 'he's composing his first piece of music!'

Music is part of every human culture—from the drums of Africa to the chants of medieval monks, from the symphonies of Mozart to the latest beat from the disco. Of all the capacities of the mind none develops earlier. In terms of human evolution it is probable that humans played music before they learned to communicate in speech or calculate with numbers. Music has the power to 'speak' to us in a way that no other medium has, even if children sometimes 'speak it' in a rather loud way.

Mothers use it to sing their children to sleep. Armies march to the sound of the drum. Each religion has its sacred music, every country its national anthem. We dance to music, express our love and our grief through music. And music is the first of the intellectual capacities that your child develops.

Studies of human development suggest that all children have some 'raw' musical ability. This natural response to rhythm and melody has its genesis in the rhythm of the mother's heartbeat, and in the child's early attempts to understand the melodic sounds of speech. Certain parts of the brain play important roles in the perception and production of music, largely located in the right hemisphere. This intelligence is highly developed in certain individuals. Yehudi Menuhin was smuggled in by his parents to hear orchestral concerts when he was three. The young boy was so entranced by the sound of the violin that he wanted one for his birthday—and a teacher. He got both, and by the time he was ten he was an international performer. He was musically gifted, but he needed help to make the most of these gifts. How would you know if your child was musically gifted?

A musically gifted child will show a strong interest and delight in musical sounds. This interest may be shown before she learns to speak. Before her second year she may be accurately singing songs she has heard. She can often imitate a song after one hearing, and have what is called perfect pitch by the age of five. Some can sight-read music by that age, and have begun to play a musical instrument for themselves.

All children are able to make up their own songs, but most stop doing this by the time they reach school age. The musically gifted child will continue to make up songs in a playful and creative way. She is also good at listening to music. She doesn't just hear the tunes, but can differentiate between musical instruments, and can identify the rhythm and the melody (or tunes) in music. She will be able to talk about the different sounds she hears, and can say how one piece of music differs from another.

Most children may not be musically gifted in the sense of being able to play a musical instrument well, but all have the capacity to appreciate music and to benefit from being introduced to music at home. Your child's response to music is ready-wired into her brain as a unique form of intelligence. Chapter 6 explains how you can help develop in your child this gift of musical intelligence.

Did you know ... ?

The idea that music can help you learn is an old one. In Ancient Greece audiences would attend a festival called the Panathenaea every four years. During this festival a presenter would chant the whole of the *Iliad* from memory to the heartbeat rhythm of a softly played lyre. Records show that many in the audience could remember long passages from it afterwards.

Physical intelligence: developing mind and body

'I wish my body would do what I tell it to!' said an exasperated child after she had tried to catch a ball and dropped it. It is not always easy to get our body to do something we want it to. To move the body we have to use the brain. Only a small portion of our physical movements, such as sneezing or yawning, are involuntary. The body is an instrument that for most uses takes effort to master. So how do we do it?

Control of body movement is localised in the motor cortex of the brain. One of the strange facts about the brain is that control of movement in right-handed people is situated in the left half of their brain (and for left-handers in the right hemisphere of the brain). When this area of the brain is damaged we can lose the ability to control our movements. Even if we have the physical capacity to move, it is an area in the brain that enables us to take the action. Fortunately we don't have to think about every action we make. The brain gets used to doing the thinking for us, it feeds the information when we want to do something automatically through the spinal cord to the relevant parts of the body. Different parts of the motor cortex are responsible for different muscular movements (which is why your child finds it difficult to rub his tummy in a circular movement while patting his head).

These pre-programmed movements are what we call 'know-how'. We don't have to think about them to do them, but we can improve them through practice. We also improve what we do through the use of tools. In using tools, such as pens, brushes, knives and forks, two parts of the body are of special importance—hand and eye. It is through co-ordinating these that we learn to use tools in ever more skilful ways. It takes time, as Jodie, aged seven, struggling with her handwriting, says: 'I know what to do, but my hands just won't do it!'

Physical intelligence is involved in more than the everyday problems of doing tasks at home and school. It is involved in all forms of play and sport. Whether we are hitting a ball with a tennis racquet, miming an action or using the body to express emotion (as in a dance), we are using physical intelligence. It is involved in all art activity, when we draw, paint or make a model. It is involved in devising an invention, mending a machine or cooking a meal. Some of us are better than others at doing these things. But it is an intelligence we all have, and can all develop—even in those who say they cannot mend a fuse, iron a shirt or boil an egg!

For some children their physical intelligence is what will give them their greatest success and source of pleasure in life. They may learn best through physical, tactile and kinaesthetic means. Like Alex, aged six, who said to me, 'I cannot tell you but I can show you how I did it.' Or like the car mechanic who needs to get 'the feel' of the engine before finding out what's wrong, or the cook who prefers trial-and-error with real ingredients to sticking to a recipe.

> **Did you know ... ?**
> In a typical class of thirty children more than twenty
> will be able to take in information in three different
> ways—visually (though seeing), auditorily (through
> hearing), and kinaesthetically (through touching). Two
> or three children will have problems learning in any
> of these ways. The rest, about six of them, will have a
> strongly favoured learning style, either visual, auditory
> or kinaesthetic.

Children for whom the physical is their preferred method
of learning need to move, to feel, to touch and to do—and
if they have no opportunities for this at home or school can
feel left out, confused and bored. Chapter 7 considers ways
to help all children learn more through their physical intelligence.

Personal intelligence: being aware of ourselves

In the beginning humans were probably not aware of themselves as persons. They were only aware of what happened
to them and around them. Their unconscious minds did all
the work, without the need for conscious understanding. A
young baby is much the same, reacting to what happens to
him without knowing who he is or that he is his own unique
person. Among the many amazing discoveries a young child
makes is the discovery that he is a person separate from
others. That is why a mirror can be a very educational toy
for a baby, for one day he discovers a fact that is endlessly
fascinating—that the person in the mirror is not just anybody,
but is himself. For some this is the beginning of a life-long
love affair.

The development of the human mind is partly the development of the 'self', my idea of the person who is me. Personal
intelligence is that part of the mind that tells us who we are.
When humans grasped that they were separate and unique
persons they not only became aware of 'what is out there?'
but also interested in 'what is in here'. When Tom, aged ten,

was asked to think about what went on in his mind he wrote, 'Isn't it strange that the only mind you really know about is your own mind. You never know for sure what is going on in anyone else's head.' Part of the fascination of being a parent, carer or teacher of a child is that there is always something new to discover about what is (or is not) going on in your child's head.

Adult (pointing to a child's head): What is going on in there?
Child: Sorry, there's no one in at present. Call back later.

Sometimes children think of their minds as if there was a little 'self' inside them telling them what to think and do. The strange thing is that there is no 'self' in there at all, only neurons sending messages round the brain. The self is one of the most marvellous of human inventions. We create the idea of our self by linking together all our bodily and mental activities. This self is often experienced as an inner voice. This 'thinking voice', when it is aware of itself as an 'I', is an expression of personal intelligence. With young children this 'I' is usually identified at a physical level:

RF: Who are you?
Paul (aged four): I am a boy.
RF: What kind of person are you?
Paul: I have brown hair.

Older children begin to assess themselves as a self in relation to others:

RF: What sort of person are you?
Jason (aged eight): I'm bigger than other kids.
RF: What is special about you?
Jason: I can run faster than other kids.

As they get older children begin to develop systematic beliefs about themselves:

RF: What sort of person are you?
Miranda (aged twelve): Well, I'm quite a nice person.
I'm not selfish. I am willing to share things with others.
I only really get cross when no one listens to me.
RF: What is special about you?

Miranda: Well, nobody else feels things or thinks things like I do. At least I've not found anybody who does!

Personal intelligence allows a person to understand and make the most of himself. It enables your child to draw upon the other forms of intelligence to gain knowledge of himself. It allows him to be aware of his feelings and of his bodily states. It helps him understand who he is and what he can do. More importantly, it helps him to understand what he needs to do to become more successful. Personal intelligence is an important element in self-control, or rather in learning when to control yourself and when to let go. This sense of self-awareness varies between people, but we all have the capacity to know ourselves, and to know ourselves better.

Chapter 8 shows how you can help your child develop his personal intelligence.

Did you know . . . ?
People who talk personal problems through to themselves are often better at solving problems than those who do not talk to themselves. In children 'talking to yourself' is an expression of personal intelligence and can lead to increased self-awareness.

Social intelligence: being aware of others

'Why can't I have what I want?' yelled a fractious two-year-old. 'Because your sister wants it and it's her turn,' came the mother's reply. 'Why can't it be my turn *all* the time?' protested the child.

In the daily drama of family life such conflicts are bound to occur. A family can be a maddening crowd. Our strongest emotions—anger, jealousy, love and despair—are evoked by our experience of living with other people. The way we understand and deal with these conflicts, and develop our understanding of others, is the work of social intelligence.

It is not difficult to see why social intelligence was important for humans. In prehistoric societies the skills of hunting and living together in groups required the participation and co-operation of large numbers of people. Social intelligence has developed through our need to solve the problems of living together—the need to balance our own needs with the needs of others, to be able to resolve disputes and to benefit from what others have to offer. These are constant challenges. As Nadia, aged four, said after she had fallen out with her friends, echoing a feeling people must have had throughout history, 'Everything would be all right, if it wasn't for other people!'

A factor that makes humans special is their long period of childhood, and the close attachment of a baby to the person who acts as her mother. Childhood is a crucial time for learning how to love and how to form relationships with others. If there is no experience of mother-love in a young child's experience, then her social development, her ability to form relationships with others, can be severely impaired. We learn through love and early relationships that the self is not alone, that we are connected to many sorts of people—family, friends, those who help us in the community, and others for whom we feel some kind of attachment. For some this feeling for others can be very wide. When Judy, aged five, was asked who she was going to pray for, she replied, 'I am going to pray for everyone—and I hope they pray for me.'

Social intelligence is shown in being aware of others. Its activity occurs mostly in the frontal lobes of the brain. If those areas suffer damage a person's personality can change, as in some forms of senile dementia, and the ability to understand and relate to others can be lost. People with a well-developed social intelligence are aware of how others feel, and know their moods, desires and intentions. They have good social skills. They get on well with others and are seen to be popular. Sometimes they become the sort of leaders and organisers whom others want to follow. As Paula, aged eleven, said about her friend, 'I like Liane, she seems to know what I want better than I know myself!'

Social intelligence utilises other forms of intelligence in gaining knowledge about and in relating to other human beings. It is a capacity we all have, but is differently developed in all of us. Chapter 9 shows how you can help to develop the social intelligence of your child.

Did you know . . . ?

There are twice as many negative emotions, like fear, jealousy, grief, anxiety and guilt, as there are positive ones. There are many ways to be unhappy, but not many ways to be much happier. Those who get on well with others have fewer negative emotions and are generally happier than those who do not. Social intelligence, insofar as it helps one get on well with others, can help your child have a happier life.

Philosophical intelligence: thinking about the meaning of life

The wonderful thing about young children is that they are natural philosophers. They want to know the meaning of things, and when they are young they are not afraid to ask. This is natural and universal.

In whatever country and whatever time, children have always asked awkward questions. They are born without experience of the world. For them it is a buzzing, blooming place full of large, strange people, events and changes. They are born without any maps or guides. Their parents and carers are their first guides. Just like tourists in a strange country, they will have questions they want to ask. Some of these will be about everyday things like 'What is that called?' 'Why is she doing that?' 'Where is he going?' These are factual questions to which there is often a simple answer, which is right or wrong.

Other questions that children ask will be harder to answer. These will be about what things mean and why life is like it is—for example, 'Why do people die?' 'Why do people hate each other?' 'What is God?' These are questions about human life, and how we think about life. Such questions not only puzzle children, they have been puzzling philosophers for thousands of years. They are common because we all have the capacity to ask philosophical questions. It is just that we may not do it very often, and as we get older we may stop asking these kinds of question. Children too will stop if not encouraged. In school, teachers say that as children get older they usually ask fewer questions, and some stop asking questions at all. This may be because they are discouraged from asking questions at home, or in class. If no one is interested, then why ask questions? As Charlotte, aged eleven, said, 'I stopped asking questions. Everyone seemed to know the answers except me, and no one wanted to listen.'

One of the problems with children's questions is that sometimes there is no easy answer, or there may be a whole range of possible answers, or the answer may not be known by us or by anybody. Here are some questions asked by four- and five-year-old children. Some of them are scientific in that there is a factual answer, others are philosophical in that they are about the nature of life and our beliefs about life, and for these there may be no easy answer.

- Why do hairs grow out of grandma's nose?
- Where do people go when they die?
- Why is it wrong to steal?
- Can rabbits think?
- Is magic real?
- Do snails love each other?
- Are there really angels?

How do we respond to these questions? Chapter 10 explores ways of responding and looks at what you can do to develop your child's philosophical intelligence.

Did you know . . . ?
When the great philosopher Kant was asked, 'What is philosophy?' he replied, 'Go away and do some and you will find out.' He believed that all people have a God-given capacity for asking philosophical questions, and an ability to use their powers of reasoning to find out answers for themselves. This capacity for philosophical thinking he called 'reason'. It is an ability all people have, though not all use.

HELPING YOUR CHILD TO LEARN

The following chapters explore in turn each of the intelligences. They explain what the intelligence is and how it can be developed. A three-step approach to helping your child is outlined in each chapter. What your child needs first is INPUT. His brain, mind and senses are wired ready for stimulus. The input you give him can be something that you do or say to stimulate his thinking, such as asking a question, reading a story or playing a game. The second stage is OUTPUT—that is what your child does in response to the stimulus, which may be the thinking, doing or discussion that takes place. The third stage is SELF-CONTROL—that is what your child learns or becomes aware of as a result of what he has heard, seen and done.

Some teachers, parents and carers get frustrated when children don't seem to take in or remember what they have been told. The trouble is that simply telling children only provides INPUT which by itself is not an efficient way of learning. Better learning occurs when there is some OUTPUT from the learner, an active or doing element, for example in solving a problem or answering a question.

Adult: You never seem to learn from what you are doing.
Child: How can I learn if I'm busy doing it?

But input and output, suggesting what to do and the child doing it, are often not enough for learning to 'stick'. What is needed is a third element, whereby the learner takes control of his learning, translating ideas or experiences into his own words. SELF-CONTROL means the sense your child makes of the input, what you have said or done, and the output which is what he has said or done. A child achieves self-control or mastery of what he has learnt when he can put it in his own words, show you or explain it to you.

Adult: Can you show me how to do it?
Child: I need to show myself first.

Showing others and helping them to learn is never easy. There may have been parents or teachers who tore their hair in the past, trying to help you to learn. Sometimes being a parent helping his or her own child may be the hardest kind of teaching of all. One parent explained the difficulty as follows: 'You love them so much that you try too hard and they reject you, and when you don't try hard enough they ignore you.'

We all dream of having children who get on with it and do well, and when they don't we fear the worst, so we nag them and push them. But sometimes this leaves them feeling less than inspired. Below are key ideas in helping your child to learn. At the end of each of the following chapters you will find summaries of seven key ideas or steps to building each of your child's intelligences. If only one of the steps works for you and your child it will at least have helped in making the most of your child's mind. The Chinese say that a journey of a thousand miles begins with one step. Work on one small step at a time. There is no one easy way that will unlock your child's potential. It will be the combination of many small steps repeated over the years that will bring success. At Joe, aged eight, said when struggling with a problem, 'If only there was a secret switch in the brain which you could turn on, which said 'BRAIN POWER'.

SEVEN STEPS TO HELPING YOUR CHILD LEARN

- Little and often is most effective—
  don't overdo it   INPUT
- Make learning fun if at all possible, fun for
  you and for her   INPUT
- Explain what you are doing and why, clearly
  and slowly   INPUT
- Involve the learner actively, don't do it all
  for him   OUTPUT
- Be patient, ask questions to check he
  understands   OUTPUT
- Pause to allow her time, prompt if she
  needs help, praise her efforts   OUTPUT
- Encourage the learner to explain,
  say or show what he has learnt   SELF-CONTROL

NOTE: The *Encouraging adult and inhibiting adult* diagram on p. 21 is reprinted from *Teaching Children to Think* by Robert Fisher, published by Stanley Thornes (1995), which discusses in more detail the nature of thinking and thinking skills. Reproduced by permission.

2   A Way With Words

developing linguistic intelligence

'What is the use of a book', thought Alice, 'without pictures or conversation?' Lewis Carroll, *Alice's Adventures in Wonderland*

Stories are not just something to read, they're something to talk about. Jane, aged 8

Jane is a child who is good with words. She expresses herself well in words and is confident about reading and writing. She is doing well at school in reading, writing and speaking. She can be expected to do well at exams and go on to a successful career, but she may not. She has linguistic intelligence, but she still needs help in developing it.

The poet T. S. Eliot was another such child. At the age of ten he created his own magazine called *Fireside*. In a three-day period during the Christmas holidays he produced eight issues, each one including poems, adventure stories, news, gossip and humour. In his childhood effort lay the seeds of future genius. But he needed much help and encouragement from home and school before he fulfilled his potential.

Brian is not such a lucky child. He is hesitant and nervous when he speaks. He has few books at home and doesn't say much to his mum and dad. Although he is six he can read only a few simple words. His writing is poor, and he finds it difficult to spell. He, like Jane, has linguistic intelligence, but he will need a lot more help from others to make the most of his gifts. If Brian gets that help and learns to help himself he may be just as successful in learning and in life as Jane, or more so. Both Brian and Jane are at risk of not fully developing their linguistic intelligence. But what is linguistic intelligence, and how is it best developed?

WHAT IS LINGUISTIC INTELLIGENCE?

Linguistic intelligence is the intelligence of words, and it develops from an early age. While still in the womb a baby will learn to recognise his mother's voice. From four days old he can recognise the speech patterns of his mother's language. Before his first birthday he begins to associate words with meanings. By 18 months he is beginning to develop a vocabulary which, by the time he is two years old, will have grown to include up to 2,000 words. How do children achieve this amazing grasp of language so quickly?

We know from brain studies that we are born with specific areas of our brain responsible for different aspects of language. If this part of the brain is damaged we can lose our ability to understand what words mean, or how they are said or spelt. Linguistic intelligence is located in the left area of the brain, but connects with areas of intelligence in other parts of the brain. We can use language to talk about maths, music and other forms of intelligence, but our ability to use words comes from this particular intelligence.

Why are words so important? Most of human thinking relies on words. Words help us to express our thoughts and ideas (or concepts), and enable us to communicate them to others. Without the words we are unable to say what we mean. Your child's ability to use words and to communicate what he knows through speaking and listening, reading and writing will be one of the keys to his success in learning and in life. But your child will need help in developing his ability to use words. As Kerry, aged six, says, 'Sometimes the words just won't come, and they won't come if they're not there, no matter how hard you try.'

Here are some examples of using linguistic intelligence for real-life problem-solving:

- Mary very much wanted to go on a particular holiday

but first had to persuade her family that they wanted to go too. She told them all about why they should go. They did not seem keen. She listened carefully to their reasons and then explained why each member of the family would enjoy the holiday. They finally agreed. Unfortunately during the holiday they had very bad weather. Linguistic intelligence helps in persuading people but cannot control the weather!

- Tony needed to buy a new cooker in a hurry. The one at home had finally died, and they needed a new one quickly. With his family's help he scoured consumer magazines for reports about recommended cookers to buy. They compared offers being advertised. Their research paid off. They found a cooker recommended as best buy in the consumer magazine at a good price in a local store. Unfortunately it was white, when they really wanted a green one. Even good research does not guarantee you get what you really want.

- Tracy was angry. She had bought an expensive watch with one year's guarantee and it had gone wrong after one year. She was told it would cost almost as much to repair as it had in the first place. She wrote to the makers, but they said her guarantee had expired. She wrote again, and persuaded the makers to replace the watch. By the time the new watch arrived she had bought another one, but her letter had worked—she had got her watch replaced.

DEVELOPING YOUR CHILD'S LINGUISTIC INTELLIGENCE

A normal child is born with a linguistic intelligence that gives him the potential to learn from birth any human language. What develops this intelligence is the stimulus that he receives from his parents and carers. The more words and ideas a child hears, uses and understands the more his verbal intelligence will develop.

This development begins with a baby listening to words and babbling in reply. It continues to develop through all the experience of speaking and listening, including speaking to oneself. Paula, aged eight, refers to this kind of inner speech when she says, 'Sometimes my best conversations are when I talk to myself . . .'cos there's no one to interrupt!'

Some children develop a way with words more quickly than others. They may talk more, show interest in new words and be actively encouraged to read and write at home. No matter how quickly or slowly your child's language develops, you can help him make more of this intelligence.

If your child	What you can do	What your child can learn
Is shy about speaking and hesitant when speaking in front of others	Encourage him to talk individually about what interests him	Speaking to one person helps you become more confident in speaking to others
Has problems in paying attention and listening when others are talking	Say how it feels not getting listened to, play listening and speaking games (see below), praise when he listens well	You find out more if you listen carefully to what others say
Doesn't like reading and has difficulty with the printed word	Find interesting books, read them to your child, and then read them together	Discovers that reading can bring interest and enjoyment and that you can learn with help
When it comes to writing says 'I can't write' or 'I don't know what to write'	Find a real reason to write, and someone who wants to read what your child writes	Writing has a purpose and value when it is done well and shared with others

HOW DOES LINGUISTIC INTELLIGENCE DEVELOP?

A baby is born with a brain poised to speak. All it needs is words to get it going. Part of the language area of the brain is programmed for speech and the control of speech muscles. But there is a large area which is uncommitted and needs to be filled with experience, particularly language experience. That is where parents and carers play their important role. The young child learns by imitation, by hearing and comparing the sounds that adults make and the words they say. Sometimes, of course, it doesn't come out quite right. Claire, aged three, heard her mother talk about 'stroking the cat. So Claire called it a 'stroky cat'.

Your child may say many odd things in trying to imitate you. That's fine, it shows she is learning—by imitation (and by sometimes being corrected) and by being rewarded. Parents tend to reward the sounds they like by paying attention, smiling and responding. Words they recognise and sentences they want to hear are rewarded in this way, and other words and sounds are ignored.

In the first six years of life most children learn to speak the first 3,000 important words of their home language. Many can achieve that amazing task by the age of four or five. They learn this mainly from their experience at home, through talking to their parents and sharing language experiences with them. If they live in a house where two languages are spoken they will learn both. If three languages are spoken they will learn three. The amount of time parents spend talking with their children, and the quality of that talk, are of vital importance and are the most crucial elements in predicting a child's success at school, because most thinking done in school is done in words. As Joe, a bright child aged nine, said about doing well at school, 'You have to be good at talking if you want to be good at thinking.'

Like all intelligences, our senses of language develops through use, through hearing words, seeing words, speaking words, reading words and writing words. Children's brains are wired to respond to words, and to think creatively about words, even words they have never heard of. This can be seen by giving any young child the 'wug' test. Say to the child: 'Here is a wug. Now there are two of them. There are two –' The child will quickly give the answer 'wugs', not because she has heard of wugs, or has been told the rule of adding an 's' to plurals, but because our brains are wired to understand the rules of sentences and phrases (syntax) and how words are built out of smaller bits (morphology). What the child needs to trigger her understanding is experience. What your child needs are the best kinds of experience for developing her natural instinct for language.

Although linguistic intelligence develops most quickly when young, it can be developed at any age. Some people are 'late developers', such as the woman who begins a course of study after bringing up a family, or the person who, once retired, writes a book that he always felt he had in him, or a person of any age who begins a political campaign to argue a case or to right some wrong. This intelligence can be strengthened at any stage in life, but the best time for developing it is in the early years when the brain is most flexible and most sensitive to influence. The challenge in a busy family life is to find opportunities for doing so.

In the average family the most frequent opportunities are found in telling each other what has been happening. 'What's the news?' 'What have you been doing?' 'What has happened to you today?' are all invitations to exercise linguistic intelligence.

The following is the developmental path of this intelligence:

Basic linguistic intelligence	*understands simple words *can speak simple sentences *has basic communication skills
Developing linguistic intelligence	*has an expanding vocabulary *is able to tell stories and jokes *is learning the basics of reading and writing
Well developed linguistic intelligence	*reads for learning and pleasure *writes for different purposes and people *communicates well in a variety of situations

49

Linguistic intelligence develops in situations where children are given the time and opportunity to express their ideas in words. For this a child needs help through having some stimulus (input) like being asked a question, some activity (or output) such as being encouraged to report her news and the chance to exercise some responsibility (control) over her means of expression such as being allowed to say as much or as little as she wants. This process, and your part in it, can be summed up as follows:

INPUT:	you stimulate your child by	giving your child words to use and reasons to speak, listen, read and write.
OUTPUT:	what your child does	talks and listens, reads to learn and writes for a variety of people and reasons.
SELF-CONTROL:	enabling your child to	communicate with confidence how she wants, to whom she wants, when she wants.

Did you know . . . ?

Between birth and four months babies can distinguish 150 distinct sounds that occur in all languages, but by the age of ten months they can distinguish speech sounds only in their home language.

Help your baby learn the speech sounds of her mother tongue by talking to her, reading to her, and singing to her. Hearing language will help your baby to recognise and distinguish speech sounds long before she knows what the sounds mean.

Children develop linguistic intelligence when they:

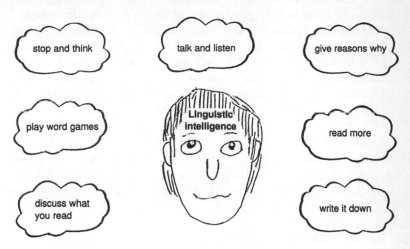

stop and think

talk and listen

give reasons why

play word games

Linguistic intelligence

read more

discuss what you read

write it down

WHAT YOU CAN DO TO HELP

There are various ways in which you can help enrich your child's linguistic experience.

From an early age children should hear daily news at home and also learn the stories of their society. Nursery rhymes, fairy stories, religious stories and folk tales all provide food for linguistic intelligence. A young child comes to learn that words can be used to solve problems and starts to exercise this intelligence by her own efforts—like Lucy, aged three, who taught her teddy all the words she knew. 'I've taught my teddy to speak,' she said, 'but he's so shy, the only one who can hear him is me.' Once your child has learnt to talk he can then talk to learn.

Talking and thinking

> 'The time has come,' the Walrus said,
>   'To talk of many things:
> Of shoes—and ships—and sealing-wax –
>   Of cabbages—and kings . . .'
>   Lewis Carroll,
>   *Through the Looking-Glass*

Learning to talk is an amazing achievement. A normal child will begin to say words by the end of his first year. By the age of two he will begin to say simple two- or three-word sentences, and will be starting to learn a most complicated system of grammar. By the time he is five he will be fluent in his native language. He will love to sing rhymes, recite stories and act them out alone or with friends. His brain will be 90 per cent grown, and his speech organs well developed. Before entering school the child will have picked up thousands of words and learnt how to use language to organise his life. But the quality and variety of his speech will largely depend on the help parents and carers have given at home. A baby can make all the noises of all the languages of the world (and sometimes does!), and could learn any language in the world. But would he learn a language if never spoken to?

In 1799 the Wild Boy of Aveyron was caught in a forest in France. He was 11 or 12 but had never, it was thought, spoken with a human. He showed so little reaction to what was said to him that they thought at first he was deaf, and it took years to teach him the simplest words. His lost childhood years could never be recaptured. In 1972 a 13-year-old girl named Genie was discovered to have been kept a prisoner in a room and never spoken to by her family from the age of two. By the age of 16, after intensive teaching, she could still only speak simple sentences at the level of a two- or three-year-old. These children had of course been deprived of more than language, they had also been deprived of emotional support and love which hampers the learning of any child. But they do show that a child, if deprived of all experience of human talk, would never learn to speak, and that the first decade of life is a crucial period for developing linguistic intelligence.

It is important not only to speak to your child, but to speak in sentences as often as you can. It gives the child more to listen to, more to learn and provides a good model for his own extended talk. For many children talk at home is limited to a few routine phrases, usually copied from parents or brothers and sisters. When they are learning to speak children will not know what a sentence is, or that language is made

---

Did you know . . . ?

When the child psychologist C. W. Valentine decided to write down everything that a 2½-year-old said in one day he didn't know what he was letting himself in for. One day's talk, when published, took up 27 pages of a learned journal.

If you have a young child, why not record in a journal some of the things your child says   it may be interesting to look back on in years to come!

---

of sentences, not isolated words. You can help your young child by expanding on what he says, and offering him fuller versions of what you think he is trying to say—for example:

Child: Gone shops?
Mother: Do you want to go to the shops with Mummy?

Child: Dog tired.
Mother: The dog is tired and sitting down for a rest.
   (Or alternatively—'Mum is feeling dog tired too!')

• There is no more important activity than having a sustained conversation with your child. Such conversations, tuned to what interests your child, are essential for his intellectual growth. This means more than giving him the one or two-word answers that are all some children hear from their parents, as in the following:

Child: I'm going to play with my cars.
Adult: OK, dear.
Child: And I'm going to do my painting.
Adult: Good idea.
Child: And I'm going to kill myself.
Adult: All right, dear.

This shows one way of not engaging in conversation with a child, by ignoring what he is saying (for more examples of such exchanges see *Not Now, Bernard* by David McKee). Another way that does not help your child is to over-run him, by finishing off what he is saying for him and not giving him time to answer—as in the following example:

Adult: Where do birds build their nests?
Child: Well ... erm ...
Adult: In the trees, dear, don't they?
Child: Yes ...
Adult: Right in the tops of trees.
Child: Yes, they build them in ...
Adult: What kind of bird are they?
Child: I've seen them before ...
Adult: They're sparrows, dear, aren't they? Sparrows.
Child: Yes, and we ...
Adult: We've read a story about sparrows, haven't we?

It is easy for adults to dominate conversation with children. What children need is time to think, time to work out what to say and time to ask their own questions—not to be bombarded all the time with questions from adults. A bright child is a thinking child. So when talking with your child allow her time to think.

How long do many parents allow for thinking when speaking to their child?

Most parents and teachers leave about one second for children to respond to a question. If you allow five seconds of thinking time after asking a question or making a comment, your child will have time to think. Sometimes children need time to sort out their ideas, to put their thoughts into words, or to decide what they really want to say. Likewise your child should not always get an immediate answer or response from you. Thinking children have thinking parents. So if you sometimes respond by saying something like, 'That's interesting, I need to think about that,' and pause for thought before you reply, it will have a double benefit. It will allow you time to get your thoughts together before responding, and also it models what you hope your child will learn to do—that is to stop and think before she speaks.

So when talking to your child, give her time to think, and time to respond to you. Think about what your child says, and sometimes say you need to think before giving a response. Remember that thinking is a kind of inner talking. If you think first it gives you time to rehearse what to say. It gives you time to think of alternatives, and to put your ideas into words. As Peter, aged eight, said, 'If you talk to yourself first then you know what to say.' The key idea, like all our key ideas, is applicable to a child of any age: encourage her to 'stop and think'. This means not hurrying her for an answer, or saying or doing the first thing you or she thinks of, but giving her time to think and talk it through to herself.

KEY IDEA: TEACH YOUR CHILD TO STOP AND THINK

Talking to your child is a two-way affair. Encourage her to be an equal partner in contributing to conversation. Try not to dominate. Treat your child with the respect that you would show any other person, and this will make it more likely that you will achieve a balanced conversation.

The great advantage you have over your child is that you have had much more experience of life. You know more answers to questions and have more to talk about. What your child has to talk about is her experience, and this may be very limited. The best way to encourage conversation is to share experiences with your child and talk about them together. This could be playing a game, going shopping or visiting local places of interest like a park. When you are with your child be observant and describe things properly. Try to find time to challenge your child to say more. Don't simply accept the easy answers that she gives. Ask her what she means and what she thinks. It is not always easy, as in the following exchange overheard in a dress shop:

Child: Want that one.
Mother: Do you mean you would like that cotton dress with the striped pattern and bow at the back? The one made in cotton and costing £15?
Child: No, the other one.

It is not always easy to get a child to say more. As Richard, a quiet boy, said, 'I only speak when there is something I really want to say.' So how do you, if you need to, encourage your child to say more?

The following are some *door-openers* that can encourage a child into conversation. They aim to open the door and offer a child the chance to talk.

'Tell me more'
'What did the man say?' 'Why did she do that?' 'How did it work?' are the kinds of 'tell me more' question that invite your child to expand on what she has said by asking a question.

'And . . .'
'I see', 'Really?' 'Oh', 'Hmmm?' 'Go on', 'Is that so?' 'Did you?' 'And . . . ?' are examples of verbal encouragement that help sustain your child's talk.

'What was it like?'
'Is it like another one you know?' 'How are they similar?' 'How are they different?' all invite your child to connect and relate her ideas with other things she knows or can remember.

'So what next?'
'Can you explain that?' 'What does it mean?' 'How do we know?' all challenge your child to think and say more, for example, about possible consequences or the next step in what happened.

A child who says; 'when's dinner?' may be asking for the time, may be indicating her hunger, may be showing she is bored, may be wanting to go out, and so on. Sometimes we need to check we know what children are saying, by encouraging them to say more through body signals like looking, or inviting them to say more.

KEY IDEA: HELP YOUR CHILD TO TALK AND LISTEN

Using door-openers to invite your child to say more may be important, particularly for a shy child. But of equal importance to speaking is learning to listen. A bright child knows how to listen.

Children first learn their language by listening. A young child will come to understand more than he can say. The first words spoken by nineteenth-century writer Thomas Carlyle were: 'What ails thee, Jock?' Obviously young Thomas had done a lot of listening before that was spoken. Learning to listen is as important as learning to speak, for it is through listening that a child learns what speaking is and how to speak well. The child who has not listened well will make errors in pronunciation. Like the young child who suddenly said, 'I want a rape, I want a rape!' The child's mother was bemused until she remembered there was a bowl of grapes on the table.

The most important step in helping your child to listen is to check his hearing. Problems such as glue ear can lead to hearing loss and learning difficulties. So have your child's hearing checked at a health clinic, and never leave an ear problem untreated. You can detect some hearing problems yourself, for example by checking if your child responds to loud noises or to his name when called. Another important element is to speak clearly to your child. If you mumble, so will he. As you speak to him so he will learn to speak to you.

If you want your child to listen to you then you must listen to your child. To show you are listening you need to respond to what he says. The trouble with listening is that it can be hard work. As we listen, thoughts keep breaking in, other things grab our attention. A child once wrote a poem about the experience of *not* listening to his teacher, which begins:

> Miss Smith thinks I am listening
> But really I am surfing in Hawaii
> I am scoring the winning goal
> I am going to a party
> I am flying to the moon
> I am travelling on a super highway
> I'm not here now
> I'll be back soon . . .

There are several clues that show if someone is not listening—the fidgeting or fiddling, the bored, faraway look (the curtains are open but there is no one in!) or the wayward gaze. Your child may show you that he is not good at listening. So how do you help him to be a good listener? Here are some games which can help improve listening skills.

Stop and listen

Try this at any time, in any place—the street, the supermarket, the house or garden. Stop everything, close your eyes and listen. What sounds can you hear—traffic, people, birds, natural sounds, machine sounds? Which sounds are closest, which are farthest away? Can you hear yourself breathe? Is there ever absolute silence?

Sound quiz

Ask the child to close his eyes and listen. Have several objects at hand, such as pencil, spoon, glass, paper or musical instrument. Make a noise, for example by tapping the spoon against the glass, or pencil on the table, rustling paper, clapping hands, ruffling curtains, opening a door, turning on a switch, and so on. See if your child can identify the sound. Take turns to play.

End the rhyme

Say a nursery rhyme, poem, popular song or limerick. Leave off an end rhyming word. Can your child finish the line with a word that rhymes?

Chinese whispers

This is a game for a group of children. Sit in a circle. Whisper a sentence in the first child's ear, so that no one else hears. He whispers it to his neighbour, and so on round the circle. The last child says the sentence she hears out loud. Has the whispered sentence changed on its journey? A harder alternative is to whisper a story and see how it changes in the telling!

Obey my command

Here the players must remember and obey a series of commands which must be fulfilled in the right order to win. For example: 'Listen carefully. You must bring a spoon from the kitchen, open and close the bedroom door, then stroke the cat.' Enliven the game by pretending the child is a robot, or a genie of the lamp. If he succeeds it can be his turn to give the commands. Young children can try three or four commands, older children can try seven or more.

Get it taped

Make a tape of sounds for your child to identify, such as footsteps, a fridge door closing, electric mixer, tap dripping, the voice of his favourite TV character and so on.

The tape-recorder can help a child's listening skills. Children can be fascinated by hearing the sound of their recorded voice. Use it to record and play back your child's earliest babbles. As he progresses in speaking, encourage him to record a conversation, read his favourite verse or both of you read a story together. Let him interview a relative or friend. Encourage him to send a recorded message to someone overseas. Take the tape-recorder on holiday and record some first-hand impressions or sound effects.

Draw your child's attention to any strange or interesting sound, and also help him appreciate the strange beauty of silence. As we shall see, listening carefully is a key in learning to read, and helps in the development of all forms of intelligence. For more on listening see p. 187, and remember that listening is a skill that improves with practice.

Watching TV does not help your child develop listening skills, but listening to the radio or a tape-recorder can. Dutch researchers wondered whether their children, who watch a lot of German television, would begin to learn some German words from it. They found that their children learned no German words unless they had learnt the words first from a parent or teacher. Another interesting piece of research concerned a boy named Jim. Jim was a normally-hearing boy whose parents were totally deaf. He heard no conversation from his parents but was put in front of the TV for hours on end. His parents thought he would pick up speaking and listening from TV. Jim was two-and-a-half before he spoke his first words—repeated from a television jingle. When his language skills were tested at the age of three it was found he knew few words. What he needed were regular speech therapy sessions. After six months of intensive help he progressed to a mastery of speaking and listening typical of his age.

Television gives children knowledge about the world and the culture they live in. But TV viewing can be harmful if it consumes all your child's spare hours. Studies show that continual background noise from TV at home can delay young children's development of spoken language. Research suggests that prolonged viewing by young children can encourage attention-deficit disorder (ADD), a condition in which the child finds it very difficult to concentrate on any one thing for longer than a few seconds (the average length of time an image stays still on TV). Television does not require careful listening or sustained attention on a particular image, nor does a child need to read, talk or play while the TV is on. Many children watch TV for more hours than they are in school. Like sweets, the passive and undemanding pleasures of TV can become addictive.

Try to limit your child to a maximum of three hours' watching a day, and establish certain times of day as TV-free zones. Some parents forbid breakfast-time or day-time viewing. Others do not allow TV in the child's bedroom. Try to ration viewing time, plan with your child his week's viewing ahead, set maximum viewing hours and evening deadlines. The same goes for computer use. Both TV and computer can stimulate your child to ask questions and set him thinking, but he needs you to help. Ways to help your child make the most of TV include:

Asking him to justify his viewing
Encourage him to say why a programme he wants to see is worth watching. If he says he likes or dislikes a programme, ask him why. If you want him to watch a programme give him the reasons why you think he should.

Talking about the programme
Discuss with your child what you plan to see, what you are seeing and what you have seen. Increase her vocabulary by checking that she understands some of the words that are being used (the ones you want her to understand!).

Discussing the production
What kind of programme was it? Was it a good programme?
What was good, or not good, about the story, scene, events,
acting, and so on? What marks out of ten would you give
the programme, and why?

Sorting fact from fiction
Help your child sort out the real from the imaginary, truth
from opinion, fact from fiction. When is it supposed to be
taking place, where, who is involved and why is it happening?

Extending his interest
Plan to enrich the content of a programme, whether it is
on wildlife, sport, show business or current affairs, with
books, pictures, newspapers and magazines to look at. In a
TV drama or 'soap', ask him to predict what will happen
next.

Being critical
Encourage your child to be critical about what he sees, for
example discuss the exaggerated claims of TV adverts,
stereotyped images and hidden persuaders. Help him to
realise that not everything is what it seems.

Whenever you are setting guidelines for your child, whether
it is about watching TV or about any other aspect of her
behaviour, the golden rule is to *give reasons* for the rules you
impose. If you want your child to behave in some way, say
why she should. If you are forbidding something, say why.
Likewise, if your child wants something, like to watch a TV
programme, ask her to say why. For example: 'Give me one
(or two or three) good reasons why you should stay up to
watch this programme.'

If you want your child to be reasonable, to know what
she is doing and why, then you must show her what being
reasonable means. It means having reasons for doing things
and saying what those reasons are. It can be time-consuming,
for every good reason can be challenged, as in the following
family dispute about which TV programme to watch:

61

> *Parent*: We are going to watch this programme because three of us want to and only you don't.
> *Child*: But why is three wanting something better than one wanting something?

It takes time to raise a bright child, and part of that time is spent in giving your child reasons for doing things and explaining why your reasons are better than her reasons. Ultimately, the reason why she should do as you say is that you are the parent and she is the child. You are responsible for her safety and welfare. So to be a parent who gives reasons is not to give up your responsibility as a parent, or to allow your child to do what she wants, but to treat your child as the kind of thoughtful and reasonable person you hope she will grow into.

KEY IDEA: ALWAYS GIVE REASONS, AND ASK FOR REASONS WHY

Word play

'The trouble with books is that they are full of words,' said a six-year-old struggling to read. The French language has a vocabulary of nearly 100,000 words, but this is less than half the number of words in the everyday vocabulary of the English language. There are an awful lot of words to learn, but they are important for developing linguistic intelligence for words are the tools of thinking. The more words your child knows, the easier it is for her to express her thoughts and ideas. Without the words she cannot fashion her ideas, and her thoughts are dumb. So feed your child's mind with words, but make it fun. Turn your word play into a game.

The first and most important word game is the naming game. In building your child's word power it makes sense to start with naming words, or nouns, since these label the people, places, animals, things and ideas that your child can identify. So help your child label everything she sees, hears, touches, tastes and smells, and also those important things she cannot see like feelings, and abstract ideas like time, space and eternity. It helps her remember if she not only says it, but also sees it, or experiences it through one of the senses. Your child knows what an apple is, but try the taste test: can she tell the difference between a Granny Smith and a Golden Delicious?

Parent: Adam named all the animals in the Garden of
    Eden.
Child: Where did he get the names from?

A young child's discovery that everything has a name is the discovery of what language is all about. Help give your child the names of everything that interests her. Name the flowers in your garden, the food that you eat, the goods in the catalogue. Naming games like 'I Spy' can begin at 18 months. Don't be afraid of long words. When I asked a four-year-old what his favourite long word was he said 'phosphorescent'. He wasn't sure what it meant, but then neither was I.

What is the longest word, the most interesting or the most beautiful word that your child knows?

After nouns come verbs, the action words. Try to keep the 'say and see or do' approach. Talk about what you are doing while doing it. 'I'm going to cook the dinner now. Do you want to help me make a mixture?' My younger son is a good cook, and it all started with him 'making mixtures' as a young child in the kitchen. Talk to your baby about what you are doing. I used to have long conversations with my sons when they were babies . . . Remember they understand much more than they can say, and it can be very therapeutic talking to a captive audience!

Add adjectives, adverbs and prepositions. Use words that describe things (adjectives) like the 'shiny, furry, silky-smooth' coat of your dog, and adverbs to describe verbs like how fast you run, and prepositions to describe the places of things. Children can get confused about grammar. When I asked some eight-year-olds what grammar was, one child replied, 'I know what "grammar" is. She's married to grandpa.' It is not only children who are unsure about grammar. If you are not sure about advising an older child about grammar, buy one of the many children's grammar books— for yourself!

More important than knowing the parts of speech or rules of grammar is helping your child to develop a wide vocabulary. Look for opportunities to introduce new words, and take time to share your interest in words with your child. But be prepared for some surprises. Once when a teacher was listening to her children report their news, one five-year-old announced: 'My brother found a contraceptive on the patio.' The teacher paused. A child's hand went up, indicating she wanted to ask a question. The teacher, dreading what she was going to hear, nodded for the child to ask the question. 'Please, Miss,' said the child, 'what's a patio?'

Make words a part of your child's everyday life. Have a pinboard in the kitchen to pin up memos, notices, letters, adverts, calendars of events, cartoons and anything of current interest for your child and family to read. Put a pinboard in your child's bedroom for him to do the same with pictures, cuttings, posters and his own writing and drawing. Have some play with words each day, for example:

Stories, rhymes and songs
A child's interest in words is often stirred by rhymes and stories, by the topsy-turvy world in which owls sail away with pussy-cats, and cows jump over the moon. Research has shown that hearing and learning nursery rhymes is important in developing later skills of reading and writing. This is partly because hearing how words rhyme teaches young children a lot about the sounds of language (see p. 68).

Jokes, puns, and riddles
Has anything funny happened to you today? Tell your child about it. Encourage him to share his funny moments with you. Share your child's interest in jokes, puns and riddles. What riddles does your child know? What is his current favourite joke? What tongue-twisters can he invent?

When I asked a seven-year-old for his favourite joke he replied:

What do you have to know before you can start training a pet?
Answer: More than the pet!

Some jokes make you laugh and some do not. Some people are good at remembering and telling jokes, some are not. A joke is a verbal game that exercises linguistic intelligence. What makes us laugh is the creative connection in a joke between two unexpected ideas. To appreciate the joke we must see the connection. Riddles also work this way. The following riddle was the favourite of an eight-year-old:

Question: What pets make the most noise?
Answer: Trumpets

Riddles are a very old and universal kind of word game. Research suggests that the more your child plays with words and sounds, the better success he will have in learning to read and write at school. Such games range from the simple 'I Spy' with young children to challenging verbal games like 'Scrabble' for older children.

Did you know . . . ?
One way linguistic intelligence shows itself is in the ability to make up new words. Our language is being continually expanded with the invention of new words, and great writers have often used words they have created in their writing. Roald Dahl is a good example of a writer who loved to create new words. Shakespeare did it too: the longest word that he used in his plays is 'honorificabilitudinitatibus' (in *Love's Labours Lost*, Act V, Scene 1, Line 44). We think it is one that he made up. Try with your child to make up some new words (read Lewis Carroll's poem *Jabberwocky* for inspiration).

The following are some more word games that help stimulate verbal intelligence:

- *Letter games* such as seeing how many things you can see beginning with a chosen letter or with young children a chosen sound).

- *Word games* such as 'Twenty Questions' or 'Animal, Vegetable or Mineral?'
- *Phrase games* such as 'Initials' in which players try to create a funny phrase from given initials (e.g. Neil could be 'Never Eat In Liverpool'), or from initials on car number plates.
- *Sentence games* such as tongue-twisters (e.g. Piglet's 'Help, help, a Heffalump, a Horrible Heffalump' or 'The sixth sheikh's sixth sheep is sick').
- *Story games* such as a 'round robin' story: one person begins a story, then stops where he wants to, and the next person must carry on and turns are taken until the story ends.
- *Memory games* such as 'I went to market and I bought . . .' or 'In my suitcase I packed . . .' The first person names an item, the next player repeats this and adds another item, and so on.

Your child's linguistic intelligence develops through his understanding of words, which is why asking questions about words he uses can be so important. Test your child's understanding of a word by asking, 'What do you mean by that?' 'What does that word mean?' or 'Is there another word which means the same?' Have a good dictionary in the house to check on words yourself. Buy a picture dictionary for a young child, or a picture dictionary of foreign words for an older child. Encourage him to try the word games that appear in comics and magazines. Remember that word play builds word power. Paul, aged seven, had an inkling of this when he said, on seeing a big dictionary, 'If you knew all these words you'd know everything.'

<u>KEY IDEA: PLAY WORD GAMES</u>

Another useful word game for a child is to learn words and sentences in another language. Your child's brain has a special capacity for learning languages. This capacity decreases with the passing of years, so the best time to acquire a second or third language is in the early years, between three and six years old. The best way of teaching another language is 'mother's method', that is to speak to your child regularly *in that language only*. This is more effective than the later translation method. Begin with simple everyday sentences rather than a lot of random words, for it is on these basic units that he will be able to build in later years. From the age of seven learning another language becomes hard work, but all children will enjoy learning some strange-sounding foreign words, especially if you keep it fun and try to make it a game.

Read all about it

'If one cannot enjoy reading a book over and over again, there is no use in reading at all.' Oscar Wilde

William Saroyan, the American writer, had a shock on his first day at school. His kindergarten teacher baffled him by writing three strange shapes on the board: C-A-T. 'That,' she said, 'is cat.' At that moment Saroyan decided she must be mad. A cat—*his* cat especially—was all black fur and green eyes. What was this woman trying to do to him?

The shock for the young Saroyan was to discover that words are a code. What interests a child when learning to read is what the words mean, not the letters from which they are made. Knowing what words mean (the vocabulary) is important, but so is the code. The code is made up of letters. These letters stand for spoken sounds, so in learning to read, knowing how letters sound (phonics) is important. And words when written or printed in a book are visible signs, so being able to recognise them by sight (having a sight vocabulary) is important too. Learning to read is the work of the mind, of ears and eyes. We need to help our children hear the different sounds in words, see these sounds in letters and write them.

meaning of word + sound of word + sight of word = reading
   (mind)   (ears)   (eyes)

A good early reading activity is the word-change game. Begin with a word like 'fat', and by changing one letter each time see how many different words you can make—for

---

Did you know . . . ?

All the words in English can be written in 26 letters, and pronounced using only 43 basic sounds (called phonemes). These 43 sounds are all contained in the following list of words (in each word *one* key sound is underlined):

c<u>a</u>t, <u>b</u>oy, <u>d</u>og, b<u>e</u>d, <u>f</u>ish, get, <u>h</u>en, pi<u>g</u>, <u>j</u>ug, <u>k</u>ey (or <u>c</u>at), <u>l</u>og, <u>m</u>an, <u>n</u>et, h<u>o</u>t, <u>p</u>an, <u>q</u>uick, <u>r</u>ed, <u>s</u>un, <u>t</u>ap, c<u>u</u>t, <u>v</u>et, <u>w</u>in, fo<u>x</u>, <u>y</u>et, <u>z</u>ip, <u>ch</u>in, ri<u>ng</u>, <u>sh</u>ip, <u>th</u>in, <u>th</u>em, c<u>a</u>ke, s<u>ee</u>d, t<u>i</u>me, h<u>o</u>me, c<u>u</u>te, s<u>aw</u>, c<u>ar</u>, <u>ou</u>t, <u>oi</u>l, b<u>oo</u>k, m<u>oo</u>n, h<u>er</u>, h<u>or</u>se

To help your young child learn these sounds, write them down one at a time, pronounce each one distinctly and encourage your child to repeat it. Once he can do this, see what other words your child can think of, say or read with each key sound. Find words with the sound coming at the end or middle of words (use a movable alphabet of lower case letters to help you). Do not bother with letter names as it is the sounds that are important.

---

example: bat, bet, bit, but, bun, bin, sin, sit, kit and so on. Try to follow the process of think, sound (speak and listen) and see (write and look) so that your child is processing the words in three ways—mind, ears and eyes.

Some children learn to read simply by being read to, following the words and learning them. These are 'natural readers'. Not many children are like that, but those who are can begin to read at the age of three. Most children find learning to read a hard task and take years to develop the reading habit. Try to get into this habit from an early age. Choose a time to read when you are both relaxed, and only read when you can both give full attention to the story.

Children learn most easily from those they love. Sharing

stories with your child is part of loving her, an opportunity to spend time in close, personal and creative contact. A story book is the perfect opportunity to get together. A lucky child will have a parent who reads to her every day. For how many years should this last? There are some parents of fifteen- and sixteen-year-olds who still read to or with their child. Recently a twenty-one-year-old went into hospital for an operation. The first thing she did while recovering was to ask her mother to read 'Goblin Market', a story poem by Christina Rossetti, to her. It had been one of her childhood favourites. A married couple in their seventies still read to each other in bed at weekends. Their children have long gone, but as they say, they just kept on reading.

Research shows that a child's progress in reading is related to the amount of time someone has spent reading to her at home. How long should parents spend reading each week? Children who show good progress in reading have parents who read to them at least sixty minutes a week, in short, regular sessions, for example for about ten minutes six times a week.

If children have books which are read, laughed at and discussed, they will learn that books can be interesting, fun and full of information. By having stories read to them they learn to enjoy books and in time will want to read them for themselves. But what books are best?

Better than any booklist is your child's response to the books she likes. If in doubt ask your child. Visit a bookshop or library and let her choose. There is no point in forcing her to listen to or read something she does not understand or enjoy. Ask for advice from a librarian or teacher. Try to interest your child in the books you like. Don't be afraid to buy books you think she will like, even if she cannot read them. Katie was only three weeks old when her aunt sent her a gift—a 200-page book of Arabian legends. Katie's mother thought this was a dotty thing to do at the time since her baby could hardly focus her eyes, let alone look at a book. Yet thirteen years later the book had a treasured place on Katie's shelf, because it was the first book she had ever owned. As she says herself, 'One day I might read it.' So never be afraid of giving a child a book she can grow into: one day she might read it.

69

Read the books and stories that you enjoy and think are worthwhile, or favourite stories and picture books your child chooses for you. Try to introduce different kinds of story—fables, myths and folktales. Try writing a story of your own to read to your child—she will think it is good! When reading aloud to your child find the most comfortable place to read—on a sofa, in bed, on the floor. Have fun with stories, laugh at the funny parts. Make the story more interesting by using different voices for different characters. Stop from time to time to see if your child can guess what will happen next (see below for questions to ask to get your children thinking about the stories you read).

Sometimes tell rather than read a story to your child. If you think you'll forget a story you mean to tell, jot notes down beforehand. Try making up parts of stories, or the whole story, to make it more interesting. Sometimes stop and ask your child to add to or continue a story that you are making up.

Read poems that you enjoy. Young children should hear nursery rhymes some time every week. Buy your child some good poetry books and try to encourage her to memorise and say her favourite poems and rhymes. Also share some non-fiction books that interest your child—boys often prefer these. Have some good reference books ready to look things up when needed. If you have a computer, show her how to use it to find out facts and information. Find some fun fact books to share, such as a book of records or amazing mysteries.

What is important is that once your child has begun reading you should hear her read regularly at home. Many research studies have shown that, no matter what kind of teaching of reading goes on at school, the most effective way to boost reading ability is for parents regularly to hear their children read at home. Just sixty minutes a week could make all the difference to your child's progress in reading.

Here are some ways in which you can make it less difficult and more pleasurable, for both of you.

- *Keep it short*, don't try to do too much. Just ten minutes a day reading and talking about it is quite an adequate programme. If you miss a day it does not matter.

Did you know . . . ?
In the tenth century a Queen of Wessex had four
sons. She knew that one day one of them would be
king. Her dearest wish was that they should learn all
the arts of kingship, including being able to read. So
to encourage them she read from her most treasured
possession, a large illuminated Bible. Only one of her
four princes showed any interest. The large coloured
pictures fascinated him. Of the four, he was the only
one who learned to read. It was seeing these pictures,
and talking about them with his mother, which,
according to legend, set him on the road to reading.
This lucky boy was Alfred, later one of England's
greatest kings.

- *Choose the best time*, when you are both relaxed. As one
  child told me, 'Before we do our reading Mum has to
  have a stiff drink.' Don't drag her away from something
  she finds more interesting, or if she's really not in the
  mood. Ask, 'When would be a better time?'
- *Let your child do most of the work*, and give her time to
  get it right. The ideal is for the child to correct her own
  mistakes. Give her time to pause, there is no need to
  hurry. Don't encourage wild guesses, help her to listen to
  the sound of the words and follow the story.
- *Read together*, sit close to your child and pay attention
  to what she is reading. Read the page to your child first
  if this helps, or read alternate pages.
- *Praise and encourage.* Never criticise her ability, or compare her with other children. Your child is unique. She
  may be maddening, and driving you to despair, but she
  deserves your best effort. As one child complained, 'I wish
  my parents could be my children, then they'd realise it's
  not easy being a child!'

The HEAD START approach to hearing a child read is
PAUSE-PROMPT-PRAISE.

Pause—give her time to think if she is stuck. Reading is

a problem-solving activity, so encourage your child to try working things out for herself—'stop and think'.

Prompt—give her a clue to any words she does not know, then pause for thought (offer help).

Praise—praise her for trying hard or reading well (reward effort).

How do you tell if a book is too hard for your child to read? If there is more than one word in a sentence he cannot read (about one word in 15), it is probably too difficult for him, though not for you to read to him. If he gets stuck on a word don't make an issue of it. Give him time to think, prompt him by saying the first letter or by re-reading the sentence, then say the word if he cannot and carry on. Letting him listen to the whole sentence to see how the word might fit may help him to guess the word. It does not always work as this example shows:

Child (reading the story): The cowboy fell off his . . .
(The word is 'horse' but the child is stuck. The parent allows a pause for thought, then repeats the sentence).
Parent: The cowboy fell off his . . .
(The parent pauses again and when the child is still stuck says the sentence with the sound of the first letter of the word as a clue).
Parent: The cowboy fell off his . . . h . . .
Child: . . . house!
Parent: The cowboy fell off his *house*? Do cowboys fall off houses?
Child: Yes. Perhaps he was painting it and fell off his ladder.

There are of course many other things to read apart from books. Some parents worry that their child is reading too many comics. Research shows that good readers tend to read a lot of comics, just as many poor readers do. Good readers read more of everything, whether they are children or adults. Reading comics or anything else will not prevent them becoming good readers. What is important is that they do a lot of reading. So what should they read?

What else should they read?

- comics and magazines;
- notes, memos and letters you write to them or write together;
- shop signs, adverts, notices, and street signs;
- shopping lists, recipes, and menus;
- instructions on packets, cartons, boxes, etc.;
- labels on bottles and packets, ingredients, instructions and special offers;
- books you make together, such as holiday scrapbooks or story books;
- newspaper headlines, reports, cartoons, and news stories;
- travel brochures, mail-order catalogues, programmes;
- information in telephone directories, Yellow Pages, etc.;
- family photo albums, scrapbooks, postcards;
- TV, teletext, computer game texts and CD Roms.

If your child is a reluctant reader, try to find something to read that is linked to his interests, hobbies or the TV he watches. Unfortunately children do not always want to read about their interests. If a boy or girl is mad keen on football he or she may want to play it, not read about it. This is not surprising. Many people who enjoy eating do not necessarily want to read about it. However, having an interest is a good starting point, and your child will *sometimes* want to read about what interests him.

Try to share your enthusiasms, but don't expect your child automatically to like what you like. Give him a chance to choose his own reading-matter and to tell you what he thinks about it. One mother was telling her five-year-old daughter a bedtime story about a young princess who befriended a frog. The princess was so kind to the frog that she agreed to take it to bed with her. In the morning she had a surprise. The frog had turned into a handsome prince, who asked her to marry him. As the mother was reading this she noticed a look of incredulity spread over her daughter's face, and said: 'Don't you believe that?' 'No,' came the reply, 'and I bet her Mum didn't either!'

Try to see the world through your child's eyes. He is sur-rounded by the printed word—in the supermarket, out in the street, on adverts, posters, signs and wrappers. We take for granted what these words say and mean. To a young child print is a constant challenge, a problem to make sense of. As with books, your child can turn a 'blind eye' to this bombardment. He needs you to help him make sense of some of these messages, to point out words of interest and to help him unlock the secrets of the written word (see p. 292 for more ways of helping your child read at home).

KEY IDEA: READ TO YOUR CHILD AND HELP HIM READ

A small proportion of children with reading problems have sight problems, which may be in evidence if he often rubs his eyes, squints at the page, covers one eye, or turns his head sideways to read. If so he may need to have his eyes tested. The ability to discriminate the sounds and shapes of words depends on speech, hearing and eyesight. If your child has a problem with any of these, have it checked at a clinic. This is important, for when children begin to fail they lose interest. What we need to do is to keep their interest in reading alive. One way to do this is to discuss with your child what you read.

Questions for thinking

> *I keep six honest serving-men*
> *(They taught me all I know):*
> *Their names are What and Why and When*
> *And How and Why and Who.*
> Rudyard Kipling, from 'The Elephant's Child'
> from *Just So Stories*

What questions should we be asking our children about their reading? The following is a list of some questions that can be asked about any reading material, fact or fiction, book or news story. Good readers ask themselves questions about what they read, such as, 'What has happened?' 'Why did they do/say that?' 'What will happen next?' These are questions that help you think about what you read. If you use questions such as these with your child, it will encourage her to ask herself questions as she reads.

Rudyard Kipling's questions are useful ways to begin in asking questions about what your child thinks about what you read to her or she reads to you:

Questions to ask about stories

- *When?*   When did it take place?
  How long ago was it?
  What happened before?
  What will happen next?
  What does 'once upon a time' mean?

- *Where?*   Where did it take place?
  What kind of place was it?
  Is it a real or imaginary place?
  Can you picture it?
  Where might it have been set?

- *Who?*   Who wrote it? Who is in it?
  Who is the most important character?
  Who else is important?
  Can you picture the character?
  What kind of person is he or she?

- *What?*   What kind of story is it?
  What happened?
  What could/should/might have happened?
  What did the characters think/say/feel?

75

What did they think/want/hope would happen?

- *How?* How did it happen?
  How did it begin?
  How do you think it will end?
  How did it end?
  How would you have ended it?

- *Why?* Why did it happen the way it did in the story?
  Why was it written?
  Why is it written like that?
  Who is telling the story and why?
  Why read it?

The following are some of the questions that a parent asked a six-year-old after reading the story of Cinderella to see what the child remembered and to help her think more about the story:

Parent: What kind of story was this?
Child: It's a fairy story?
Parent: What is a fairy story?
Child: It's a story where dreams come true.
Parent: How might the story have ended?
Child: Cinderella might not have married the prince.
  She might have grown up to be mean and ugly like her sisters.
Parent: Why might she have grown up to be ugly?
Child: Because when no one loves you it makes you feel ugly and then . . . you look ugly.
Parent: What character would you have liked to be in the story?
Child: (after some thought) One of the mice.
Parent: Why?
Child: . . . Because I like cheese!

What this excerpt shows the parent doing is following up her child's answer with the question 'Why', inviting the child to say more. There is a difference between a child just reading the words and forgetting them or not understanding what they mean and reading for meaning. A good reader is a fluent reader, which means the child can read the words and understand them. It is only by talking with your child about her reading that you can tell if she is reading fluently. For more on discussing stories with your child see p. 277.

KEY IDEA: QUESTION AND DISCUSS WHAT YOU READ

Write on

When the writer Evelyn Waugh was asked the secret of his success he said, 'I put the words down and push them about a bit.' There is much that you can do to help your child be a writer, to get him to put words down and 'push them about' a bit. William Hazlitt said that the more a person writes the more he or she can write. Children learn to write by reading and by writing. Which comes first, reading or writing?

Children in a Montessori nursery will learn to write before they learn to read. At first they learn to control the muscles in their hand, through playing with shapes, jigsaws and other puzzles that develop the hand skills needed for writing. Once they have the manipulative skill to control a pencil they learn to draw round stencils and trace with a pencil. Later they will trace letters made of sandpaper and learn the sounds that letters make. In this way, through training the senses of hand and eye, and learning the sounds of letters, the child is ready to write. Maria Montessori writes of the need to *involve* the child and encourage him to persevere over puzzles that involve the use of hands and eyes, and illustrates this by telling of a boy aged two and a half who kept up a game with letter shapes for three quarters of an hour (or 'pushing them about a bit', as Waugh would say).

For a young child, learning to write begins with playing with his hands, eyes and brain in order to move, manipulate and test the physical limits of things. The necessary control of hand muscles for writing comes through drawing, painting, scribbling, Lego, jigsaws, play with Plasticine, catching a ball, using knife, fork and spoon, dressing, cutting and sticking scrapbooks and so on. One young child loved to tear pages of coloured magazines into small pieces. 'She's only testing the physical limits of things,' said her parent to a dissaproving onlooker. Later the child found the process of using a pencil quite easy, and now works as an editor on a glossy magazine (which from time to time she says she still feels tempted to tear into small pieces).

According to the Montessori method a child naturally moves from writing to reading, usually at around the age of four or five. If a child is interested in words he should be given every opportunity to draw or scribble with pens, pencils, crayons or chalks. Letters are made up of straight lines and circles. Straight lines are horizontal (lying down) or vertical (standing up). Point out horizontal and vertical things. Collect circles and round things. Teach your young child to draw a circle from the two o'clock position clockwise and anti-clockwise. Practise other patterns—loops, arches, curves, diagonals, hooks, zigzags, any pattern he can invent or copy from you. Draw the patterns of real things like driving rain, billows of smoke, dotty ladybirds, curved moons, spiral snails, pin-people, animal tails and kisses (xxx).

Buy letters such as an alphabet tray (letters that fit into a moulded tray), and magnetic letters to stick on a fridge or other metal surface. Spell out your child's name in letters. Write your child's name, and let him trace it in different colours to create a rainbow effect. Teach him the small (lower case) letters first, rather than capitals. Check which kind of writing style they use at the school which your child does or will attend. The first word written by my children, wrote Maria Montessori, 'aroused in my little ones an indescribable emotion of joy.'

For some children reading comes first. They may find the manual skill required for writing much harder than reading words on a page. Do not expect your child to write at the same level as he can read. Writing is a more demanding task. Be grateful for his progress in either skill and help him when you can. Sometimes, if children are not taught how to write, they will try to work it out for themselves. Gary, aged five, worked out his own method for writing. He held his pencil quite still while moving the paper round to make letter shapes. An ingenious but cumbersome method. It was time to show him an easier way to write. He didn't need to be told what to do, but given practical activities so that he could come to know in himself what writing was and whether he could do it.

If your child is unwilling to write, act as his scribe and show him what writing is by doing it for him. Let your child dictate his stories, letters or ideas for you to write. Simply say, 'You tell me what to write down and we will read it back together.' Don't be surprised if he finds it difficult. It took people many thousands of years to learn how to read and write. Your child is trying to fit thousands of years of human development into only a few years, so be patient.

Handwriting, like spelling, is a skill that needs to become automatic. Using a computer frees a child from the chore of handwriting. To write well, either on the screen or on a page, requires much practice. The mark of successful learning is the gradual mastery of the skill, through practice and guidance, trial and error. Expect your child to make mistakes. Praise effort. Remember what is important is the message, not how it was produced. Many great writers, like doctors, have very poor handwriting. Many make spelling mistakes. What they have all had is a reader who is sympathetic and involved in what they are trying to say.

From childhood into adolescence your child should be writing more—more clearly, more fluently and more quickly. He should be developing a 'best hand' for handwriting that is easy to read, and a 'fast hand' for quick notes (the sort of notes your doctor writes that are hard to read). To create a fast hand means joining as many letters as possible. Older children often like to test their speedwriting skill.

Here is a test of speedwriting you or your child might like to try:

Speedwriting test
Write a sentence that contains all the letters of the alphabet, such as 'The quick brown fox jumps over the lazy dog', as often as you can in one minute. When you have finished count how many letters you have written. The sentence above ('The quick brown fox . . . dog') contains 35 letters. The number you write, which somebody else can read, is your speedwriting score of words per minute. For a child of 8–10 years less than 80 words per minute is not very good, 100

words is fair, 120 is good, and over 175 is very good for an adult.

Another sentence which contains every letter of the alphabet is 'The five boxing wizards jump quickly'. After speed-writing try an older child on a speed-typing test.

Remember, no writer can write as fast as he or she can think. The aim for your child is that her ability to write should allow her to capture her thoughts and put them down on paper. The need is for fast, fluent writing, not slow and painstaking neatness, but it may take a long time to develop. Children who have messy, poorly co-ordinated handwriting may also have problems in spelling, so how can you help with spelling?

Questions about spelling that parents often ask include:

'Why does my child misspell words even after I've shown her the right way?'

'Why do some children find it easy to spell while others don't?'

'Why is it that good readers are sometimes poor spellers?' Spelling is a very different skill from reading. Many of us can say we can read anything, but few of us can say we can spell anything. In reading we can guess at some words, and leave words out. If we make a mistake in reading nobody knows, but in spelling mistakes on paper are there for all to see. In reading we get a lot of help from other words in a sentence, but we get no such help in spelling. Spelling is different from and harder than reading. That is why some good readers are not necessarily good at spelling. Your child is not odd if she can read but not spell. The trouble with spelling is that there are many possible ways of spelling any word. What to us is obviously the right spelling may not be at all obvious to your child.

We all have words which we find difficult to spell. Spelling is not 'child's play' for any of us: we can all make mistakes. Words can go rusty if they are not in regular use. Our ability in spelling is not an indication of intelligence, nor is poor spelling due to laziness. We can try really hard and still spell words wrongly. We have different ways of remembering the words that we spell. The words that trouble you may not

Did you know . . . ?
There are thousands of ways of spelling the name
Shakespeare so that it still sounds like Shakespeare.
William Shakespeare spelt his name in various ways—
eleven in all. There is no authentic way of spelling
Will's name. Here are some alternatives:

Shakespeare   Shakspayr   Shakespear
Shackspur   Shakespiere   Shaxpur   Shaxspeare
Shakespere   Shaxpere   Shaksper   Shaxpeire
Schakspier, etc.   *Shespeer*

*How many different ways can you find of spelling
your child's (or your own) name that sound right?*

trouble others in your family and your ways of remembering
words may not be the same as theirs. Which words cause
you problems in spelling? How do you remember the spelling
of problem words? What can you do to improve spelling?

Many schools use a routine called Look-Cover-Write-
Check, which aims to give all children a way to learn how
to spell 'problem' words, with mixed results. The trouble is
that if children do not see the point of a drill or routine they
are unlikely to practise it on their own sufficiently for it to
become automatic. It is best if children are shown the different ways we learn to spell, and encouraged to find their own
successful methods of remembering spellings. What is needed
is the multi-thinking HEAD START approach, where the
learner is encouraged to stop and think and use all her facul-
ties of intelligence to aid her learning.

Here is what a teacher using this approach might say to a
child struggling to learn how to spell a word: 'Let us try to
learn this word in every way we can think of. You can learn
it with your eyes by looking at it carefully, closing your eyes
and trying to picture it in your mind. You can learn with
your ears, by spelling it out and listening to how it sounds.
You can learn it by hand, when you write it down. You can
think about the bit of the word that is hard to spell and think

of a trick to remember it. Let us see if we can find the best way for you to remember it.'

What this teacher is doing is trying to help the child find a strategy, the best strategy for the child, in learning to spell, through a thinking approach using visual (looking), verbal (saying), or physical (writing) means. The main strategies to think about are 'see, say, do, and review':

- *See*
  Look at the word and try to get a picture of it, or as one teacher says: Take a photo of it in your head! Cover it, and try to write it from how you remember it looks.
- *Say*
  Look at the word, read it and say it slowly in syllables (e.g. 're-mem-ber'). Spell it out in letters, and listen carefully. Spell it again without looking at the word. Check to see if you were right.
- *Do: write and check*
  Copy the word several times (in joined writing if possible), then write it without looking at the word. Write it carefully. Check to see if you got it right.
- *Review: think it through*
  Ask yourself: What part(s) do you spell wrong? Think about the tricky bits (underline them, or highlight them in colour). Now you don't have to learn the whole word, only the tricky bits!

One personal trick that helps some people remember the difficult words they need is through mnemonics (the 'mn' could stand for 'memory nudge'). For example some people remember how to spell 'necessary' by remembering the mnemonic: 'never eat cake eat salmon sandwiches and remain young'. Some people remember to spell 'stationery' by thinking of the problem 'e' for 'envelope'. Some children remember to spell 'Wednesday' by saying it as it sounds ('Wed-nes-day'). One child remembered one of her problem words, 'people', by inventing the mnemonic 'people eat oranges, pigeons lay eggs'.

Learning some spelling rules may help. The trouble with the English language is that some words do not follow the rules. There are a lot of rules to learn and they can easily confuse a young child. Some rules, like 'q' is always followed by 'u', may be useful. If in doubt the motto is 'Ask the school', and look out for exceptions.

Do not despair if your child cannot spell. Napoleon never learned to spell correctly, and his writing was awful. The playwright George Bernard Shaw always found spelling difficult, but being a poor speller did not affect the quality of his writing. Some children get very worried about their spelling, others not at all. As one boy said, 'I know I'm no good at spelling, but I'm all right. I've got a machine to do it.' Of course he was referring to his laptop computer, with its spellcheck facility.

Other aids to spelling include dictionaries. These are difficult to use if your child has problems with alphabetical order. Using the telephone directory, an address book or index will help with this. Why not buy an A–Z address book, and use it to store the words that your child asks to spell. You can also include any mnemonics to help the memory. Play a quick dictionary game—ask your child to open the dictionary anywhere, say a word and ask, 'Do you need to turn forward or back?'

Good writing and spelling develop if there is a reason to write. All writers need encouragement, be they best-selling authors or infants struggling with their first words. Develop the writing habit by trying to provide some reasons for writing at home.

Here are some ideas for developing the writing habit for a child who can write.

- *The story of my life*
  Every family has a history and every child his or her own life story. Use photos, drawings and mementos and record in writing the time, place and events that happened.
- *Calendar*
  Older children can fill in a daily calendar, for example a calendar of TV programmes to watch. Create a calendar for a young child, for example from a large notepad.
- *Diary*
  A holiday diary is a good way to show the value of keeping a diary. Buy a diary each year for your child—one day he might write something in it, as you once did.

- *Invitations*
  Ask him to write in the greetings or invitation cards to send to friends and family.
- *Letters*
  Write a letter to your child. Encourage him to write to family and friends who are far away, or to add something to any letters you write. Try to link your child to a pen-friend.
- *Memos*
  Write memos to your child. Encourage him to write lists of things to remember. Give him a private book for his own memos, thoughts or stories.
- *Stories, poems and songs*
  Encourage your child to write a story for a younger brother or sister, or to send to a friendly relative. Collect the stories, playscripts or poems he writes in a scrapbook, or pin them up.
- *Local guide*
  Create a local guide for your area for visitors, or to send to a penfriend, giving descriptions of local places of interest, illustrated with photos, pictures, drawings and maps.
- *Create a magazine or newspaper*
  Why not try to create your own newspaper or magazine? Begin by identifying a purpose and audience for your publication, for example a magazine about a favourite hobby, or a Christmas newsletter to send to family or friends. Plan what it could include. Think of a title and how it will be put together, and write on!
- *Competitions*
  Competitions from television, newspapers, magazines and comics can also create reasons for writing. Hold your own competition—for example, how many uses can you think of for a brick? (a creative ten-year-old may think of up to 30)—with a prize or reward at the end.

There should be many outlets for your child's creative writing, both at home and school. More and more child authors are getting published. Dorothy Straight was aged four when she published her book *How the World Began*. Janet Aitchison was five when her story 'The Pirate's Tail' was published

---

Did you know . . . ?
Sometimes those with very good linguistic intelligence
do not do well at school. The poet Dylan Thomas
was one such child. He liked to play truant from
school. One afternoon, when he was 'bunking' off, he
was caught by one of his masters. 'Where are you
going?' he was asked. 'To write poetry,' said Dylan.
'Well,' said the master, 'make sure you don't get
caught!'

---

in a magazine. Jayne Fisher was nine when a series of stories
she wrote about fruit and vegetable characters, called *The
Garden Gang*, was published, illustrated with her own felt-tip
drawings. What is common to all these children is that being
given encouragement at home, and a reason to write from
an early age, had helped to reveal their creative gifts.

KEY IDEA: INSPIRE YOUR CHILD TO WRITE FOR REAL REASONS

SEVEN STEPS TO LINGUISTIC INTELLIGENCE

- Encourage your child to stop and think, and think things through.
- Help your child to talk more and listen carefully.
- Give reasons for what you say, and ask your child for reasons.
- Play word games, introduce new words and increase your child's word power.
- Read to your child, and encourage him to read books, comics, magazines.
- Discuss what she thinks of stories, poems and other kinds of reading.
- Inspire your child to write stories, letters and personal memos for real reasons.

3   Number Sense

developing mathematical intelligence

A child of the new generation
Refused to learn multiplication
He said, 'Don't conclude
That I'm being rude;
I am simply without motivation.'
                                    Anon.

If numbers make you numb what do more numbers make you?
                                    Child, aged 10

Jane was out shopping with her mother in a supermarket. She followed her mother round, not allowed to touch anything or ask any questions, while her mother busied herself looking for things on her list. Suddenly her mother saw something that was not on her list. It was a rack of maths workbooks. Happily she picked one from the shelves and put it in her trolley. The book was full of sums which she would get Jane to do later. She had wanted something to help Jane with her maths. What she did not realise was that the supermarket contained more important basic materials for maths learning than any workbook she could buy.

Maths is about the world we live in. Maths is about what we see and handle. Maths is about living and helping us to solve the problems of life. Maths is shopping for a dozen eggs and two and a half kilos (five and a half pounds) of potatoes, sharing chocolate with friends or seeing what size of shoe you need. Maths is sorting your pocket money, buying something and seeing what's left. Maths is about seeing how much to save each week to buy yourself that gift you always wanted. Maths is counting out and planting seeds in the garden. Maths is weighing the flour you need for baking. Maths is checking the football pools, measuring the material for a dress, shopping for the best bargain, and many other daily activities.

Many parents feel anxious about maths. It is the only area of school work which causes a recognised 'phobia', called 'maths phobia'. For some parents maths is the subject they hated most at school. It is a subject in which many feel a failure, a secret garden to which they could never find the key. The good news is that it need not be like this for your child. Even if you were never any good at maths, or your child is not taught maths the way you were, you can help him find the key to the garden. Whatever bad memories you may have, you can start afresh at maths, and help show your child some of its magic.

WHAT IS MATHEMATICAL INTELLIGENCE?

A man called Mr X has a strange condition of the brain. He cannot tell the difference between odd and even numbers. He knows that five plus seven do not equal nineteen, but thinks two and two are three. He thinks a year contains about 350 days, that an hour is made up of about 50 minutes and that a dozen is somewhere between six and ten. Mr X had a bad fall and lost much of the left hemisphere of his brain and suffers from a rare neurological condition called acalculia which disrupts his understanding of numbers.

There is a region in the brain that acts like a primitive calculator, and gives us the ability to use numbers with precision. We are all born with this number sense. This bit of brain, located in the inferior parietal cortex just above and behind each ear, gives us the ability to understand numbers. It enables us to estimate that seven times eight is somewhere around 50, but it takes years of practice to know the accurate answer is 56. Babies are born with a rudimentary understanding of number, but it takes years for their innate mathematical intelligence to develop. For this to happen they need help at home and school.

Humans are not alone in having some innate knowledge of numbers. Experiments with animals show that rats, pigeons and chimpanzees have a very primitive sense of number. Babies as young as five months have the logic to work out that one and one are two. If you show a baby two puppets, then cover the puppets with a curtain, and remove one of the puppets, when you lift the curtain the child may well look for the missing puppet. There were two puppets, there is now one puppet, there should be one more puppet. We do not know for sure but it seems from such experiments that young children's brains are wired for the simple logic of addition and subtraction. This is equally true of boys and girls.

Mathematical intelligence gives your child the ability to understand numbers and to describe the world with numbers. One way we describe the world is through measuring it, such as the measures we use in a recipe. Another way is through understanding the relationship between shapes, such as the shapes that make up a pattern for a dress. This number sense is involved in many aspects of running a home and in most jobs. We need to know about numbers, shapes and measurement in the home, in banks, shops and all kinds of service industry and also in engineering, technical jobs and using computers.

Mathematical intelligence is involved in solving many practical problems in life. For example:

- Danny is saving up to buy a new bike. He knows the price and how much he has saved. All he must do is to work out how much more he needs, then he'll know how much to ask for on his birthday.

- Carla wants to go with her friends on a journey to a distant part of town. She must work out the train times so they know when they will arrive and when to leave to ensure they catch the last train home.

- Tony is going to buy a new computer. He has information on many different models. They are different prices, with different extras and some special deals. He needs to compare the models carefully if he wants the best model his money can buy.

Did you know . . . ?

When the philosopher Bertrand Russell began to study geometry at 11 he wrote: 'This was one of the great events of my life, as dazzling as first love. I had not imagined there was anything so delicious in the world.'

There are some children like Bertrand Russell who are natural mathematicians, born with a wonderful capacity to understand numbers, just as some children are natural readers. Such mathematical children can be of any personality and either sex. They love numbers (they often have their own favourite number like 3 or 7). They can add, subtract, divide and multiply at an early age. They will ask mathematical questions like, 'What happens if we put 6 instead of 3?' They search out answers for themselves and enjoy working with large numbers. These children need a good stock of problems and challenges to stretch their minds, and this can be tiring for those at home and for teachers in school. The sort of people who require a well-developed mathematical intelligence include scientists, engineers, police officers, lawyers and accountants.

Most children, however, are not natural mathematicians. They have a number sense but find maths hard, and need help at home to develop their mathematical intelligence. How, then, does this intelligence develop?

DEVELOPING YOUR CHILD'S MATHEMATICAL INTELLIGENCE

Mathematical intelligence begins with the baby handling objects she can see and touch, and in recognising the visual patterns around her. Before they can crawl babies will start sorting things to fit into their mouths. They begin solving problems about which shapes can be put together. Gradually they come to understand that numbers can be matched to real objects, that two things are not one or three, and that numbers can be used for many purposes. By the age of three they will have had much mathematical experience through trying to make sense and order out of the buzzing, blooming confusion that surrounds them, trying to answer such questions as: What are these things? How many are there? Where do they belong?

Later they will learn number facts, for example how different numbers can be added together to make ten. Then other basic operations like multiplication, such as four lots of three objects make twelve—or as a child once said when being shown this with Smarties, 'There should be twelve, but I ate one.'

Children learn that maths is not only about numbers, but also about solving problems in real life through measurements—as the child said who was counting the miles on a car journey, 'Why is the last mile always the longest?' And about using real objects of different shapes (geometry)—or as a young child said, 'Why is the circle you draw never as good as the circle you can see?'

All children will learn some maths through the natural exercise of their intelligence, but you can do much at home to make the most of their ability—even if you are not much good at maths yourself.

If your child	What you can do	What your child can learn
Says he hates maths and can't do it	Help him use maths to solve problems at home and help with homework	Finds he can succeed with maths and sees how it can help in everyday life
Works on maths but sometimes finds it hard	Help her to practise puzzles and problems with numbers and shapes	Confidence in using numbers and shapes to solve puzzles and problems

Is good at numbers and solving problems in maths	Encourage him to do logic and number puzzles, and to help with maths at home	Success in maths brings interest and enjoyment in using numbers and solving problems

HOW DOES MATHEMATICAL INTELLIGENCE DEVELOP?

Most people think maths is about arithmetic, which is the study of numbers and operations such as adding and dividing. Maths is much more than this. It is a way of describing the world and how each part is related. These relationships are shown in numerical symbols which describe truths about the universe in which we live. Mathematicians begin by asking questions about the world—about the patterns of spiders' webs and the distance to the stars, the shapes of seashells, the swing of a pendulum, the leaves on a branch, the flight of a dart, the best shape, the exact amount, the right pattern. Numbers are just part of the special language of mathematics, and like learning any language it is best done through using it, and learning it starts at home.

INPUT:	what you do	You stimulate your child by taking an interest in numbers, patterns and shapes, sharing in your child's maths homework, and maths at home.
OUTPUT:	what your child does	Your child sees maths is useful in the real world and gains experience in using numbers and shapes.
SELF-CONTROL:	what your child learns	Your child becomes confident in using maths and sees the point of maths in the real world.

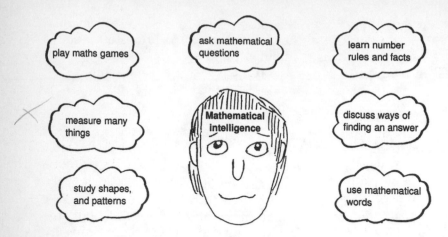

Ways to develop mathematical thinking

WHAT YOU CAN DO TO HELP

For success in maths your child must develop two separate abilities which are involved in all mathematics—rules and reasons. One aspect of maths is rules. In maths we can prove things are right or wrong if we know the right rule and follow it—for example, that in multiplying any whole number by 10 you simply add 0 to the number. The rule is logical, it can be proved and it always works. Your child will need to learn certain number facts and rules, such as multiplication tables and how to work out the area of a square.

Computers and calculators are very good at applying rules. But to know when to apply a rule requires reasons. Children often go wrong in maths (and in life) when they apply the wrong rule, or do not know which rule to apply. Reason tells us when to apply rules, and it helps us understand how to work out the rules for ourselves. More important than knowing rules is your child's ability to see relationships, to reason and to solve problems for himself.

The following example illustrates how knowing a rule does not guarantee a right answer:

> *Adult*: If I have five and give Mary five, how many have I left?

Child: Ten.
Adult: Why ten?
Child: Because five and five make ten. That's easy.
(The child knows the rule 5+5=10, but in this case
applies it wrongly)

Mathematicians speak of pure and applied maths. Pure maths
is about following rules, working out problems in a logical
sequence, using abstract symbols. A child uses rules of pure
maths when doing a page of sums. Applied maths is about
solving problems in the real world. Applied maths is what
we need to use when we are shopping, cooking, making,
decorating, budgeting and working out a route on a map.
You can help your child learn the rules he needs to know,
but the practical side of using maths to solve real problems
is probably where you can help your child most at home.

Even if your child is not very good at maths he can still
enjoy it, and you can help him to put the meaning into maths
by making the most of your mathematical home. Running a
home requires a lot of maths work, to furnish it, maintain it
and pay for it, a lot of number work, measuring and shapes.
The home is the place where the child learns his first maths.
It is the place where the experience of maths is most real,
because it is about maths in real life. Children learn their first
maths the way they learn to talk and read, that is through
talking, listening and daily experience—like adding scores in
games or measuring out the ingredients of a recipe.

Maths at home should be fun. Having fun with maths
doesn't guarantee that your child will be a maths expert but
it will provide a climate in which learning is most likely, and
one in which positive attitudes to it can be developed. Playing
games, doing puzzles and investigations are ways in which
learning maths can be made more enjoyable.

Playing games

'I cannot do it without counters', says a character in
Shakespeare's *The Winter's Tale*

Games are a good way of having fun while doing some maths.
Games arouse a natural curiosity. How do you play? Get

your child to teach you how to play a game. It will help sharpen his logical skills if he goes through the rules with you step by step. How do you win? Discuss the problem-solving strategies needed to win. Is it a game of luck or skill? If it is luck, then what are the odds of winning? If it involves skill, what skills does it involve? Are any of these skills mathematical? (If they involve logic, numbers, measurement or shapes then they involve maths.) Games that are of mathematical interest can be divided into two kinds—visual games and number games.

1 *Visual games*

Visual games help teach your child about relationships between line and space (see also p. 134). They help develop spatial awareness, as well as strategic and logical thinking. Maths, like art, helps us to explore and find out more about the world we see. The simple question, 'What can you see?' can also be a mathematical question about shapes and spaces, and can lead on from shape to number. With any interesting picture you can ask questions such as:

- What shapes can you see?
- What lines can you see?
- What patterns can you see?
- What spaces are there?
- How big are they?
- How far away are they?
- How many can you see?

Every picture, every scene is a mathematical puzzle of shapes and space. With young children visual games begin with simple activities like 'Hunt the Thimble' and shadow games (fingerplay shapes made on the living-room wall). 'I Spy' games, using picture books or the scene around you can include not only letters but shapes, such as 'I spy something round', 'I spy something flat' or 'I spy a rectangle'. As they get older visual games can increase in complexity, using *maps* ('Can you see where we are?' 'Can you see where we are going?'), *directions* (as in a Treasure Hunt, following directions to find where the treasure is hidden) and *plans* (computer games like Sim City where the challenge is to plan your own city are ideal for this).

Here are more ideas for playing games to develop ability to visualise mathematical shapes:

Shape Patterns, with sets of shapes such as equilateral triangles (triangles with sides of equal length), making pictures with them of humans, dogs, flowers, etc. For example, make a star with 12 equilateral triangles of the same size (put six together to make a six-sided figure or hexagon, and use six for the rays of light). You can also make larger triangles with them, using 4, 9, 16, 25, 36, etc. (These patterns are square numbers, i.e. $4=2^2$ $9=3^2$ $16=4^2$ etc.) Older children will be able to make patterns with geometrical instruments—for example, compass patterns—or using the draw facility on a computer. Encourage your child to talk about the patterns he makes, using the questions above.

Tangrams, the Chinese puzzle of seven shapes, can be used to create a myriad other pattern shapes. Tangram pieces originally formed a square. Versions are available from games shops, or make your own version. (See Tangram p. 115.)

Origami is the Japanese art of paper-folding, which often demands great intricacy and skill. Many books show how to fold paper into simple models. Start with everyday objects like hats, darts, boxes, envelopes, boats and birds. The value of origami is not just the fun of folding but lies in talking about the problems being posed and the shapes being made.

Mazes fascinate children of all ages. Draw them yourself, or find examples (e.g. p. 96). Visit a turf or hedge maze. Encourage your child to invent his own mazes. Some people say that if you keep to the left you will get out of any maze. Is this true?

Shape puzzles can be obtained in many forms, as construction kits, Rubik's cubes or in book form—for example, as dot-to-dot drawing puzzles.

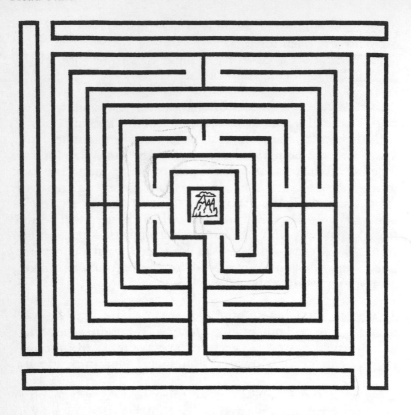

Can you find your way through this maze to the mountain in the middle, and then out again?

Board games of increasing complexity, from simple games like Snakes and Ladders and Ludo, to games of spatial logic like chequers (draughts), Mastermind, Othello and chess.

Outdoor games include jumping games like hopscotch, target games like darts (ideal for teaching parts of the circle), and sports like tennis and football (point how these pitches are divided into regularly-shaped areas).

Dance and gymnastics use shape, space, balance, patterns and rhythm, as do all arts and crafts. In fact there is maths involved in any physical movement. Whether it be in cooking, needlework, woodwork or any physical activity, talk about its maths with your child.

Pencil and paper games like noughts and crosses are shape games that create logical puzzles, such as, What is the best first move? The following pencil and paper games are played with a square of 16 dots:

Dotty games

Start by drawing a playing field of 16 dots, four in each direction.

```
.    .    .    .

.    .    .    .

.    .    .    .

.    .    .    .
```

Game 1: *Linking*
Take turns. Link any two dots that are next to each other, side by side, above or below. A dot may be linked with only one other dot. The winner is whoever makes the last link.

Game 2: *Right up*
Take turns. Start at the dot in the lower left-hand corner. Link with a straight line as long as you like to another dot either right *or* above it. Each turn draws a line either right or up. The winner is whoever lands on the dot in the upper right-hand corner.

Game 3: *Any way*
Take turns. Join any two dots with a line (across, up, down or diagonally). A line must never cross another line, or close a shape. Your line must be drawn from either end of a line already there. Straight lines only. The winner is whoever draws the last line.

Game 4: *Four square*
Take turns. One player marks **X**s, the other uses **O**s. Mark any dot with an **X** (or **O**). The winner is the player who can mark four dots that would make a square (if connected). The winner connects his or her dots into a square.

Once you have played these, try adding more dots, and make up your own rules.

These games involve thinking about shapes, they involve the use of logic and strategy (thinking in a series of logical steps). The value of playing these games is in thinking, imagining and talking about them. Can you, or your child, find a strategy for winning?

2 *Number games*

Every game that involves scoring is a number game. Get your child to keep the score whenever you play—on paper, mentally, or with a counting frame. The following number games are enjoyable ways to help familiarise your child with the number facts she needs to know:

Table buzz is a fun way to learn multiplication tables. Choose a number between 1 and 9, for example 3. Each player says the table in turn, saying 'buzz' for each multiple of the chosen numbers, as follows: 1, 2, buzz, 4, 5, buzz, 7, 8, buzz, and so on. Go on for as long as you can. Later try two tables at once, such as 3 and 5, saying 'fizz' for one and 'buzz' for the others, as follows: '1, 2, fizz, 4, buzz, fizz, 7, 8, fizz, buzz, 11, fizz, 13, 14, fizzbuzz! 16, 17 . . .' and so on.

Number plate sums is a car game. Young children add the numbers on the number plate of a car they can see—for example $375 = 3+7+5=15$. Older children can multiply them—for example $375=3\times5\times7=105$.
The highest (correct) total wins.

Target games. The Eggbox Game is popular with young children. Open an eggbox, write 1–6, or 1–12 inside, one number on each of its egg containers. Try to bounce a table tennis ball or throw small objects into the open box. You score the number on the container the object lands in. The winner is the player with the highest score at the end of a given number of throws. For older children darts is a good target game for scoring.

Guessing games. The player who makes the best guess wins the competition, for example by guessing the weight of the Christmas cake, a bag of potatoes, a pair of shoes; or the number of matches in a box, chunks of pineapple in a tin, sweets in a bag; or the height of the ceiling, the fridge, the door. Guess, then measure and see which guess is nearest.

Calculator games can be fun. In the game *Twenty-one* the first player presses any number from 1–9. The second player then adds any number from 1–9 to it. Players then take turns to add a number from 1–9, but each number can only be used once (a good idea is to write numbers down as they are used, to prevent disputes). The player who brings the total to 21 wins; any player who goes over 21 loses. *Race to 100* entails using two dice to add or multiply numbers thrown to see who reaches exactly 100 first (take turns throwing dice and score on a calculator). Take your calculator shopping, and ask your child to help you check those store bills—that too can be quite a game.

NOTE: A calculator is an important mathematical instrument that every bright child should own. It will not tell your child the rules or reasons for what it does, your child needs to exercise her mathematical intelligence for that, but it will allow her to use and play with large numbers.

Dice games. Simple physical objects like dice have been used for centuries to play games using numbers. With young children play adding-up games with dice using Lego bricks, counters or coins, collecting the number that you throw on the dice, and saying (or writing down) your total. First person to 20 wins. Later play the games in reverse, starting with 20 objects and taking away the number shown on the dice. First

to get exactly 0 wins! Older children will not need objects but can play with numbers alone. In *Number Bingo* draw circles with numbers in between 2 and 12, throw 2 dice, add the numbers. If the total is one of your numbers you can cross it out. First to cross out all his or her circles wins. Then try with three dice and numbers up to 18. Later you can include multiplying as well as adding the numbers on the dice. The following is another good dice game for playing with numbers:

Pig

Pig is a simple and exciting game for any number of players. All that is needed is a die, and a pencil and paper if you want to write down the score.

Players take turns in throwing the die. Players can throw the die as often as they like during each turn, adding on to the total score shown on the die each time. A player can end her throws whenever she likes, adding her score for that round to any score she has already made. *But* if a player throws a 1, her entire score for that round is lost, and her turn ends. When a 1 is thrown the player can shout 'PIG!'—it doesn't affect the game, but it usually makes you feel better. A player wins if he or she reaches a score of 100 or more points. Once you have played with one die, try playing with two or more, and try making up your own rules.

Card games. Play *Making Tens* using a pack of cards with kings, queens, jacks and 10s removed. Spread cards face down on the table. Take turns to pick up two cards. If they add up to ten you keep them, if not they are turned down.

When all cards are picked the person with most pairs wins. In *Sevens* each player is dealt five cards from a pack (with court cards removed). Each player must try to make 7 with cards in her hand (add, subtract, multiply or divide). Lay these cards down, then take the same number of cards from the pack. The player who makes most sevens wins. Play games like this and make up your own rules. Older children can practise maths through scoring proper card games like cribbage.

Domino games. Dominoes provide good opportunities for playing with numbers with young children—for example, can you make a long line of dominoes where all the matching edges add up to six?

KEY IDEA: PLAY MATHS GAMES WITH YOUR CHILD

Whatever the learning game, for your child to enjoy it try to let her win more times than you!

Games like these, and others below, will not make your child a gifted mathematician, but they will provide the good foundations from which mathematical skills develop. As Jamie, aged six, said, 'I don't like sums, but I don't mind adding up when it's part of the game.'

Making sense of numbers

Teacher: What are four twos?
Child: Eight.
Teacher: Yes . . . but only just!

A mother was counting along with her three-year-old child. 'One, two . . . What comes after two?' she asked. There was a pause. 'Too many,' said the child. Until she went to school any number above two was for that child 'too many'.

Some children as young as three can count an impressive string of numbers, but there is more to understanding numbers than saying their names. Jane was such a child. She could count to ten before she was three, but when shown three buttons did not know which number they represented. A young child needs help to convert the labels of 'one-two-three-four' into an understanding of the 'twoness' of two, the 'threeness' of three and so on. He needs help to develop a 'feel' for numbers, so that he can see them and touch them as well as say them, and practice in using them as well as saying them. The 'feel' for numbers is developed through saying and showing, for example asking: 'Show me what it is' and 'Tell me what you mean'.

Did you know . . . ?
The Greeks thought even numbers were feminine and odd numbers masculine.

In the physical world numbers are everywhere. There are daily opportunities for counting with young children—stairs, cutlery, toys, buttons, fingers, sliced bread, biscuits, money. Numbers are in nursery rhymes and stories. Numbers are in objects around you—the clock, page numbers, front doors, clothes sizes, packets and bottles. If you talk about numbers it is likely your child will talk about them too. Some children become fascinated by numbers and enjoy counting things, looking for patterns and learning number facts. Others by the age of five cannot count, and may not know how the postman knows which house to bring a letter to, or how mother knows which bus to catch.

One of the characteristics of mathematical intelligence is the ability to see patterns and relations between things. Try the following Number Patterns activity to encourage an older child to make patterns with numbers:

Number patterns

Choose ten or twelve random numbers and write them down.

Study them and see what links you can find between any of the numbers.

What patterns can you make with them? (for example,

by putting them in order, by making sums from them, sets from them—such as odds/evens, primes, etc.).

How many different patterns can you find?

Counting

Counting is the most basic number operation. The Four Rules of Number—addition, subtraction, multiplication and division—are all forms of counting. Start by teaching your child how to say the number, then give or make him a number ladder. A *Number Line* is a long strip with numbers written on it in order. This can be stuck vertically (like a ladder) or horizontally (like a frieze) on your child's bedroom wall. Start with 1–10, move on to 1–20, then 1–100 and so on. Parents of young children often concentrate on the numbers from 1–10, but bigger numbers are just as important. Other counting aids include a clock, beads on a string, an abacus, a calculator and of course fingers and toes (how many fingers and toes are in your family?).

Number patterns can be made by playing with a set number of objects. For example, how many different patterns can you make by arranging five objects? (Can you find ten different ways?) Games like Snap can easily be made using numbers and matching patterns of dots drawn on card. Board games and bingo will also help develop number recognition.

Once your child can count he can start learning to tell the time, to say what page in the book he is on or to read the thermometer. Such numerals are called *cardinal numbers*. Even more important are *ordinal numbers*. When the clock strikes it strikes in order—*first* stroke, *second* stroke and so on. Ordinal numbers show the order of things. This can be confusing to a young child. Jill had just counted five buttons. When her mother asked for two, Jill offered her the second button. What Jill needed was more experience in matching, sorting and ordering numbers before she moved on to the next stage—counting on.

James had five sweets, was given three more and asked how many he had. Instead of saying he had 'six, seven, eight', James started counting the whole collection over again from one. He had not learnt how to count on. Here the Number Line can be of great use. Once a child knows about ordinal numbers and counting on he has got a basic understanding of addition. Subtraction concerns the difference between numbers, and this can be done through 'taking away' one number from another, or counting on from one to another (the way shop assistants often give change). Again the simple facts of subtraction are best learnt through see, say and do, using real objects first, then numbers on the Number Line. When it comes to sums different methods can be used. Find out if the method your child's school uses is the one you learnt at school. To avoid confusion, help your child learn the school method.

Whatever your child's age, mental maths is very important. The following is a mental maths game that can be played with children aged seven upwards. *Secret Numbers* is a 'mind-reading' game which encourages logical deduction as well as understanding of numbers:

Secret numbers

A person volunteers to think of a secret number between 0 and 100.

The rest of the players have ten questions to try to discover the secret number.

The person with the secret number can only answer 'yes' or 'no'.

NOTE: With a younger child the number limit might need to be lower, like 0–20; older children good at maths might try 0–10,000. It is a good idea if the person who chooses the secret number writes it down, to prevent possible changes of mind during the game. After playing a few times, talk about which questions best help to narrow down possible answers.

The Four Rules of Number are easy to show on a Number Line. Adding three and two is simply '3 count on 2'. The addition sign '+' is simply a short way of describing this process. The quick way of adding equal numbers is called multiplication.

Learning tables

Multiplication is made much easier when a child knows the basic multiplication facts—the 'times table'.

Help your child to learn her tables by *seeing* them (on a tables square or on cards), recording them so that they can be heard, *hearing* them (on a tape-recording of the table being learnt), saying them (chanting or singing them), *doing* tables sums and *reviewing* (identify the table facts your child finds hard to learn and make up a rhyme to help her remember—for example, 7×7=49 THAT'S FINE! 8×8=64 WHAT A BORE! 7×8=56 FIFTY KICKS! Once she knows her tables try doing them backwards—'How many 7s in 35?' Teach your child that the answer is the same no matter which way round the numbers are 3×7=7×3. This almost halves the number of facts needing to be learnt (see *Homework*, p. 17, for more on learning tables).

Dividing begins with sharing out real things like sweets, and can be shown by equal subtraction which is counting back a number in equal steps.

If your child is trying to do a sum in her head, encourage her to make a rough estimate of the answer. The ability to 'guesstimate' an answer with any accuracy only comes after a lot of experience. It is particularly important in sums involving place-value. A man once received a gas bill of £9999— all that was wrong was the place of the decimal point between £ and pence. It is not at all obvious to a young child that 27 should be 'two tens and a seven'—why not two and seven, or seven tens and a two? For centuries children have been helped to 'see, say and do' place-value with the help of an *abacus*. Remember, in the number 210 the 2 is not really 2 at all but 200, the 1 is 10, and the zero is no number at all (it is just there to keep the numbers in their place!). No wonder children get confused with the tricks numbers can play.

Did you know . . . ?
Winston Churchill's father, Lord Randolph Churchill, although Chancellor of the Exchequer never understood decimals. He later complained: 'I never could work out what those damned dots meant!'

Decimals simply continue the hundreds, tens and units place-values to tenths, then hundredths, then thousandths, etc. If we had eight fingers our numbers system would probably have been based on 8 (what mathematicians call 'base 8'). Because we have ten fingers our number system 10 is the key number in decimals and the metric system. Your child still needs to understand numbers in other than the base 10 system—for example, what does this sum mean . . . ?

$$
\begin{array}{r}
16 \\
+\ 5 \\
\hline
24
\end{array}
$$

The sum looks strange, but not if told it means 1 week and 6 days, add 5 days makes 2 weeks and 4 days. Because there are 7 days in a week, we start a new column of figures when we reach 7. This means the sum is in base 7. With minutes and seconds we work in base 60, hours in a day use base 24. So putting numbers in the right place begins with tens and units, and is only one kind your child must learn, and decimals are only one kind of fraction.

Question: Where does 10 plus 3 equal one?
Answer: On a clock, if you add three hours on to 10 o'clock you land on 1.

Once the Number Line is understood it can be extended to include fractions between each whole number. Fractions can be shown on rulers and tape measures, measuring jars and height charts.

Problems about fractions are problems of real life, such as sharing sweets, dividing a bar of chocolate or cutting a cake. A boy in class was once asked by a school inspector interested in his knowledge of fractions how he would find half of five potatoes. The boy answered, 'Mash 'em!' Fractions are best understood by measuring things, like time. Fractions can be made smaller and smaller until there seems to be nothing left. Can you get less than nothing?

For centuries mathematicians could make no sense of numbers less than zero. To almost everyone in the Western world numbers started at 1 and continued in one direction—

upwards. Numbers counted things, and you could not get fewer things than one. It was not until relatively recently that mathematicians have accepted negative and imaginary numbers. However, at the age of four, Paul Erdos remarked to his mother, 'If you subtract 250 from 100, you get 150 below zero.' He had discovered negative numbers, that you can carry on counting down as well as up. Many children without the extraordinary mathematical talent of Erdos can respond creatively to such thought-provoking questions as: 'You know 10, 9, 8, 7, 6, 5, 4, 3, 2, 1, 0 . . . What comes next?'

The following is how a discussion with eight-year-old Jake continued after I had asked this question:

Jake: One?
RF: You mean it goes one, nought, one, two?
Jake: Yes.
RF: So what follows one . . . nought or two?
Jake: It isn't one. I don't know.
RF: Well, what is one take away two?
Jake: (Writing 1−2=1, then 2−1=1) The answer is one.
RF: How did you do it?
Jake: You take one from one number and add it to the other.
(After several attempts at trying to write this Jake suddenly writes 1−2=−1)
Jake: It's take away one.
RF: What is one take away three?
Jake: It's take away two. You go take away one, take away two, take away three and so on.

Jake had extended his understanding of the number system himself, through responding to questions, being given time to think out his ideas and someone to offer clues and help test his ideas. All that was needed was for his natural number sense to be stimulated by questions.

Children are fascinated by numbers large and small. Try asking your child questions like: 'What is the largest number you can think of? 'What is the largest number in the world?' (And if he gives an answer: 'What is one more than that?') *The Guinness Book of Records* is a wonderful Book of Numbers, offering a feast of record-breaking large numbers, minuscule numbers, decimals, fractions, measurements and shape. A great book for some children to be read at bedtime.

Did you know . . . ?
If you lived for a million seconds, you'd only have lived for 12 days (you can check this with a calculator). There are up to half a million hairs on a human head (to check this you will have to count!).

One of the problems with numbers is that we read them from left to right, which gives us the highest value number first (say these numbers to see what I mean: 9, 29, 69, 129). But when we come to do calculations like this:

$$155$$
$$+\ \underline{\ 69}$$

we work it out from right to left. A child with a real flair for maths can of course work it out just as easily from left to right, but for some children this can be confusing, especially if they have not listened too carefully to their teacher, and have missed the basic point. What can seem so obvious to us who have had years of experience in adding from right to left may not be at all obvious to a child. That is why talking through the steps of arithmetic problems can help children who are confused or who have a block when faced with sums. If they think they know how to do it get them to teach you. This is called 'overlearning', and as any teacher knows there is no better way of learning something really well than to teach it.

The trouble with most maths workbooks is that much of the work may not be interesting or creative. This is where you can help at home, even with number sums. Get your child problem posing. For example: 'If the answer is 12, what is the question? How many other questions can he think of with 12 as the answer?' Or you could ask your child to write down some creative answers to arithmetic questions such as:

$$? + ? = 12$$
$$? - ? = 12$$
$$? \times ? = 12$$
$$? \div ? = 12$$
$$? + ? - ? = 12$$
$$? \ ? \ ? \ ? \ ? = 12$$

Number puzzles can be fun for children. They can be found in many magazines and puzzle books. A popular number puzzle is 'Think of a number . . .' It shows children some of the mystery and magic of maths, and is a good way to introduce them to the notion of a formula (or algorithm) and to algebra.

Think of a number

1 Think of a number. Double it. Add five. Add twelve. Take away three. Halve it. Take away the number you first thought of. The answer is seven.

2 Think of a number. Double it. Add the number you first thought of. Double it. Add the number you first thought of. Divide it by seven. The answer is the number you started with.

3 Think of a number. Double it. Double it again. Add the number you first thought of. Divide it by five. Your answer is the number you started with.

Of course using a calculator makes the working out of these steps easier. Children can also construct their own 'Think of a number' puzzles, when they see the principle of doing and undoing an operation, for example: 'Think of a number, add one, take away one; you've got the number you first thought of!' Or of course the ultimate joke: 'Think of a number. That's the first number you thought of!'

KEY IDEA: LEARN NUMBER FACTS AND RULES THROUGH DOING MENTAL MATHS

Investigations: finding different ways

There is more than one way of doing any sum. There is no one 'right' way of doing any sum. Different methods suit different people. Your child will have to learn the methods taught in school, but when working things out in her head she will want to do it her own way. Once they are confident in their own way of working things out children are often fascinated to find how many different methods of doing a sum can bring the same answer. To a child who thinks the answer is easy it can be quite a challenge to be asked to work it out in a different way.

For example, consider the problem: 20 is to 30 as 10 is to – ? Choose an answer from the following: a) 5 b) 10 c) 15 d) 20 e) 25.

The answer given by a thirteen-year-old was 'Ten'. Instead of simply giving her the correct answer, her father asked her why she thought that the answer was ten. She explained her answer as follows: 'Twenty is to thirty as ten is to ten. If you add ten to thirty, you get forty; and twenty is half of forty. If you add ten to ten, you get twenty; and ten is half of twenty. Am I right or what, eh?'

It is very tempting to correct the mistakes of others, particularly children. However, many problems have more than one possible answer. In the example above the answer could be 20, for 30 is 10 greater than 20, and 20 is 10 greater than 10. But neither 10 nor 20 was the right answer according to the textbook. What do you think *is* the right answer?

Even if they are wrong, it is always a good idea to try to get children to unpack their thinking. Here is another problem to investigate yourself and then with a child:

A cock and bull story

In a barn there are some chickens and cows. Altogether there are 24 feet. How many chickens and how many cows are there?

NOTE: This problem needs you to make several assumptions. First, that there is more than one cow and one hen. Second, that all cows have four legs and all hens have two feet—and not as some children argue, that there might be a three-legged cow or a one-legged chicken. Finally, that all the feet in the barn belong to cows and chickens—no other creature is hiding in there!

See p. 112 for the answer to this problem.

Life is full of situations in which several right answers are possible (for example: the five coins in my purse total 75p. What might they be?), and although there might only be one right answer there are often different ways of arriving at it. Solving problems in maths, as in life, requires making assumptions. Often mistakes are made when we make the wrong assumptions, which is why investigating different ways of tackling a problem can be so helpful.

KEY IDEA: DISCUSS DIFFERENT WAYS OF WORKING THINGS OUT

Measuring up

Measurement cannot always be exact: we don't aim to get a recipe right to the nearest grain. Allow some leeway in your child's efforts when trying to measure something. Encourage the skill of estimating—how many walnuts in a jar, how many peas in a pod, how many cups will the bottle fill? Teach the important concept of 'betweenness'. Ask: 'What is the answer between?' If you ask the time and get the answer 'It's between five and ten past', the answer is entirely correct.

Man's first measurements were based on the human body—foot, spans, etc.—and this is a good way to start with children. Help them get the 'feel' of measurement, to get the 'feel' of the weight of a packet of sugar, the litre of water and the length of the room in strides. Never measure for your child what he can measure for himself. 'I like this,' said Larry, aged four, as he filled the litre bottle once more, 'because I can do it.'

Learning about measurement can be split into three stages:

1 With young children it begins with *comparing lengths of and sizes of things*. Which is longer/shorter, larger/smaller, more/less, most/least, etc. Compare lengths and sizes in

---

Did you get the right answer? Did you assume that there was only one right answer? There are in fact several possibilities. Any of the following pairs are possible:

Cows	Hens
2	8
3	6
4	4
5	2

Each of these combinations would produce the right answer of 24 feet.

(If this problem is too easy, ask older children to work out how many cows and chickens there are in a barn where there are 30 heads and 68 feet!)

two ways—'How much longer?' and 'How many times as long?'

2 Using *home-made units*, for example measuring length using parts of the body, hands, feet; or for capacity spoon-fuls, cupfuls, jugfuls; for weighing: any heavy object; for time: a sand timer. Show your child that something bigger is not always heavier. Does changing the shape of a lump of dough alter its weight?

3 *Use of standard measures* with ruler, scales, timers, etc. Have good measuring instruments in your home, and show your child how they are used. Check the weight printed on cans and packets. Guess the weight of something, then check to see who is nearer. Help your child take and record his own measurements:

Did you know . . . ?

Prehistoric man tried to keep accurate records by making notches on bones. Later, bones were replaced by tally sticks. Up until 1826 tally sticks were used by the Court of Exchequer in England to record the taxes people paid. Piles of these old sticks were stored beneath the Houses of Parliament, until in 1834 it was decided to burn them. They were duly stuffed into a stove in the House of Lords and the fire lit. Unfortunately it was not only the tally sticks that burnt: the wooden panelling caught fire, and flames spread. The Houses of Parliament were entirely consumed by the fire.

Investigating me
Ask your child to estimate various body measurements, for example:

- How tall are you?
- How much do you weigh?

- How wide can your arms stretch, your hand stretch, your stride reach?
- How long is your foot, your leg, your arm?
- Distance around your waist, your neck, your head?
- How long can you hold your breath?
- How many times does your heart beat in a minute?
- How many times longer is your body than your head?
- What is the length of your ears, your nose?
- How wide is your mouth, your eye, your face?

Estimate first. Then measure with a centimetre tape measure or ruler (or one marked in inches). Keep a record of your growing child and help him to check on his growth.

Take an interest in graphs and statistics, in record achievements. Find out your child's record achievements—how high to jump? How fast to run a given distance? How strong (how hard a push on the bathroom scales)? Or an old favourite— how long can he keep silent? Remember to encourage your child to estimate first. As Janie, aged eight, said, 'You don't have to think about something to measure it, but you do have to when you measure it in your mind!'

KEY IDEA: ESTIMATE AND MEASURE MANY THINGS

Getting into shape

> *Geometry teaches you how to bisect angels.*
> Child, aged eleven

We live in a three-dimensional world full of shapes, but we have to learn to see, and to interpret what we see. For this your child needs the experience of seeing and the language of description. Young children will need a supply of interesting shapes to play with, to be encouraged to talk about what they are doing and eventually to describe what they are thinking rather than what they are doing.

How many different squares, rectangles and triangles can you see in the room where you are sitting? How many squares, rectangles and triangles can you see in the picture of a Tangram opposite?

The tangram comes from China where it is known as ch'i ch'ae
pan *or 'Seven-Board of Cunning'.*
The tangram set consists of seven pieces formed by the dissection
of a square:

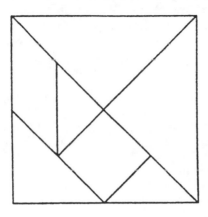

Using these seven pieces it is possible to construct an almost
infinite number of amazing shapes.

A two-year-old, given the right experience, can identify a
tractor in a field. This is a task which requires complex visual
discrimination. To investigate what she sees a child needs to
be able to describe to others what she sees so that they too
can see it. Prepositions like 'before', 'behind' and 'beside' are
needed for this, and eventually these can turn into precise
mathematical descriptions called co-ordinates which are
essential in understanding graphs as well as in map-reading
and technology.

Follow the bear is a useful activity with young children—
for example, tell them the story of a little bear that climbs
out of a hole, over a log, under a branch, around a rock
and so on. Ask the children to act out the same movements
themselves using chairs and tables as forest objects. Stories
such as *Bears in the Night* by Dr Seuss or *Rosie's Walk* by
Pat Hutchins give opportunities for use of prepositions and
developing positional vocabulary.

For older children Arthur Ransome's book *Swallows and*

Amazons describes an interesting positional technique for getting a boat into a narrow channel at night. Many computer programs involve finding ways through imaginary positions or ways to create complex pictures. Ask your child to describe what she sees and does, asking for example: 'What is the exact position?' 'What is the direction?' 'Where is it located?'

Investigate shapes. Play 'I spy with my little eye a circle/square/triangle/rectangle/oval, etc.' When asked to describe an oval a child said, 'It's a circle which someone has sat on!' When asked how he knew that, the child replied, 'Mummy told me.' Lucky child had a mother who pointed out oval things to him—eggs, grapes, lemons and oval balloons. The world is full of regular shapes—circles, squares, triangles and rectangles (squares that have been stretched); it is also full of odd shapes—hands, feet, leaves and shells, all good to make prints with. Jigsaws are full of odd shapes. Make patterns of shapes by drawing and colouring, build shapes with bricks, Lego and modelling clay. As your child grows older, help her recognise more shapes—diamonds, crosses, rings, stars, cubes (dice, sugar), spirals (screws and shells), as well as pyramids, cylinders and cones (packets and containers).

Symmetry is another important concept to investigate. Show how two halves must be exactly alike in shape to balance (like the wings of a paper aeroplane). Symmetry is essential for balance in dance, sports, design and in nature. Investigate which letters or numbers are symmetrical (for example, A, N, 8, 66 or 00). Make symmetrical models or cut symmetrical shapes from folded paper. Is your body symmetrical? Stand by a mirror and see!

Area is also about shapes and what is inside them. Count the number of tiles needed to cover the kitchen floor (is there a quick way of doing it?). Show how to measure the floor for a new carpet, the material needed for a dress, the grass seed necessary for a garden lawn. Talk about the play area, the penalty area (on a football pitch), your local area. How big is your local area? Imagine you are flying above your house. What shapes and patterns will you see?

Show how shapes fit together—tiles, bricks in a wall, a bees' honeycomb. Talk about patterns. Encourage your child to draw her own designs, by hand and on computer. Get an older child a geometry set to help make compass patterns, to design transport or fashions of the future, to draw a desert island or plan a dream house. Try to show in your investigations that maths, in the words of Bertrand Russell, 'possesses not only truth, but supreme beauty'—beauty in numbers and in shapes. For more on the study of shapes and patterns see p. 174.

KEY IDEA: STUDY SHAPES AND PATTERNS

Homework: how to help

> *By and by comes Mr Cooper ... of whom I intended to learn Mathematiques ... After an hour's being with him at Arithmetique, my first attempt being to learn the Multiplicacion table, then we parted till tomorrow.*
> Samuel Pepys, aged 29, diary entry for 4 July, 1662

Learning tables
Sometime at primary school your child is going to be asked to learn multiplication tables, sometimes called the 'times tables', along with other number facts in maths. Your child's school may ask you to help at home, or to learn a times table like the 'five times table' for homework. The best way to help, as in spellings, is little and often. If your child has not been given a sheet, write out the relevant table or number facts and utilise all his modes of learning in the *see, say, do, review* pattern for five or ten minutes:

- *See*
  Get your child to look carefully at the number pattern or table to be learnt (visual intelligence).
- *Say*
  You, your child or both of you say it out loud and then to yourself. Repeat as often as you need. Say the whole table, that is 'once five is five, two fives are ten ...' and so on. Not just the answers '5, 10, 15 ...' etc. (use verbal intelligence).
- *Do*
  Cover the numbers and ask your child to say the table or

117

sum from memory, giving help if he gets stuck, or to write them out from memory (physical/kinaesthetic intelligence).

● *Review*
Once your child is confident at saying the table from beginning to end, ask different parts of the table—for example, 'What are seven fives?' 'What are three fives?' 'What are nine fives?'

Remember that part of the purpose of review is to praise success, as this is the best kind of motivation. If this does not work and your child is struggling or reluctant, then try a reward system such as a treat for every time a table is learnt. Make the practice regular—a short time every day is best—and do not move on until he is confident in what he has learnt. Do not forget to revise previous tables as well as learning new ones. No matter how well the information is memorised, if it is not used it will fade. Do not be surprised or irritated if your child forgets what he has previously learnt—we all forget what we do not practise. What is true for us the older we get is also true for our children—'Use it or lose it!'

Did you know . . . ?

In any group of 30 or more randomly chosen people, or children in a class, what is the chance that two of them will have the same birthday? Strangely the answer is more often than not. Mathematicians who have studied probability theory (and birthday parties) have proved this to be true. Try some research yourself. Ask people when their birthdays are and stop when you find two with the same one.

The following are some questions to help extend your child's thinking about his maths homework. The aim is not to ask your child all the questions, but to ask different kinds of question on different occasions both to show your interest and to support his mathematical thinking. It is better to have one question that provokes an interesting answer than to ask many questions and get little response. Here are some homework questions you could ask:

Maths homework: some questions to ask

- How are you going to tackle this?
- What do you need to find out, or to do?
- What kind of maths is it?
- What method are you going to use?
- What do you think the answer will be?
- Can you explain what you have to do (or have done)?
- What did you do last time? What is different this time?
- Why not make a guess and check if it works?
- How did you get the answer?
- What are you going to try next?
- Have you checked your answer? Why, or why not?
- What have you found out?

Tests and exams
Throughout school your child will be faced with tests and exams. Some parents will think their children are being tested too little, and some that they are being tested too much. Try to show your concern and interest, but not your anxiety— like a fever this can be catching, or in the words of a twelve-year-old 'a real wind-up'. What, then, is the best way to help?

The best way is to practise short tests at home in the comfort of your own kitchen or at the dining-room table. The school may give you maths problems at the right level to practise at home. The whole point of assessing the progress of children is for them to do the work on their own. See how far your child can get without your help. Try to keep the test short. Then let him do something restful or relaxing. Do not have a coaching session immediately after a test, save this for another time.

If my child is stuck, how do I help?
One of the interesting things about maths is that it can be done in different ways. This is helpful to remember when your child gets stuck or has a problem. Sometimes it helps for a child to work out a problem in different ways, using

different mental processes—the physical, verbal, visual and symbolic. Questions to ask might be:

'Can you show me how to do it?' (physical)
'Can you tell me how to do it?' (verbal)
'Can you draw it or see how it looks?' (visual)

We know that memory is helped if we can use our different senses, what is called a multisensory approach. Without the use of different ways of processing knowledge, maths experience can remain muddled and fragmentary in your child's mind. Most textbooks emphasise the symbolic (using numbers and signs). Teachers rarely have enough time to talk through maths with individual pupils. What children get at school, hopefully, is systematic instruction in the use of mathematical methods (called algorithms) for finding answers. These they need to practise, and this practice should include homework. The risk is that these lessons may not be clearly understood (even when your child is getting his sums right!) and may remain meaningless. As one child complained, 'I do these sums but what have they got to do with me or anything!' What we can provide at home is time for talking maths.

Talking maths

A child when asked what a circle was replied: 'It's a round straight line, with a hole in the middle.'

When asked, 'How are you at mathematics?' Spike Milligan replied, 'I speak it like a native.'

One way of coming to understand maths is to learn its language. You may not think of maths as a language but in many ways it is. Most maths problems become easier if you know how to translate from maths to English and vice versa. The maths sign = translates as 'is the same as', + means 'added to' and so on. The best way to learn the French language is to live in France. The best way to learn maths is to live with it and to experience it around you. It is through experience, repeated and talked about, that your child will gain an understanding of basic maths. This means not just learning but 'feeling the language', through activities such as comparing sizes, building shapes, counting and matching things. At home we can help our child work on the visual, verbal and physical levels of learning through the mathematical experience of our daily lives and then later at the symbolic level through helping with homework.

Children often do not find it easy to talk about their thinking in maths. As Charlotte, aged eight, said, 'I know what I mean, but saying it is hard!' At first, speaking about and listening to maths words needs to be linked to practical work, such as shopping, cooking or playing games, so that your child can see what the words mean in real-life situations. Later you can try oral methods alone, for example in telling stories, in recounting family news ('I bought two drinks at 50p each. Do you know what *twice* 50p is?') or talking about future plans.

The questions you ask are important in helping your child understand mathematical ideas, and to practise using mathematical words correctly. What your child needs are not the same kinds of question all the time but different kinds of question, including question that require higher levels of thinking. If you can get used to asking the full range of questions you will find your child giving more complex answers that explain what she is thinking.

The following are different kinds of mathematical questions to challenge your child's thinking in maths:

- *Memory questions*
  What is 6 add 3?
  How many days are in a week, month or year?
  How many centimetres in a metre (inches in a yard)?
- *Problem or puzzle questions*
  How long is your bed?
  How many different shapes can you see in this picture?
  I have 27p in my purse, what coins do you think they could be?
- *Estimation questions*
  Estimate the number of sweets in this jar.
  How much do you think you weigh?
  What do you think the answer is going to be, roughly?
- *Process questions*
  What is the best way to find out the answer?

Can you explain how you got your answer?
Is there another way of doing it?
* *Follow-on questions*
What other shapes can you see (or numbers can you find)?
What does that tell us about other numbers that end in zero?
Is the sum of angles the same in every triangle? Why?

KEY IDEA: ASK MATHEMATICAL QUESTIONS, AND TALK MATHS WITH YOUR CHILD

'I'd understand maths better if I understood what the words meant,' complained Beth, aged eight. Maths is about numbers and shapes but it is also about words. Sadly, children are often expected to write maths and do sums before they have had time to imagine or discuss what the words mean. An understanding of mathematical language is essential for mathematical thinking. If a child does not have the vocabulary to talk about multiplication, division, perimeter, area or number, this will block her understanding of mathematical ideas. The trouble with everyday language is that children do not always know the specific mathematical meanings of the words they are using. Sometimes teachers assume children will pick up the mathematical meanings of words along the way, or assume they know, and do not explain them.

Initially children will hear their teachers use and repeat words during practical activities with real objects. Usually they will begin to pick up the words and try them out too. But sometimes they don't, or they have not grasped the mathematical meaning of the word. A group of children were having a lesson on volume, using containers and wooden cubes to solve problems and correctly filling in the answers on their worksheets. At the end of the lesson I asked one of the children what the lesson was about. He said he did not know. I asked him if he knew what 'volume' meant. He said he did. I asked him to tell me. He said, 'It's the knob you turn on the telly to make the noise louder or softer.'

A useful book to have at home is a mathematical dictionary. This will tell you, and your child if she gets stuck, what different mathematical words mean. Maths is a language and if you are talking maths at home it is good to use proper mathematical terms whenever you can. Why call something a ball when you can call it a sphere?

Appendix B contains a list presenting most, but not all, of the important mathematical terms a young child will encounter in school. She will be introduced to new words in maths at school, so useful questions to ask your child's teacher might be: 'What new words in maths are being introduced or used this year?' 'Are there any mathematical words that my child does not understand properly?' 'What is the most useful thing I can do to help my child in maths?'

What can talking about maths at home achieve? The following are some of the things that talking about maths with your child can achieve:

- *Applying what your child is learning to practical situations*, like working out shopping bills, measuring the right amount, drawing the right shape and solving practical problems—for example, how much, how far, how old, how many, etc.

- *Thinking mathematically* through the use and understanding of mathematical words, speaking maths, using maths words to describe things and as a tool of discovery—for example, what are the mathematical facts on that packet of cornflakes?

- *Estimating amounts*, for example how many books will go on those shelves, how much sugar in that recipe, how many miles will the journey be, how long will it take, how fast can you run?

- *Solving problems*, through investigating situations and discovering solutions—for example, what is the best route to take, what present could we buy from the catalogue given the money we have, how do we share our TV time fairly?

- *Playing with maths*, through games which include scoring, or predicting moves—for example, when playing Snakes and Ladders ask your child to work out which square she will land on after throwing the dice.

- *Mental arithmetic*, by chanting a multiplication table or having a quick mental quiz—for example, on a car journey choose a target number and ask your child to find a car number plate that adds up to it.

- *Meta-mathematical thinking*, which is thinking and talking about what we have learnt from what we have been doing, helping the child see where she has achieved success and how she could help herself become more successful in maths.

KEY IDEA: USE MATHEMATICAL WORDS, AND CHECK YOUR CHILD UNDERSTANDS THEM

The trouble with maths is that for almost all children mathematical understanding is slow to develop. Because as adults we have been doing the sums we need when we go shopping or measure things in the home, it is easy to forget how long it took us to master even the most basic of calculations—and even adults can get stumped by quite easy calculations. Learning to think in maths requires endless practice in different situations and lots of talk—and home is the best place to start. As Nick, aged eight, put it, 'Home is where you have time to think.'

SEVEN STEPS TO MATHEMATICAL INTELLIGENCE

- Play maths games, such as board games, with your child as often as you can.
- Teach your child number facts and rules, encouraging him to do it mentally if possible.
- Discuss different ways of working out the answer.
- Encourage your child to estimate and measure many things.
- Study shapes, patterns and designs.
- Ask mathematical questions and talk maths with your child.
- Use mathematical words and check your child understands them.

4   Finding Out
developing scientific intelligence

The most beautiful thing we can experience is the mysterious. It is the source of all true art and science. Albert Einstein

I like finding out, but it's not always easy. Jane, aged 6

David is staring intently at a spider as it crawls up a window pane. He watches the spider's movement, and begins to wonder about it. Mum is ready to go shopping. 'Come on David!' she shouts. 'Stop wasting time!' 'There's a spider, Mum,' says David, 'come and look.' Mum thinks that David is wasting time. What's the point of looking at a spider? She pulls David away, there is shopping to do. David soon forgets the spider. He continues to look at things carefully from time to time, but there is no one at home insterested in what he is looking at or thinking about. David comes to think, like his Mum, that there is not much point in sitting watching something, unless it is on TV.

Jane has seen a butterfly through the window, fluttering in the sunlight. She stares transfixed, marvelling at its unsteady flight. Mum is ready to go shopping. 'Come on, Jane,' she says, 'it's time to go.' 'There's a butterfly, Mum, come and look, quick!' Mum puts her shopping bag down and stares with Jane through the window. A butterfly flutters by and is soon gone. 'Let's look for some butterflies on the way,' says her mother. Although they look they see no more butterflies that morning. 'I'm glad Jane saw that butterfly,' thinks her

Mum. Later she borrows a book on butterflies from the library which they look at together. When Jane does her next painting it is of a butterfly.

Despite his lack of encouragement David might still grow up to know a lot about science and the world around him, and Jane may, in spite of every encouragement, not take to science. She was lucky, though, in having people at home who took an interest in what she saw and thought, and in her scientific interests. This did not mean that Jane was fed with scientific facts, but that she was encouraged to observe, to question and to find out about the world around her. She was being taught to make the most of her scientific mind. So what is this scientific intelligence?

WHAT IS SCIENTIFIC INTELLIGENCE?

Scientific intelligence is our capacity to investigate the world and enables us in a systematic way to find out more about it. It begins with a curiosity about the natural world which all young children have, but which is easily lost as they get older. One of the benefits of having a child to care for is that they can help us to recapture that curiosity about everyday things such as shells, leaves and stones (biology), and about what things are and how they work (physics), and what happens when you mix things together (chemistry), which we had when we were very young.

The positive aspect of a scientific mind is that it gives us the ability to discover more about the way the world works; its negative aspect can take the form of seeking knowledge for its own sake and forgetting the importance of human values and relationships. Knowledge can be a dangerous thing, as Adam and Eve found out, unless we use it to serve human ends. We find out for the pleasure that knowledge gives, but also because it can help us lead better lives.

Scientific intelligence can help in the solving of human problems, for example:

- Sam walked into a cupboard door. There would soon be a nasty bruise over his left eye. But he knew what to do and why. A cube of ice placed quickly on the bruised area would keep the bruising down. He knew that the cold ice would restrict the blood flow in the capillaries, and the bruising would be far less.

- Jane wanted to cook her pasta as fast as possible. She was late and her dinner guests were waiting. Instead of putting salt into the water to boil, she waited until the pasta water was boiling. She knew that adding salt to water would slow down its rate of boiling (salt water boils at a higher temperature). Adding the salt later would mean quicker cooking time.

- Ben was invited by a friend to try a drug which he was told would make him feel 'real good'. Ben had been told by his parents not to take drugs, but it was not this that put him off. He had learnt about the ill-effects of drugs on the body, and the likelihood of becoming hooked. It was knowing these facts that made him say 'no'.

DEVELOPING YOUR CHILD'S SCIENTIFIC INTELLIGENCE

Your young child has a lot to learn about all sorts of strange objects like sand, stones, shells, leaves, buttons, seeds, balloons, TV remote controls, Velcro, glue, and countless other objects which all have different properties. As he finds out about stickiness, fluffiness, smoothness and so on he develops many beliefs (mini-scientific theories) about the world. Not all his beliefs will be right.

As a child I believed that electricity ran like water—after all, I had heard about the electric *current*, and about currents in a river. But I could never understand why, when you take a bulb out of its socket, electricity doesn't flood over you like water. My belief was so strong that even now, when I change a bulb, I have an irrational fear that a flood of electricity might pour over me. It hasn't yet, but it might.

Developing scientific intelligence means asking questions about the world, and finding out through observation, experiments and theories that help explain what we see. We seek to prove that ideas about the world are right by finding evidence. We can then make predictions and test the truth of our theories. Some children show more interest in the physical world than others. But every child can become more scientific in his thinking if he is encouraged to ask questions, observe and experiment and test his ideas about things that interest him at home.

If your child	What you can do	What your child can learn
Shows no interest or curiosity about the world or in finding out	Share your own interest in and curiosity about the world	That the world is a more curious and scientifically interesting place than he first thought
Has problems in sustaining interest in scientific matters	Introduce and discuss new books, visits and experiences that may stimulate interest	Discovers that finding things out can bring interest, enjoyment and success in learning
Is keen on science and good at finding out about and explaining things	Discuss and question what he knows and challenge him to find out more	There is no end to scientific enquiry and the pleasure to be gained from finding things out

HOW DOES SCIENTIFIC INTELLIGENCE DEVELOP?

Scientific intelligence does not develop by chance. It took thousands of years to amass the knowledge that scientists have today and your child has a lot to learn. You help her not by feeding her with facts but by helping her to be curious and to think scientifically. She not only needs to learn what we know, but also how to discover new knowledge and find out for herself.

The process of developing scientific thinking involves giving your child the sort of experience that will encourage her to find out more (input), as well as helping your child to learn through active investigation of the world around her (output) and supporting her efforts to understand what she has seen or done (self-control). This process can be summed up as:

INPUT: You stimulate your child by helping her to look carefully at things, by asking questions, encouraging new ideas and helping her think of ways to test ideas.

OUTPUT: Your child learns to observe things carefully, ask questions, think new ideas, look for evidence, use fair tests, and say or show what she has found out.

SELF-CONTROL: Your child has evidence to support her ideas, understands what she has seen, can explain it, and has the confidence and ability to find out more.

Did you know ... ?

All great scientists have a question, or a number of questions, to which they would like to find the answer. A question that interested the German astronomer Kepler was on what-shaped path planets travelled through space. One day he dreamed up the idea that the orbits planets travelled on were an elliptical shape, but then dismissed this idea as a 'cartload of dung'. It was only years later that he realised, and showed, that this hypothesis had been true.

Do you have any questions to which you would like science to find the answer?

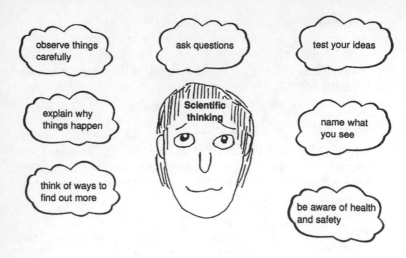

Ways to develop scientific thinking

WHAT YOU CAN DO TO HELP

To prepare your child for success in a complex scientific and technological world does not require hi-tech experiences in childhood. An enquiring mind and everyday activities are better preparation for developing the analytic and creative skills needed to cope with the problems he will have to face. Giving a child the latest computer technology and scientific gadgets, and letting him get on with them, may be helpful but is not enough. The most up-to-date computers and technological toys will soon be superseded. What will not change will be your child's need to use his brain, his ability to perceive a problem, analyse it and apply creative strategies to finding solutions. Your role is to help develop your child's creative thinking, as well as his confidence, through meaningful activities that exercise his scientific intelligence and help him understand how scientists find out about the world.

Scientists work like detectives. They carefully gather and share information on everything they can find out about their area of study. They create scientific theories based on interpreting and explaining their information. Amy, aged four,

130

when faced with something she did not understand said, 'What do you *do* to find out?' What scientists do is to follow scientific methods of investigation. How do we help a child like Amy use her intelligence in scientific ways and scientific methods to find out about the world?

First—take a closer look

About 2,000 years ago Pliny the Elder noticed during a storm that he saw a flash of lightning before he heard the crash of thunder. Both actually happened at the same time, so he discovered from this observation that light travelled towards him more quickly than sound. (We now know you can estimate how far away a thunderstorm is by counting the seconds between seeing a flash and hearing a bang—3 seconds = 1 kilometre or just over half a mile).

Scientific thinking begins with observation. As one mother put it, 'Having a child gives you the chance to stop and look at things. You miss so much, so much beauty and interest in the world unless you take the time to look at it with them.' In helping your child to look carefully at what she sees you are forming the basis of a scientific attitude. Most of our knowledge about the world comes through the eye. We say 'I see' when we mean 'I understand'. The more skill your child has in looking carefully at things the more she will be able to learn and to understand. As John, aged five, explained it, 'When you really look, you can see.'

If you doubt the importance of seeing, try blindfolding yourself and trying to find the correct money to pay the milkman, or finding the right packet in a crowded kitchen cupboard—and boiling an egg can be a real challenge! A good way to show children the importance of seeing is to blindfold them and play 'Blind Man's Buff' or 'Pin the Tail on the Donkey'. More ways of developing seeing as a skill are described on p. 134, and more on ways to develop visual thinking will be found in Chapter 5. The purpose here is to show how you might help your child to use her eyes to find out more about the world, to form the habit of looking, and to be able to attend fully to what she is seeing.

The reason why it is important for your child to take a *closer* look at things, is that we find out more by paying closer attention. Normally we don't look at things in close detail. We don't need to. The brain processes only a small fraction of the information it receives from the eye. The impressive thing about the retina of the eye is how much information it *can* process. Billions of photons of light strike it every second, the equivalent of about 100 megabytes of information. The optic nerve cannot handle all that information; it processes less than 5 per cent of it at any one time to the brain. It processes the main features. It says the sky is blue, and does not record every variation in the colour of the sky. This means we can go through life seeing things without the need to look closely or sift every bit of information about them.

This makes optical illusions possible. It explains why 'eye-witness' accounts of any one incident can vary so dramatically. It explains why your child can see something but not remember much about it, not remember shapes, colours or details. 'I can't remember,' said Anna, when asked what she had seen that morning, 'I didn't look at it properly.' Taking a closer look means helping your child to look at things, as Anna says, 'properly'.

Did you know . . . ?
When people are presented with an object they have never seen or heard before it can be very difficult for the brain to make sense of what it sees, if there are no background clues. When Christiaan Huygens became the first man to see through a telescope the rings that circle the planet Saturn, he could not 'see' or interpret what he saw as a ring.

Where seeing really takes place is in the visual cortex at the back of the head where cells process different aspects of the scene our retina has recorded milliseconds earlier. Some of these cells handle basic features like shape, colour and movement, while others deal with more subtle variations. These cells need time to be activated, and for the optic nerve to relay information about what is being seen. That is why seeing 'properly' takes time.

The more time and effort your child puts into looking, the more she sees. You need to help her to do this, to focus on the whole thing so that she really takes in what it is, the shape, the texture, the colour, and then to look more closely at the details. Try this experiment:

- Ask your child to draw a leaf. Does she draw something vaguely leaf-shaped and green? Now look at real leaves, as many real leaves as you can find. How many different kinds and shapes of leaf are there? How many different colours can leaves be? Are any two leaves exactly the same?

- Ask your child to draw a tree. Does she draw something like a lollipop, with a straight pencil-shaped trunk and a blob of green on top? Now look at real trees. Do they grow straight? What kinds of shapes and colours can they have? How many different kinds of tree can you find?

- Ask your child to draw a flower. Does she draw a straight stem, with a blob of coloured petals on top? Now look at real flowers. What different kinds can you find, different shapes, colours and details? Take two flowers of the same kind. In what ways are they the same? In what ways are they different?

Every year the seasons are the same, but every year a young child sees them with new eyes. Help your child become sensitive to the environment around him. For example: what season of the year is it now? How can you tell? How can your child tell? If it is early in the year, help your child hunt for the first signs of spring—the leaf buds forming on the trees, the first bulbs pushing through the earth, the lengthening days and activity of birds. Every season has its changing sounds, smells and sights, even in the middle of a city. Not only is each aspect of nature ever-changing, but so is your child's human and physical environment. Help your child to notice and be sensitive to the changes around him. Scientific observation begins in looking at the ways things change, wondering why and trying to find out.

Take a young child to a local park to observe flowers and

trees. Look out of your window to study the patterns of stars, and the shape of the moon. Visit an animal sanctuary, local zoo or pet shop to study baby animals. Grow plants from seeds and cuttings on your window-sill at home. Look at clouds in the sky. What shapes do you see, what movement, what changes?

Buy your child a magnifying glass or hand lens. It may not hold his attention for long, but try to encourage some focused attention on the details of things magnified in size. Carry one on outings. Look at an ant in the cracks of the pavement, the bee on the rose, the path of a snail, the grain of wood, some objects found in the earth. 'To see the world in a grain of sand . . .' said Blake. Everything you see is a world in itself, yet all the parts are in some way connected. Your child begins by looking at separate things, and later can discover the connections.

Try making collections which show the endless variety of things—stones from the sea shore, leaves from different trees, pressed flowers, shells, conkers, acorns, feathers, fungi and so on. Make your outings scientific journeys, choose something that you will research, observe, collect, record (with camera, tape or video recorder). This is one way that scientists work. Darwin discovered his theory of evolution by travelling the world looking carefully at things like the bills of birds and the shapes of feathers, recording them, noting similarities and differences and wondering why things had changed and evolved that way.

The following are some ways to improve your child's skill in seeing:

- Play games such as 'I spy'.
- Spot similarities and differences in colour, shades and shapes.
- Look close up with a magnifying lens.
- Look far away using binoculars or a telescope.
- Draw something as accurately as possible.
- Look briefly at an object or picture, hide it and try to describe it.
- Use accurate describing words—for example, tiny, minute, enormous, gigantic.

- Look from different viewpoints—for example, above, below, side on.
- Play with visual puzzles like jigsaws.

No two days are exactly alike. There is always something to say or to experience about the weather. Buy a thermometer, show your child how it works, test the temperature of the air or heated water. Ask your older child to guess the temperature (make an estimation), then measure to see whose estimate was nearest (test the hypothesis). Look at a barometer. What does it say? Is it right? How do you check or test it is right? Create a gauge to measure rainfall (when you are expecting some heavy rain). Having looked at something the next step will be to ask about it. Why does it rain? Where does all that rain come from? Where does it go to?

Science begins with everyday experience, with looking at and thinking carefully about the things around you, with asking questions and trying to find out more. For example, if you fill a glass of water to the brim and look at it carefully you will see that the level of the water peaks *above* the level of the brim. Why? From observation and experience come questions, and from experiment comes discovery and new knowledge. This is the way that scientific intelligence works, and it can be developed before your child enters school. From this foundation he may continue to develop and enrich his life with a fund of knowledge that will never stop growing. You are never too young or too old to discover something new.

KEY IDEA: ENCOURAGE YOUR CHILD TO OBSERVE THINGS CAREFULLY

Stanley Kubrick's classic film *2001: A Space Odyssey* begins with a sequence that shows a good illustration of scientific intelligence at work. The opening scenes show primitive cave-dwellers struggling for existence in a barren rocky setting. One of them sees a bone lying on the ground. He picks it up and looks at it carefully, as a child would, studying its shape and feel. The man's brow furrows. Perhaps he is thinking, What could this smooth bone do? What could it be used for?

The cave-dweller decides to try an experiment. He throws the bone, and as it moves through the air it is cinematically transformed into a rocket ship of the future, travelling on its journey into space.

Next question, please . . .

The children had been on a walk in the park and they had some questions. Paula wanted to know why grass is always green. James asked why roses have thorns. Kim wanted to know why leaves fall from some trees and not from others. All children have questions to ask. Some children's questions do not get an answer. As one mother in a hurry was overheard saying to her son, 'Don't ask me any questions—we're trying to get somewhere!'

Everyday life presents children with some puzzling questions to answer, like these from six-year-olds: Why are leaves different shapes? What is blood for? How can electricity kill you? Why has sea-water got a salty taste? Why do stars only come out at night?

Your child's questions need an answer. You may be feeding the baby or trying to fry the bacon, and you may have to postpone the answer. Try to remember later, and re-open the subject. Chances are that your child will have lost interest in the question, which is why your immediate response is best and most important. Lucky the child who has a parent there to make the most of his occasional flashes of curiosity. Often you will not be there when your child has a question. When as a boy Isidor Rabi got home from school, the first question his mother would ask was not 'What did you learn in school today?' but 'Did you ask any good questions today?' Later Isidor went on to win the Nobel Prize for physics, and he would say it was his questioning mother who sparked his early interest in finding things out.

Teach your child that it is always right to ask a question, though sometimes he must await a better time for an answer. Sometimes your child will be ready for a long answer and sometimes all he wants is a quick response. I would say to my children: 'Do you want the long answer or the short answer?' (Now they will say to me in answer to my questions:

'Do you want the long answer or the short answer?') There is always a simple or a more complicated answer to any question. Don't be afraid of giving a complex answer to a child who is ready to listen. I once met a four-year-old who could explain in detail how an internal combustion engine worked, and was overheard saying to a friend, 'Dad's having trouble with his spark plugs again!'

The first question a child asks is usually 'What's that?' This follows the important discovery that things have names, and this need to name things and to find out the names of things will last a lifetime. Then come questions beginning 'Why'. Some you can answer, some you will not know but can find out together and some, like 'What is a number?', have puzzled philosophers for centuries. Often when a young child asks a 'Why' question it is simply a way of saying 'Talk to me about it'. Some questions that your child asks may not make sense, such as the following:

Child: What colour is Wednesday?
Parent: That's a funny question to ask.
Child: Well, everything has a colour, and I just
       wondered what colour Wednesday was.
Parent: Wednesday doesn't have a colour. Only things
       have colours and a day isn't a thing.
Child: If it isn't a thing, what is it?

As many exasperated parents know, the trouble with an

answer is that it can always prompt more questions. Children often do not understand what kind of questions they are asking. They need help in putting questions in ways that can be answered. One good way of helping your child is to ask good questions yourself. Not by interrogating your child, but by 'talk-alouds'—that is, asking yourself (and anyone in earshot) questions out loud about what you are seeing or thinking. Simply asking 'I wonder why . . .' when reading a story or seeing a picture or looking at what's cooking, will encourage your child also to ask questions, to speak up when he does not understand and to acquire the skill in asking for answers to what is puzzling about his world. You don't find out by not asking questions.

Questions to develop scientific intelligence include:
What can you see? (Take a closer look).
How has it changed? (Look for differences).
Why has it changed? (Think of reasons).

If you don't know the answer to a particular question try to find out together. Look through your books at home, try the local library or the Internet. Invest in a good set of encyclopaedias in book form, and for the computer (show your child how to look things up using books as well as the computer).

Museums can be good places for finding out some answers, even for pre-school children if you keep the visit short and look for something specific (other than the shop!). If you go, try to ensure there is some point to the visit. Think before you go what you want to see and find out. Let your child wander round at his own speed but try to stop him at least once to look carefully at what you have come to see, to ask your child questions about it and talk about what you have found out. It might be a great whale in a natural history museum, a giant jewel stone in a geology museum, or an interactive machine in a science museum. Talk afterwards about what you remember about the visit. What was the highlight for you? What was the highlight for your child? What did you see? What did you want to find out? What *did* you find out?

One of the important skills in scientific thinking is classifying what you know, putting things in categories or classes. Ask a young child if there are more animals or cats in the world. He may say there are more cats! This is because he may have seen more cats than other animals. He may not see cats as part of a larger class of animal. A seven-year-old can usually classify pictures of animals into different groups, but may have to think if you ask, 'Would there be any mammals left if all the animals in the world disappeared?' We can of course tell children what fits into each category in their lives, whether it be cutlery, the laundry or living things, but they also need to make these connections in their minds. Remember, rules can be taught but understanding can't, it has to come from the child. And often we can only tell if he understands or can work something out by asking a question.

Did you know . . . ?

Staying at home is surprisingly dangerous. Nearly as many people are killed in accidents in the home as are killed on the roads. One reason why accidents happen, so psychologists tell us, is because human attention wanders very easily. Helping your child think about possible dangers in the home may save him from an accident.

Question to ask: *What dangers can your child see in the room around him?*

The following are some ways of asking questions that will get your child thinking:

- Ask questions before explaining what is correct. For example, if your child has spilled water on the floor ask: What would be the best material to mop up the mess?
- When your child asks a question, instead of always telling him the answer, ask a question back to make him wonder (but not too hard so that it frustrates him). For example, after saying a particular insect is a bee ask: Do all bees look alike?
- Ask a question that will give a clue to finding an answer

or solving a problem, like: Have you thought of looking inside?
- If you do not know the answer, admit it. Try asking: How can we find out?
- Remember your child easily forgets, so ask questions to see what he remembers from this morning, last week, last month. Praise him if he can remember.
- Allow your child to struggle to find solutions, don't always jump in with the right answer.
- Be tolerant of wrong answers. Always offer the chance to think about it and try another answer if wrong first time—'Can you think of another answer/suggestion?'

Remember we are not trying to see how *fast* intelligence can grow but how *far*, and this takes time.

Use the TV sometimes as a means of discovery. Try to find at least one nature or science programme per week that might interest your child, which you will watch together. Talk about what you are watching. Follow it up afterwards by asking what you or your child remembers about the programme. Use birthdays or other present-giving opportunities to buy something from the toyshop that may help him finding out, such as a science discovery kit or materials from which things can be made.

KEY IDEA: ASK YOUR CHILD QUESTIONS TO CHALLENGE HIS SCIENTIFIC THINKING

In school children will be doing a lot of 'listening to science' in lessons. What they can do at home is 'talking science'. This means encouraging your child to talk about what she sees, smells, tastes and feels; to ask questions about the world, and to try to explain why things happen the way they do. In doing so your child is not only finding out about the world, but also learning how to find out. To be scientific she needs to have something to talk about. You can give her something to talk about by being a scientist and trying your own experiment.

Try an experiment

Sometimes your child will ask a 'What will happen if . . .' type of question, such as:

- 'Can you keep a snowball in the fridge?'
- 'Do eggs float?'
- 'Can you freeze milk?'

Answer, whenever you can, with 'Let's try an experiment'. Rather than tell her what is going to happen, see if she can predict what she thinks will happen. If you are going to try an experiment let your child do it rather than watch you. Remember to train your child to look carefully at what is happening, and to ask questions about it. Afterwards talk about what has happened and why it happened that way. Ask, 'Do you think the same thing would happen if we did it again?' If she is in doubt, try it again. Do not worry if the experiment fails. There is much to learn from things that don't work.

You will find many books of simple experiments in bookshops and the library that you can do with everyday objects, ideal for a rainy day. The following are examples of simple experiments to try with children under eight years old.

1 Does it rot?
Find a plastic bottle, a piece of fruit and a sheet of newspaper. Put them under the soil in the garden or in a pot. Leave them for two weeks. Dig them up and see what has happened to them. Which object has changed, which has not changed? Why?

2 Melting ice
Take three ice cubes. Put one in a cup of hot water, one in a cup of warm water, and one in a cup of cold water. Find out which melts first.

3 Stirring sugar
Find three kinds of sugar such as white granulated, a sugar lump and icing sugar. Fill three mugs with warm water. Put a spoonful of granulated sugar in one mug, a sugar lump in another mug, and a spoonful of icing sugar in the third mug.

141

Stir all three mugs. Which kind of sugar dissolves first? Why is this?

4 What floats, what sinks?

Put some water into a bath or bowl. Collect a range of different objects such as a sponge, piece of apple, paper-clip, fork, cork, slice of orange, yoghurt pot and pencil. Take each one in turn. Ask your child to predict whether it will float or sink. Place the object in the water and see what happens. See if your predictions were correct.

Not all questions are open to experiment. Some experiments are impractical, like the child who asked, 'What would happen if Grandma never cut her toenails?' Others, like 'What would happen if the sky fell down?' are too theoretical, or show the child's ideas are confused. Any child is liable to be confused about ideas or concepts that for us seem easy but for a child are difficult to understand. So it is important not to assume your child knows what things like electricity, gas or the greenhouse effect are but to give her time to sort out and explain her ideas. Children want to make sense of the world and when they don't know why things happen will

---

Did you know ... ?

The first battery was invented by Alessandro Volta in 1800. Experimenting with frogs' legs, he found that two hooks stuck in a frog's leg would make it twitch. This was caused by a flow of current when the hooks (one brass and one steel) were connected by a piece of wire. From this he found that two metals in an acid solution would create a continuous electric current—the battery.

You can make a sort of battery similar to Volta's. If you attach a piece of copper wire to a nail, and touch your tongue with both ends (wire and nail), you will feel a slight electric tingle. The metals and your saliva make a simple tongue-tingling battery.

---

invent their own explanations. One child was overheard in a nursery trying to explain to a friend where his new baby sister came from: 'I know where babies come from. They come from 'ospital. You go there and they give you a girl or boy. You can't say, they just give you one.'

One key idea that any child needs help to understand is, 'What is science?' The following are some of the key ideas and questions involved in science:

Where?   Seeing science all around you, at home, on TV, in town, country or seaside.

What?   Questioning what things are made of, what they do, what makes them work.

How?   Testing how things work, using experiments to test ideas, causes and effects.

Why?   Explaining why things happen, justifying ideas with reasons and evidence.

KEY IDEA: HELP YOUR CHILD TO TEST IDEAS AND EXPERIMENT TO SEE WHAT HAPPENS

Every scientist needs a workplace, and fortunately your home is provided with a ready-made laboratory, one in which an experiment is conducted just about every day:

YOUR LABORATORY—THE HOME!

How is your home like a laboratory? First, it has a range of equipment ideal for scientific purposes—knives for dissecting, sources of heat and cold, instruments for weighing and measuring, running water, various containers and packets of interesting natural and chemical substances. The kitchen is an ideal place to start scientific observation of ingredients and processes. It is a place where experiments in cookery often take place. You don't have to be a scientist to help your child with science but it does help if you cook, for every act of cooking involves important scientific principles. Cooking involves important ideas of quantity, measuring, sequencing steps to a problem, following directions accurately and testing hypotheses. Every cake you make with your child is an experi-

143

ment using a range of substances and processes, a hypothesis that may or may not work—and you can eat the results! As an old physics teacher once told me: 'I became a scientist when as a child I learned to cook'.

1 Food for thought

Here are some scientific activities to try with your child in the kitchen:

- See and discuss what happens when food is heated, what melts, what happens during boiling—and when it cools again?
- Find out what dissolves in water, what solutions you can make (e.g. powdered drinks). Introduce your child to proper terms like *dissolve* and *solution* which will make it much easier to talk about processes, rather than having to describe what happened each time.
- Investigate baking and the effects of yeast, of plain and self-raising flour, try baking bread rolls. Make dough with your young child, with different amounts of flour, water and salt.
- Make your own butter by shaking (churning) cream in a tightly-fitting jar.
- Experiment with bacteriological change by making yoghurt or by leaving things to rot, and prevent bacteriological change, for example by refrigeration, or by drying fruit (can you turn grapes into raisins?), herbs or flowers.
- Study a living fungus like mushrooms growing, or mould growing on stale bread.
- Show how your kitchen equipment works (emphasising the dangers and need for safety).
- Test your child's sense of taste by having blindfold tastings of mystery substances.
- Experience the smell of ingredients in common use in cooking, and describe the aromas.
- Try a tactile test by asking a child to identify various substances such as soil, sand, water, liquid soap, glue, salt crystals, soap powder, flour, pasta shells by touch when blindfolded. Compare and contrast.

- Grow seeds and plants on the window-sill, such as vegetables, flowers, herbs and trees. Remember that if your child is cultivating seeds or cuttings with close observation and care she will not only be growing plants but growing in biological knowledge.

2 Science around the house

There is something of scientific interest in every room, for example:

Electric shocks
Discuss how electricity works, show the fuses (circuit-breakers) and how you can shut off electricity in one circuit or in the whole circuit. Show the meter, and how the numbers mean money! Teach your child how to fit a plug, and what it means to be a live wire. Point out the dangers and need for safety, the function of rubber and how the fuse controls the power of the plug. Show static electricity by rubbing a comb vigorously through the hair, or rubbing a balloon hard on the chest and 'sticking' it to your clothes, point out lightning conductors on buildings. Discuss conservation of electricity—and why turning if off may be good for the earth's, and your own, diminishing resources.

Plumbing the depths
Does your child know where the bathwater comes from or goes to? Hunt the pipes, follow them back from the taps to the main. Show her what shutting off the main means. Study how the loo works, what a cistern is and the work of the ball-cock.

The heat is on
How is your house heated? Investigate the heating of your house with your child, check on the insulation, test the temperature. Show the boiler, the hot water tank, the means of ventilation, the radiator valves. Hold a strip of paper or feather above the air vent or radiator—which way does hot air go?

Your living world
What things are living in your house? Some you can see and
study, others you cannot see. Some are temporary residents,
others are permanent features of your child's life. Study the
living world of your garden, encourage your child to plant
and care for seeds, study insect life, the composition of soil,
the effects of chemicals (fertiliser or weedkiller), the naming
and classification of plants.

KEY IDEA: SEE IF YOUR CHILD CAN EXPLAIN WHAT CAUSES THINGS TO HAPPEN

3 Science on safari

A walk in the park or woods can become an adventure in
biology, a wildlife safari for a young child. On such a walk
teach the skills of observation by example. Your child will
be sharp-eyed (and sometimes sharp-witted) about the things
that are of direct concern like the way his room is arranged,
the party cake or the look on your face, but will be largely
unobservant about the world around him. Widen his world
by pointing out things that interest you. For example:

Spot the bird
Even a three-year-old can learn to recognise a wide variety
of birds (a birdwatching friend has a three-year-old who can
identify and name more than twenty birds). Once your child
can recognise a bird, sharpen his powers of recognition by
asking, for example, 'What colour is the bird's beak?' 'Is it
male or female?' If interest is shown buy a good bird book
and some binoculars, go on a hunt for particular birds and
keep a bird diary. Ornithology may become a lifelong
interest.

Flower power
As Blake said, 'The tree which moves some to tears of joy
is, in the eyes of others, only a green thing which stands in
the way'. The beauty of flowers and trees can pass children
by unless someone points it out. Some young children are
not aware that one tree is different from another. Show the

different types of tree. Press leaves, plant seeds, take cuttings. Many parents are amazed at how quickly a young child can learn to identify common trees and flowers. Part of science is knowing how to name and classify things. Once you know the name of the flower, investigate parts of the flower and the family it belongs to.

Creepy-crawlies
Many children are fascinated by animal life, including insects. Encourage them to observe the social life of ants, the dance of bees, the silver of a snail's trail, the intricate beauty of a spider's web.

Collecting things
Benefit from your child's hoarding instinct. The trouble with collecting things, like leaves, shells or stones, is that children often lost interest once they get their collection home. Help them to be systematic and scientific with their collections, sorting them, displaying them on trays, display boards or in albums, and (if possible) labelling them.

The sky by day and night
Weather is always with us. Whether we like it or not, 'there's a lot of it about'. Help keep track of the changing weather by making or buying a simple weather chart, study weather forecasts and compare them with the real weather. (There is a simple way of forecasting the weather—on any day there is more than a 50 per cent chance it will be the same as the day before!) Buy a thermometer, test the temperature (guess first and see who is nearest the right answer). Study the night sky, marvel at the stars, spot anything moving across the sky. Look at moon craters through a telescope. Can you see a planet tonight? (Venus, the brightest planet, may be visible, near the horizon.) Can you identify any of the constellations of stars? Tell your child a Greek legend connected with the stars—it will help fix the moment and the stars in his memory.

The scientific method involves observing, gathering information and using this to make predictions about the future. When observing or gathering information about things, try to encourage your child to use scientific words to name and describe what he sees. What is it called? What is a scientific way of describing it? How many are there? For example: What animal can he see? What kind of animal? What materials are his clothes made of? What is each kind of material like? What are the ingredients on the label of the food package? What kind of food is each ingredient? If he doesn't know, or you don't know, ask your child how you could find out. Where could we look? Who could we ask? How could we find out?

KEY IDEA: HELP YOUR CHILD TO NAME AND IDENTIFY WHAT HE SEES

SCIENCE IS FUN

Science is not simply something which children have to do in special lessons at school. Nor is it something which requires an expensive 'science set' to do. There may be a lot to be gained from giving your child a science book or discovery kit, but this should be in addition to exercising her scientific intelligence through day-to-day discoveries and experiences. Science involves exercising the mind in special ways of thinking—paying close attention, asking questions, making hypotheses and testing ideas. This takes effort, but it can be fun.

Almost all your child's daily activities have some scientific interest. Take a simple craft like paper-folding. Much can be learnt about flight, aerodynamics and airflow by making and flying paper aeroplanes. Crafts like making your own candles involves learning about wax and heat. Model-making will involve finding out about different kinds of material.

Children are often curious to find out how their toys are made and how they work. Talk about how their toys have been put together and what makes them 'go'. Encourage your child to learn some magic tricks and point out if you can see any scientific principles involved. For example, can you balance a potato on the rim of a glass? The trick is to push the prongs of two identical forks either side of a small potato with handles extending downwards, which should allow you to balance the potato on the rim (the forks act as a counterbalance).

There is science involved in hobbies like music, art or sport. Simple games often involve interesting physical principles— how do you maintain motion on a swing, how does a seesaw work, why should you never jump from a moving roundabout? Every physical activity involves use of the anatomy and physical functions like breathing, pulse, heart rate, muscle tension and so on. (How much air do your lungs hold? Make a prediction, breathe into a deflated balloon and find out.)

We are surrounded by inventions in which scientific principles have been used to make things that solve problems. Encourage your child to invent ideas that solve problems. Ask her to draw her ideas, for example a machine to help at home or a fun machine.

Did you know . . . ?
Inventing things can make you rich. Sylvan Goldman wanted to find a better way to carry his shopping, so he put a chair on wheels and fitted two baskets on top. It became the first supermarket trolley and earned him a fortune. Margaret Knight found another solution to the same problem. After many experiments she invented the first flat-bottomed shopping bag. Her new bag held twice as much shopping, and Margaret became a wealthy woman.

What can you or your child invent?

The future belongs to our children. What do they think the cars, houses and fashions of the future will be like? Making predictions about the future is an important aspect of scientific intelligence.

Most primitive societies had a magical view of the world. They assumed the world around them was not governed by rational laws, but subject to the whims of gods and magical powers. We should not be surprised if our children too think the world of nature magical and man-made machines to have minds of their own. As Jamie, aged three, said about his washing machine, when it had broken down, 'I know why it is broken, it just decided to stop.'

It took thousands of years for humans to work out ways in which the world could be understood through the power of human reasoning. The great strength of scientific thinking is that it can help us predict the future. We know there is a *reason* why the washing machine has gone wrong. We know that if the fault can be found and repaired it should work. We use scientific intelligence when we apply reasoning to the physical world.

Encourage your child to make predictions—for example: What will a magnet pick up? What will or will not float? Which seed will grow the fastest? What will happen if you put red food dye in the water of a vase of white flowers? What will the weather be like tomorrow? If she has good reasons or evidence to support her predictions she is being scientific; if she just guesses, or gives a magical answer, she is not. Being scientific does not necessarily mean being right. It means having reasons and evidence. Good science means having good reasons and evidence. When a young child was asked why she thought it would rain tomorrow she said, 'My teddy told me.' She was not being scientific, but she was right—it did rain. Science is not the only way to get a right answer, but is the most reliable way.

KEY IDEA: ENCOURAGE YOUR CHILD TO PREDICT WHAT WILL HAPPEN NEXT AND SAY WHY

The world is a dangerous place. The curiosity of young children can be a threat to their health and safety. Part of being scientific is being aware of the dangers of the physical world. When I was three I was fascinated by electric plugs. I wanted to find out what happened when a plug went into a socket so I stuck my fingers in a socket to see—and got a shock. Luckily I survived. An enquiring mind can lead to danger, so we must help our children to be aware of the myriad dangers that surround them. A good rule for a young child is to say he must *ask first* before he does or tries something new.

Young children are not aware of how dangerous they or their friends can be. Once a four-year-old was stopped when he was seen repeatedly banging his younger brother on the head with a toy. 'I only wanted to see if stars came out of his head,' came the reply. The child knew comic characters 'saw stars' when hit on the head, and he wanted to see them for real.

Of course we need to say not just *what* is dangerous but *why*. We cannot eradicate all danger, but we can help our children recognise hazards and risks that surround them at home, and in the wider world. 'Never play with things in the house without permission' would be a useful rule. What dangers at home can your child identify? What accidents might happen? What do you do when an accident happens?

A ten-year-old boy brought a mushroom into the class to show his teacher. He and his friend had found it growing in the woods. The boy had wanted to taste it, but his friend had been told never to eat anything from the wild without checking it first. The teacher identified the 'mushroom' as a particularly poisonous toadstool. Each year children die out of simple curiosity to see what things in the wild taste like. Another useful rule might be: Never experiment without asking first.

KEY IDEA: TEACH YOUR CHILD TO BE AWARE OF HEALTH AND SAFETY

In matters of health and safety we not only have a responsibility to ourselves and others, but perhaps to all living things. We are all part of the same world, or as one eight-year-old put it, 'If I take care of everyone I am also taking care of myself.'

But accidents will happen and there is something of scientific interest in even the most unpromising situations. A mother once found her young child in the kitchen with flour all over the floor, and himself. 'I was only experimenting,' said the child. 'Right,' said his mother, 'now let's experiment on clearing it up!'

SEVEN STEPS TO SCIENTIFIC INTELLIGENCE

- Encourage your child to observe things carefully.
- Ask your child questions about what she sees, touches, hears, feels and smells.
- Help your child to test ideas and experiment to see what happens.
- See if your child can explain why things happen.
- Help your child to name, identify and describe things accurately.
- Encourage your child to predict what will happen next and say why.
- Teach your child to be aware of health and safety.

5   Seeing More

developing visual and spatial intelligence

To gaze is to think. Salvador Dali

I can remember what I see, but not what people say. I don't know why. Jamie, aged 9

Jamie is a doodler. He is a visual learner. Tell him about something and he quickly forgets; show him a picture of it and he is much more likely to remember. He does not like to write or talk much. He likes pictures and colours. Whatever he is learning he likes to draw it. Once when he was asked what he was daydreaming about he said, 'Pictures in my mind.'

When Jamie listens to stories he likes to close his eyes and to visualise the story. He likes to draw in his spare time; often these are mazes, monsters and battles. And he uses the computer to help him draw and print off his pictures. He is good at reading maps and finding his way round, but he is not good at following directions. He can see where to go but is not good at remembering where he is told to go. Because he loves the visual he is easily 'hooked' on TV and given the chance spends endless hours watching whatever is on. For him the visual and spatial world offers a source of enrichment and delight, but it can also be a drug. What Jamie needs is visual experience that is more than tele-visual.

Jamie has visual intelligence—but what is it, and how can it be developed?

WHAT IS VISUAL AND SPATIAL INTELLIGENCE?

Visual intelligence is to do with seeing, possibly our most important means of taking in information, and is a key ability for any child. To say 'I see' is often a way of saying 'I understand'. Seeing is to do with knowing, not just with looking. A child's eye may work perfectly well, but the brain may miss or not recognise the visual signals. So a child needs to be helped to 'see' and make meaning of what he is looking at. A TV may work, but it is not much use unless it has good reception—that is the ability to decode the visual signal so that it can be easily understood by the human eye. Many problems in learning come through poor perception. A child may be able to see but his reception of what is seen may not be good. This chapter is about seeing more, that is improving your child's perception, his reception of what he sees. As one child put it when trying to work out a 'Spot the Difference' puzzle, 'Hang on, I think I need to adjust my picture control!'

It is not only what your child sees that is important but also what he remembers. Much of a child's thinking takes place in the world of remembered images. Your child has a store of pictures in the mind which make up visual memory. Having a good visual memory is important in all learning, and is especially important in learning to read and spell. A written or printed word is a kind of picture that your child needs to see and remember. Maths too demands a good visual memory in terms of numbers, shapes and patterns.

Even a simple picture presents problems that need to be solved. Mark, aged five, was painting a picture of a garden. Carefully he painted a strip of blue across the top of the paper, and then a strip of green across the bottom. He knew the sky was up there, and the grass was down there, so that is how he painted it. When his mother asked, 'But what was in the middle, Mark?' his brow furrowed. 'I don't know,' he said. To make a scene or object visible one must first be able to grasp its essential elements. Anyone who has tried to draw or to follow a complicated diagram or route knows what hard work visual and spatial thinking can be.

Visual intelligence is the capacity to see things accurately, to be able to recreate what one sees and to learn from what one sees. Spatial intelligence is involved in finding your way round, and in recognising locations of objects in space, such as a piece of jigsaw that fits, or a route through a maze. We know that the left hemisphere of the brain is used for language, and the right hemisphere for visual and spatial thinking. Damage to specific areas in the right brain responsible for visual and spatial processing can lead to failure to recognise faces, find one's way round or to notice details. Much of school requires left-brain thinking, whereas visual intelligence is right-brain thinking. The trouble with schools is that often the teaching of English, maths and science squeezes out time for the visual arts. It is important therefore to help your child have visual and spatial experiences at home.

Every child is born with visual intelligence. Some children like Jamie are visiles, which means they learn best from visual information. They need to see things to remember them. Whether visile or not, your child lives in a visual world and will need to do much of his learning through looking. He needs to develop an 'intelligent eye'. Any child can be taught to see more, and the more a child's visual intelligence is developed the more he will learn and the more visually creative he will become. This will involve visual ability like Jamie has to see form, colour, shape and texture, in the 'mind's eye', and creative ability to represent these in art form.

Some career choices such as design, engineering, architecture, art, botany and navigation depend on well-developed visual and spatial thinking. Visual spatial intelligence is needed for all forms of problem-solving which require visualising objects and patterns—for example whenever we read a map, recognise a pattern, form a mental image, or draw a picture.

DEVELOPING YOUR CHILD'S VISUAL INTELLIGENCE

Visual intelligence is about using pictures to learn. It develops through teaching your child to look at things carefully, to visualise things in her 'mind's eye' and through making her own pictures. Activities that develop this intelligence include encouraging your child to draw, paint and make models; to look at things from different viewpoints, to understand maps and use computer graphics.

Developing visual and spatial intelligence means helping your child improve her understanding of space and see more in what she looks at. Some children are more naturally attuned to the visual than others. They think in pictures, create rich mental images, like art and find the reading of maps, charts and diagrams easy. They see more in the world around than other children. But whether your child is a visual learner or not, her visual intelligence can be developed, whatever age she may be.

Here are some possible reactions from your child to visual thinking and ways you can help:

If your child	What you can do	What your child can learn
Feels she is no good at drawing or artwork	Buy her interesting pencils and sketchbooks, play art games and puzzles	Realises drawing and artwork can be an enjoyable way to communicate, slowly develops pride in her work
Shows no interest in visual images or in using his 'mind's eye' to create mental images	Invite him to 'picture this in your mind's eye' when telling a story or describing a scene	Uses mental pictures to help remember, recall and represent visual information
Is good at art and design, and has a vivid visual and spatial imagination	Give her new art materials and methods to make pictures, visit art galleries, and engage her active imagination	Understands that one learns more through looking carefully, that art gives pleasure and a sense of achievement

156

HOW DOES VISUAL INTELLIGENCE DEVELOP?

Visual intelligence develops through experience, and this experience can be enriched by what happens at home. This intelligence begins with the child looking and taking in all the different perceptions of the world around her. The brain helps the eye to distinguish different colours, shapes, forms, textures, spatial depths, dimensions and relationships. We are right therefore to offer the young child a rich visual environment. Jane is a parent who does this. She provides her baby with bright and differently coloured toys, a hanging mobile of varied shapes, and her partner Joe has painted a multi-coloured mural on the child's bedroom wall showing animals, a castle, floating balloons and a cow jumping over the moon, in strongly contrasting colours. They try to give their baby something new to look at each day.

They know that visual intelligence needs the use of hands as well as eyes, to make pictures as well as look at them. Their baby will need to develop hand and arm muscles for controlling pencils and brushes. Later their child will be able to use pictures, and her ability in drawing and painting, to further develop her visual intelligence. They will play 'art' games, look together at picture puzzles, mazes and maps in stories; imagine what people, places and things look like; and make detailed and imaginative drawings. They will try to trigger their child's visual intelligence by showing her unusual, delightful and colourful designs, patterns and pictures, and will encourage her interest in art. Their child may never be a great artist or designer but they will have done their best to develop their child's capacity to see, to represent things visually and to learn from what she sees.

The process of developing your child's visual intelligence involves: input (you providing some stimulus), output (your child doing things) leading to self-control (your child learning for herself):

INPUT: You stimulate your child by providing her with a sensory-rich environment with things that are interesting to see and touch.

OUTPUT: Talking together about different colours, shapes, forms, textures and visual information. Encouraging the child to make visual notes, draw, paint and model.

SELF-CONTROL: Enabling your child to pursue her own creative activities. Giving the opportunity for complex visual experiences, like chess, computer games, visiting art galleries.

Some of the earliest evidence of human activity comes to us from pictures drawn and painted on cave walls. Through these pictures ancient peoples could share their stories and give us mental images of times long past. Such drawings were no mere doodles but were the result of close observation of people and animals, and were a sign of growing human intelligence and culture.

In all societies children have cultures enriched by the patterns, designs and colours of their people, The crafts of pottery, painting, clothing, design and architecture reflect the natural colours and shapes of the region and the history of the people. In our society our children are informed not by a single culture or one set of visual patterns, they have access to the cultures and visual experience of the world, and of a variety of cultures. The visual richness of the world is greater now than at any time in history. We help our children by sharing with them the visual arts of other times and cultures.

Every drawing, unless it is a doodle or a scribble, is a problem-solving activity. How do you show what you want to show? Where do you make your marks? Can others see what it says? Drawing involves many thinking skills, as does the critical appraisal of works of art and design. Other forms of spatial problem-solving include visualising objects 'in the mind's eye' (can you see them from different angles?), and playing visual strategy games like draughts, chess and Othello. All of us are visual learners and learn through visual means, but all aspects of our learning can benefit from practice in visual thinking.

Here are some examples of using the 'mind's eye' for problem-solving:

- Mary is reading a book with her mother. Her mother plays 'I spy' by asking her to spot something very small in a picture in the book. (The *Where's Wally?* series of books are good for this.)

- John is about to try something he has never achieved before. He is taking part in a high jump competition. The bar has been put higher than he has ever jumped before. John closes his eyes and summons up a vision. In his 'mind's eye' he sees himself taking long, easy strides then taking off and arching his body over the bar. Having seen himself achieve his target gives him confidence. He opens his eyes and takes his position to start the jump...

- Jane has a problem revising for her exam. There is so much information to remember, and it is all scattered on different pages, in different books. She opens her book and writes in the middle of the page one word she knows will come up in the exam. Around this word she writes others she can remember. She circles them and links the circles with lines, and writes words along the lines to show how they are related. This is a mind-map she will remember if she gets stuck in her exams. Because the words make a picture she will be able to recall it to her mind's eye if she needs to.

Did you know...?
Picasso continued to develop and extend his visual intelligence throughout his long life. By his death, aged 92, he had completed 170 notebooks of sketches, drawings and experimental ideas. These he regarded as the essential raw material for his finished work.

WHAT YOU CAN DO TO HELP

Some children find it difficult to communicate in words, and much easier to describe things in pictures. Others prefer to talk, read or listen and don't like drawing. All children need opportunities to develop their visual intelligence, whether it is their preferred style of learning or not. All are capable of developing their visual skills if given help and encouragement.

The following are key ideas in helping to develop visual thinking:

Learn to look

To make sense of what we see the mind must be active. Evidence that the mind is active in making sense of what it sees is the presence of optical illusions. Look at the drawing on p. 161. The same image can represent different shapes, but only if your seeing brain can make sense of them. Your brain is saying what you see can only be what it looks like. Yet if you are told you can see the same picture in a different way, and your eyes and brain work on it, you suddenly see that it can be showing something else. Children are often fascinated by optical illusions, because they are puzzles that tease the brain and stimulate visual thinking.

Whenever you look at a picture of a landscape you are being fooled by perspective. The picture is flat, yet it seems to have depth. It is an optical illusion—the illusion that the

Children develop visual intelligence when they:

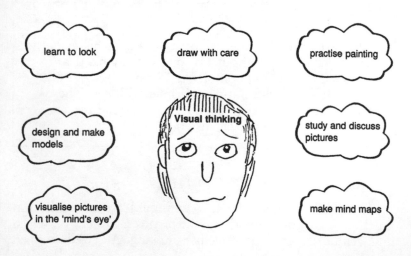

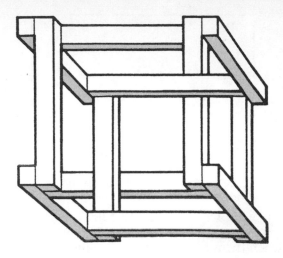

converging lines are vanishing into the distance. The wonderful drawings of Escher exploit this and other visual illusions. The brain's problem is how to make sense of a three-dimensional world using information processed through the two-dimensional retina of the eyes.

In the visual centre of the brain are different cells which deal with different kinds of visual information. Some cells deal with colour, others with different visual features like lines, edges and angles. Brain cells each take in small bits of information; what they then do is link this information together with information in other areas of the brain (such as verbal intelligence to label what we see) and memory (to see if we can match it with items we remember). The shape of an orange, for example, is recognised by one set of neurons, its colour by another, its position in space by another. What we see is created by the mind by combining these bits of information. That is why the mind can re-create visual sensations (as in dreams) when we are not using our eyes, and through visualisation (using what we call the 'mind's eye').

The trouble with visual information is that we may be missing a lot through the brain's habit of excluding information it thinks irrelevant. It edits out what it thinks it does not need and goes for what it thinks is the obvious interpretation. For example, what does this sign say?

```
I

LOVE

LONDON IN THE

THE SPRINGTIME
```

Many people do not notice the repeated 'the' in the sign.

We need to help children learn to look, to look longer, to see more and learn more from what they are looking at. We need to teach them the skills of being able to observe closely shape, size, colour, form, details, markings and so on. But where do we start?

One way to trigger visual thinking is to offer your child a rich visual environment of patterns, shapes and designs. Show him unusual and colourful pictures, patterns and objects. Remember your child can only take in so much stimulus at any one time. If you offer too much, or bombard the child with too many visual elements, this will be as much a turn-off to his visual mind as blank walls. One of the problems of modern life is that we suffer from visual overload; our mind switches off from endless images shouting at us from screens, hoardings and signs. We filter out what we don't want to see, and sometimes miss things that are important, like the flower by the wayside, or the road we meant to go down. We have no control over the visual world of public life, but we can control it in our homes.

Begin with your child's bedroom. If he is old enough, let him share in discussions with you about how to decorate it. Discuss possible colour schemes, put up a bulletin board so that posters, pictures and other visual objects can be displayed or changed easily. Offer interesting objects like shells, fossils and growing plants. Encourage the display of your child's own drawings and paintings. Offer cheap ways in which they might be framed. Find a good place to store, collect and mount photographs. Investigate different patterns and designs for things like curtains and bedcovers. Collect pictures and postcards that might one day interest your child. If you are wallpapering the room, study with your child designs and wallpaper catalogues. Involve him in discussions about how to design and decorate other rooms in your home.

One day one of our children announced he wanted to decorate his entire bedroom in blue—walls, ceiling, window and furniture. He had looked and thought about his environment, and wanted it redecorated. Should we allow this? After discussion of colour schemes and shades of blue, and agreement that our son would do half the decorating himself, we let him have his blue room. So pale blue replaced the colourful murals I had painted on his walls when he was a baby. The ceiling became dark blue, a particularly effective backdrop to the luminous paper stars patterned over it. The rich visual environment of his room became his own. After our input, and his effort, he now has his blue environment.

If you want your child to stop and think, you must give him something interesting to look at. What children need is an environment which is visually stimulating, not the bare pastel walls some parents provide. A child's senses are stimulated by contrast. Your child will spend a lot of time in his bedroom or nursery, so give it some visual interest. Stimulate your baby's senses with boldly contrasting pictures and patterns in black and white, with a mobile, mirror, and picture to look at. Hang wind chimes, coloured streamers or paper kites form the ceiling. Place interesting objects on the window-sill, and a reproduction of a famous painting on the wall. As your child moves from toddler to child encourage him to display his own artwork on the walls. Keep in mind the need to provide novelty in your child's environment, and satisfy that unspoken question of every bright child: 'What's new?'

If you go on a trip encourage him to bring home anything of visual interest, to feel, study and display. Picasso once said, 'I do not seek, I find.' Encourage your child to be a finder of unconsidered trifles, such as leaves, stones or natural objects. Discuss what is special about his finds—the colours, shapes, textures. Find treasures for yourself to share with your child. One old aunt had a fail-safe strategy for interesting young children who came to visit. She would say, 'Would you like to see what I have got in my Treasure Box?' and each time she would have something new to show, such as a piece of jewellery, an old postcard, a shell, a memento, or a small wooden animal. She showed that the small things in life can sometimes be the most important.

A good way to preserve items of visual interest is to photograph them. Add interesting photos that you take, or from coloured magazines, to your bulletin board or personal scrapbooks. Photograph your child's artworks, especially those transient ones like fancy dress, snowmen or sandcastles. Children as young as five can learn how to take good photos, and it's worth getting them their own camera (preferably with autofocus and flash). They will present their own visual puzzles. As Claudine, aged six, said, 'Why do photos never come out the way you saw them through the camera?'

KEY IDEA: TEACH YOUR CHILD TO STOP AND LOOK

Drawing to learn

'We should talk less and draw more,' said Goethe. Drawing, copying, tracing and making pictures can help a child make sense of the world around her. Drawing also enables a child to make visible what is imaginary. Drawing and artwork can help to celebrate pleasures such as birthdays or parties, or enable a child to express worries and anxieties such as the ghosts and monsters of imagination. Drawing stimulates visual intelligence, and can be a way through which a feeling for beauty, harmony and order is developed. 'When I am drawing,' said Fiona, aged five, 'I feel in charge of the world.'

Drawing is the easiest way that many children find to express their creativity. Some children are able to show complete freedom in the use of shape and colour to express their ideas. In this sense their work is like that of accomplished artists. Picasso once said, 'When I was a child I could draw like Titian, but it took me all my life to draw like a child.' Remember that the *act* of drawing, if it is done carefully, is more important than *what* your child draws. The drawings will give you clues to what your child finds interesting or important at any one time. Allow her to use drawing to stimulate her imagination and to play with ideas. There may be some surprising results. A child was asked by his teacher what he was going to draw. 'God,' replied the boy. 'But nobody knows what God looks like,' said his teacher. The boy started to draw. 'They soon will,' he said.

Did you know . . . ?
The artist Paul Klee said that drawing was the most important experience in his life. He tried to ensure not a day went by when he did not do some drawing. He said the whole of his art could be summed up as 'taking a line for a walk'.

For drawing you need to provide your child with a range of pens, pencils, crayons and paints. Try giving your child different materials on different days—for example, different sorts of lead pencil, wax crayons, coloured pencils, felt pens, chalk, charcoal, and slowly try a range of pens. Give your child a sketchbook or notebook. Provide plenty of plain paper, and a space in which to draw. Collect and store any interesting drawings your child does when young—later, when she is much older, she may be fascinated by her early scribbles, drawings and artwork.

Provide experiences to stimulate your child to draw by pointing out patterns, people, animals, cars, houses, trees, cartoon characters that might stimulate your child to draw. Teach your child to really *look*.

Take an interest in what she draws or paints but don't interrogate her. Better to invite her to discuss what she is doing by saying, 'Tell me about your drawing,' than to invite a one-word answer with a question like, 'What's that meant to be?' Darren stopped showing his drawings after his father had said about one of them, 'It doesn't look like a horse to me.' Darren stopped drawing horses, and many things that he thought about remained forever undrawn. When asked by his teacher to draw something in school Darren would reply, 'I can't draw.'

Value originality by remembering it is your child's picture, not yours. Don't expect your child to draw like you or to draw what you want. Respect her creativity, even if you can't always praise it. Remember that signs of development in drawing reflect developments in her visual thinking.

Clues to your child's development in drawing will include, for example, whether she takes an overall view of the *picture as a whole* (the 'big picture') or is just drawing separate bits stuck together (like the child who painted grass at the bottom and the blue sky at the top of his picture). Help your child to see that *details* of pattern and shape, as well as the whole object, are included in the picture. Look for how *inventive* your child is—for example, how many things can she draw starting from a single shape like a circle (a ball, a nose, a head, a hole, an apple, etc.)? Offer your child a creative drawing challenge such as a squiggle and see what she makes of it through incorporating it into a drawing.

Between five and ten years children's drawings often become a practised formula, with stereotypical people and houses. Help your child develop by pointing out different kinds of houses, or ask her to draw people not just standing there but doing things. Two ways to encourage development in drawing are:

1 Creative ideas

Being creative means drawing something someone has never seen before. Try asking your child to:

- draw something that is not visible, like a sound or a mood;
- draw the inside of a body or a machine;
- draw a map such as the map of a treasure island, or a maze;
- draw an invention that will solve a problem, like how to get up in the morning;
- draw something with her eyes closed;
- do a random drawing by 'taking a line for a walk'. What can she see in it? Can she complete it?

- design her own clothes, sports outfit or a house of the future;
- see how many things your child can draw from a circle. Try with other shapes too.

2 *Close observation*

Ask your child to look carefully at a single flower and to draw it as accurately as he can. Buy him a sketchbook and encourage him to draw when you go on an outing. Drawing from observation is a difficult skill. It is the 'doing' that counts, not the finished drawing. Expect your child to make mistakes (have a rubber to hand, but encourage him not to use it too often). Draw something from different viewpoints. Change places in the room to gain a new perspective.

Here are some more ideas to get your child drawing and picturing:

Picture a book:	Ask the child to draw his own picture of a favourite story or book.
Picture an alphabet:	Make an alphabet book with a letter on each page accompanied by a drawing by your child of something beginning with that letter.
Picture post:	Encourage your child to draw a picture to send with a letter you (or he) are writing to a friend or relative.
Picture a pet:	Ask your child to draw or paint his pet.
Picture your designs:	Encourage your child to design his own flag, sign, stamps, monsters, magic castle, clothes, badges, shoes, bag, T-shirt, car, etc.

KEY IDEA: ENCOURAGE YOUR CHILD TO DRAW WITH CARE AND ATTENTION TO DETAIL

Practise painting

Drawing is about line and shape; painting introduces the element of colour. Like drawing, a child's ability to paint develops in stages. The first stage is the play stage. The young child plays with paint rather than painting a picture, while the older child is more interested in painting than playing with paint. But the early experience of play is very important. It is by practice and experiment that a child learns how to manipulate a brush and control the flow and mixture of paint. These early experiments are crucial to later development.

Physical practice in the skills of manipulation are also very important (for more on this see Chapter 7). Your child's hands are, after his mind, his main tools for problem-solving—essential for jobs that require manipulative skills like those of surgeons or mechanics. The first phase of practice and experiment may take many years, even up to your child's eighth or ninth year.

Picasso said that all his paintings were experiments, and he maintained his playful approach to paint into his old age. For Picasso this was serious research, and for your child play with paint can be a serious activity. Even if his painting becomes an overworked and soggy mass of paper he will mind what you say. Because it is play it does not mean that it does not matter. He may be learning a lot about paint, colour, consistency and texture—whatever you may think of the result!

By the age of seven children grow more aware and self-critical. Try to guard against this growth of selfconsciousness. At this stage children often grow dissatisfied with their drawings and paintings—now is the time to help. Remember, your child needs more help as he grows older, not less.

When you do help, if at all possible help your child solve his problems for himself rather than solving problems for him. Sometimes the solution will be in persuading him to persist a little longer. Sometimes he just needs some interest and encouragement. Sometimes he needs to stop and try afresh another time. Try not to intrude if your child is working happily and spontaneously at a creative task. Once he has finished, be prepared for him quickly to lose interest in what he has done. His pleasure was in the doing, and it is up to you to value the finished product.

Did you know . . . ?
The painter Matisse was once showing his pictures in a gallery. A visitor pointed to one and said to him, 'That doesn't look much like a woman.' Matisse replied, 'It isn't a woman, it's a painting.'

Painting, like drawing, is one way your child can exercise his visual intelligence. You are not here to teach your child 'art' or painting but to broaden his experience and encourage his effort. The objects your child paints may not always be recognisable to you, but if the green splodge is said to be a dog going for a walk then that's what it is. Sometimes children will paint just one colour all over the paper. Peter, aged six, got into one of those 'blue' moods. He kept painting blue all over his pictures, more than a dozen pictures all blue. His teacher was concerned, so she asked an expert in child art what it meant. 'He likes blue!' came the reply. Excitement over one colour can be so intense that a child may want to repeat it time and again.

Some objects your child may want to paint again and again, then he will get bored and need more ideas. He may ask, 'What shall I paint?' Hopefully he will not be like Michelle, a seven-year-old who could never paint anything unless someone told her what to do. Her creativity and confidence had been sapped by an over-protective parent. Every few brushstrokes she would say, 'Am I doing it right?' She had been brought up to believe that painting, like everything else, had to be done 'right' and was not an activity she could enjoy for its own sake and her parents see as useful in exercising her visual intelligence, whatever the splodgy outcome.

If your child is stuck for something to paint, talk about things she has recently experienced and enjoyed, such as outings, stories, TV or a comic. Try drawing or painting for a purpose—for example, by making birthday cards, invitation cards or cards for festivals such as Christmas.

What your child will need is a place to work and a supply of materials. Children are usually quite content to paint with whatever materials their parents provide. It is a good idea not to give her too many materials or all the materials at once. A mother once complained, 'I've bought my son every kind of paint and paintbrush he could wish. Picasso should be so lucky, but he doesn't want to paint!' Hold back some ideas and materials for a 'rainy day' when your child is bored. Offer a few colours rather than all the paints and a few pages of paper rather than a whole sketchbook. Try painting on different kinds of shapes of paper, or use boxes, scraps of materials, cardboard and so on.

Did you know . . . ?
The youngest exhibitor at the Royal Academy
Summer Art Exhibition in London was Lewis Lyons
who, in 1967 when she was five years old, exhibited a
picture called 'Trees and Monkeys'.

There are many books which will give you painting ideas to try with your child. Here are some ideas:

Go sketching
Take a trip with a sketchbook (or camera) to a place of interest. Draw what you see, and colour your favourite sketch later.

Copy a picture
Copy a print of your favourite picture, painting, postcard, photo or magazine cutting.

Paint an object
Find an interesting pebble or object to paint, such as an old tin or tray. Varnish it afterwards to give it a glossy and protective finish.

Make a montage
Cut out pictures from magazines, arrange them and stick them on paper, then paint it as you wish.

Abstract design
Take a line for a walk across the paper in any direction so that it forms a pattern with spaces. Colour in the spaces to make an abstract pattern.

Find a space to display your child's art. Take her to art exhibitions. Collect pictures and postcards that one day you will share with your child or that you will let her look through for painting ideas.

KEY IDEA: ENCOURAGE YOUR CHILD TO PAINT

Handy crafts

Children need to learn to see line, shape and colour and also physical forms in space. They need experience of handling objects large (for example the feel of sculpture) and small (such as tiny objects that can fit into a matchbox). A good way to encourage understanding of physical forms of three-dimensional objects is for them to create some themselves, through creative craft.

All creative crafts can make a contribution to visual under-

171

standing if they involve the creative and skilful use of hand and eye. Try to encourage your child to make models to her own design rather than to a pre-set pattern—for example, her own puppets, scarecrows or sand sculpture. As she gets older, move on to more demanding handicrafts such as wood-work, knitting and embroidery, achieving higher levels of skill and attention to detail.

An age-old craft to try at home is modelling. There are many kinds of modelling materials to try, some natural like dough or clay, some artificial like Plasticine. Can your child model her own pet monster? Another activity for young children is to make a junk sculpture by gluing waste materials such as boxes, lids, tubes, cartons, cans, offcuts of wood and so on, and painting or decorating them. Can you design and make a robot? Driftwood can provide an interesting visual challenge—'What does it remind you of?' 'What could you make it into?' 'What would you call it?'

Collages are three-dimensional pictures made by pasting materials like papers, seeds, leaves, bits of fabric and other scraps with interesting textures to make a picture. These materials will encourage your child to look, touch, investigate and ask questions. Collage materials can be stuck to form any sort of pattern or picture, real or abstract. For example, ask your young child to draw the outline of any real or imaginary animal and fill the outline in with as many different scraps of coloured paper or fabric as she can. Collages can be mounted on coloured paper or a background can be added in paint.

Mobiles are free-hanging constructions, usually hanging from wire (such as old wire coat hangers). Cut and hang some decorated card shapes such as birds, fish or butterflies from the wire by different lengths of thread. As one child said on seeing his first mobile, 'It's swinging art!' Invite your young child to make her own mud city in the backyard. Make roads and streets with a spade, buildings from found objects like sticks, boxes, mud or clay. Use twigs for trees. Computer simulation games, like Sim City, also offer your child the chance to design her own city state. For older children origami, the Japanese art of paper-folding, can be a fascinating challenge. Visit a Japanese craft shop to explore origami papers and books of designs to try.

Whether it is imaginative play with a box of wooden shapes or more intricate crafts like making furnishings for a dolls' house, discuss with your child the visual elements of what she is doing—the shapes, proportion, relative size, spatial depth, encouraging her to see it from different angles and to use her imagination to think how it might look. Remember that the struggle with resistant materials is not always easy. As one glum child said about her failed model, 'Why does it never come out like it looks in your mind?'

There are many excellent craft books to be found in libraries and bookshops that will offer endless opportunities to exercise creativity, visual and physical challenge, both for your child and for you.

KEY IDEA: ENCOURAGE YOUR CHILD TO BE CREATIVE WITH CRAFTS

Get thee to a gallery

It is never too early to introduce your child to works of art, or to visit art galleries. We live in a visually rich environment, surrounded by images that clamour for our attention. The flickering pictures on the TV screen and the endless spectacle of adverts, signs and symbols create a visual overload that stimulates the eye but does not instruct the mind. If the next image is coming up in three or four seconds we need not pay much attention. Some children grow up never paying much attention to anything. They don't have to. They are used to being force-fed by the televisual world that surrounds them. Children need help in attending to what is important in their visual environment. They need to be taught how to look, to sustain attention, to take in information, to see details, to learn from what is seen. They need to stop and look.

One of the best ways to help your child attend to and learn from what is seen is to look at and discuss pictures together. This can be done through looking at picture books, looking at pictures and looking at the world around you. Your child will not see the same things that you notice and you will see more than he does, but he may see things which you miss.

That is why looking at pictures with children can be so fascinating. You are learning about the picture by looking for clues to what it is trying to show and say. What you do not point out your child may not notice, and vice versa. So share your enjoyment in looking at pictures, and encourage your child to share his.

If you take your child to an art gallery or exhibition, keep the visit short and be prepared to go at your child's pace (while trying to slow him down by stopping to look and discuss one or more 'special' pictures). Better to see and discuss a few pictures than to trail round with a bored child. Back up the visit with postcards, prints or the chance to look together at an art book.

Create your own scrapbook of postcards of favourite art works from galleries. See if your child can match up paintings by the same artist. See if he can paint or draw his own Old Master by copying a painter's style or a favourite picture. Copying can be a great way to learn about art. Artists have always copied, borrowed other artists' ideas and sometimes tried to improve on them. Picasso once said: 'Good artists copy, great artists steal.' If your child tries to copy the work of one of the great artists of the past he is following a centuries-old tradition. As David, aged ten, said, 'When you copy a picture you have to look really hard, and still you can't see everything.'

Here are some questions that you could ask your child about any picture, to stimulate his eyes and his mind:

Some questions to ask your child about any picture

- What can you see?   How many things can you see?
- What colours can you see?   How many colours or shades can you see?
- What shapes can you see?   How many different shapes can you see?
- Can you see any patterns?   What kinds of pattern can you see?
- Can you see any people?   What are they doing?
- How does the picture make you feel?   Is it a happy or sad picture? Why?

- What do you think the picture is called? What title would you give it?
- Have you seen a picture like this before? What does this picture remind you of?
- What does this picture make you think? Is there anything strange about this picture?
- Do you like this picture, or not? Why do you think so?

To read a picture we need only a seeing eye, but to understand it we need to exercise the mind. A good work of art gives pleasure *and* exercises the mind. That is why a picture of a countryside scene printed on the lid of a chocolate box is a poor work of art and a landscape by a painter like Constable can be a great work of art. The chocolate box picture can be absorbed in a few seconds. It tells us what we already know, and we have no more interest in it.

The more we look at a Constable landscape the more there is to see, to feel and to think about. There is distance, we can walk into it, explore it. When we look closely at it we see there are shadows, details, highlights of colour, and intricate skills of brushwork. When we step back an overall pattern emerges, a balance and harmony of composition. The mind remembers familiar landscapes we have seen. We now have a new landscape in our minds, one that we can return to, like an old friend, which will be there to enrich our future experience.

KEY IDEA: SHOW AND DISCUSS DIFFERENT KINDS OF PICTURE, VISIT ART GALLERIES

Using the mind's eye

The fact that the brain only takes in a few details at a time to store as memories can be shown by the following visual memory test. Try it yourself, or with an older child.

Visual memory test: Can you draw a coin from memory? Choose a coin to draw from memory. Do not look at the coin before you draw it. Draw the coin, trying to include as

175

many details as you can. When you have finished compare your drawing with the coin. What has your brain remembered? What have you left out? Compare your drawing with someone else's. Did you draw or leave out the same things?

Guide your child with prompts that encourage him to use his mind's eye, for example by saying, 'Close your eyes while I read you a story,' or 'Close your eyes and see if you can imagine what I'm going to say.' Or guide your child on a visualised journey to a place you both know. Think of a special place you both know well, like a park, beach or house. Close your eyes and describe a walk through this special place. You (and your child) try to visualise it in your mind's eye as you describe the place, and what you can see and feel.

Here are some games for exercising the mind's eye and developing visual memory:

Kim's Game
Arrange a number of objects on a tray of different sizes, shapes and colours. Give players a minute to try to visualise what is there. Cover the tray with a cloth and see if your child can visualise what was under the cloth and how many of the objects he can recall to mind.

Spot the difference
Ask your child to leave the room, and to try to remember exactly what the room looks like. While she is outside rearrange some items in the room. When your child returns, see if she can spot the changes. This game can also be played with cards (for example, changing the order while players close their eyes).

Pick your potato
Ask your child to choose a potato from a bag of similar potatoes, and to study it carefully for a minute. Put the potato back in the bag. Can she pick her potato out from all the others? Discuss why. Try playing this game with stones, buttons, leaves, or other near-identical objects.

Picture quiz
Choose a picture, preferably one new to your child. Give him the picture to look at for one minute. Take the picture away and see how much he can remember about the picture. Find out how many things he can remember and award one point for each item or feature.

Picture memory
Collect ten pictures—postcards or magazine cuttings. Number them from 1 to 10. Show the numbered pictures to your child (or other players). Hide the pictures. Call a number (from 1 to 10). Can anyone remember the picture that went with that number? How many out of ten can you remember correctly?

Pelmanism
Lay a set of playing or picture cards up for all to see. Then turn them over. Players take turns to choose a card, say what it shows and turn it over to see if they were right. If they are they keep the card.

Recall the event
After a video or a film ask your child to recall scenes or events to picture in her mind's eye or to discuss—'What can you remember about . . . ?'

Mystery object
A player is given a mystery object or picture to look at which others cannot see. She describes the object or picture, without saying what it is. Others try to visualise it and guess what it is from the description.

Mystery shape
Draw a mystery shape and ask your child to look at it and list as many things as she can think the shape might represent.

Draw from memory
Invite your child to draw something he knows well from memory (his mind's eye'). Choose a picture that interests your child (such as a magazine picture, photo or art print).

Ask him to look at it carefully using his eyes and his mind, to try to visualise the picture in his 'mind's eye'. Then hide the picture and ask him to draw it from memory, trying to recall it as accurately as possible. Together compare his drawing with the original. How could it be improved?

KEY IDEA: HELP YOUR CHILD VISUALISE PICTURES IN HER 'MIND'S EYE'

Mind-mapping

We learn a lot from pictures and images—trademarks, road signs, maps, diagrams—and children need to be taught how to read them. Your child can also learn a lot from making visual maps, designs and images to represent her own thinking. This kind of activity is called mind-mapping. It is an important skill your child can learn.

The idea of a mind-map is to show connections between words and ideas in a picture or map. Start with one word or idea in the middle of a page, draw a circle around it and then show how other words and ideas are connected with it. The best mind-maps are made on large sheets of plain paper, with plenty of space to develop ideas and additional thoughts.

Mind-maps are a good way to show what you know, to help remember information and to work out answers to problems. They are used by students studying at school or university, by executives in business and by all sorts of creative people using a tested way to improve their thinking.

The following are some mind-mapping activities to try with your child:

Local map. Invite your child to make a map of your local area, putting your home in a circle in the centre. Show places which your child knows well. Connect these places with lines.

House map. Can your child make a map of your house?

Classroom map. Can your schoolchild draw a map of her classroom or school?

Story map. Help your child to make a map of a story in words and pictures. Show the hero or chief character in a circle in the middle, and link this to other characters and events in the story.

Idea map. Start with a central word or idea in a circle, for example 'blue'. See how many ideas you can link with this central idea. Draw lines to link your ideas. Write along the lines what the link between your ideas is.

Knowledge map. Choose a topic your child would like to know more about. Using a reference book, find some facts about your child's chosen topic. On cards write different facts about this topic (one on each card), using as few words as possible (use different colours for words, pictures, numbers, etc.) on each card. When you have done ten or more cards ask your child to arrange them in any shape she wishes—a circle, line, ladder or tree. Play Pelmanism (see above) with the cards.

Problem-solving map. Write your problem in the central circle—for example 'Where to go for a holiday?' Write down all the factors that relate to your problem, such as factors that make for a good holiday. Use the map to test ideas.

KEY IDEA: INTRODUCE YOUR CHILD TO MIND-MAPPING, MAKING HIS THINKING VISUAL

Other ways of making thinking visible include drawing diagrams, plans and charts. These help to strengthen memory by using the visual side of the brain. This is very helpful for some children. As an eight-year old once said to me, 'I can remember if it is a picture, but I can't remember if it is words.' This was not strictly true, for his memory also responded to the mode of knowing we consider in the next chapter—the sound of music.

SEVEN STEPS TO VISUAL INTELLIGENCE

- Teach your child to stop and look, with a rich and varied visual environment.
- Encourage him to draw with care and attention to line, shape and detail.
- Practise painting, and develop an awareness of colour.
- Design and make models, play with creative construction toys and handicrafts.
- Look in detail at and discuss different pictures, visit art galleries and exhibitions.
- Visualise pictures in her 'mind's eye' to strengthen visual memory and imagination.
- Introduce your child to mind-mapping, help make his thinking visual.

6   Music in Mind

developing musical intelligence

Just as humus in nature makes growth possible, so elementary music gives to the child powers that otherwise cannot come to fruition. Carl Orff, music teacher and composer

Music helps you to be yourself. Jane, aged 10

Jane is a musical child. From an early age she responded to the sounds and rhythms around her by humming tunes, making up her own songs and tapping out rhythms. Hers is a world of rhythm and melody. She began to learn the recorder, but didn't like it much. Then she started to learn the piano and soon wanted a piano of her own. It is not always easy living with a musical child. Her parents didn't know whether to pay out the large amount of money needed to buy her a piano—suppose she were to give it up, as she gave up the recorder? Her music teacher said she was good, but did not know how long Jane's enthusiasm would last. Recently her parents took the plunge and bought her a piano (second-hand) for her birthday. They hope it will last.

Robert also has a musical mind although there was very little music in his house. He tried to learn the recorder when he was young, but with little success, and his parents were glad when the sound of his shrill squeaking stopped. Later he tried the violin, again with agonising sounds and equal lack of success. His teachers said he was not musical, but he persevered. As a teenager he tried to teach himself the guitar and the piano, but soon gave up. As a child he was always encouraged to listen to the music he liked, and as he grew older his tastes in music widened from pop to ethnic and classical. He is now an adult but his musical taste and intelligence continue to develop.

WHAT IS MUSICAL INTELLIGENCE?

Every child has a musical centre in the brain, but not every child has the chance to discover or develop it.

From the day they are born, and perhaps before, children are exposed to sounds and music. In houses, cars, streets and shops there are sounds, some of them musical. If they can hear, children are hearing sounds of all kinds throughout their waking lives. A child cannot help absorbing sounds from his environment. But what have these to do with musical intelligence?

Musical intelligence is the ability we all have to respond to and make sense of patterns of sound. The rhythms of life begin before birth, for in the womb the child's life begins to the beat of his mother's heart. Studies show that a newborn child can hear well enough to detect the differences between the notes C and C sharp, and between the syllables 'Pa' and 'Ba'. This implies that even in the womb musical capacities are developing. Some babies are born with the sound of soft music playing. After birth the baby will hear rhythmic and musical sounds around him, including, if he is lucky, hearing his mother sing lullabies to him.

Parents are usually content that their child has got his senses, that he can hear, see, smell, taste and touch. For the child that is not enough. He will seek every opportunity to expand his experience, and even in a pram he is busy looking and listening, absorbing the sound of rain, of water running, birds chirping, motors humming, people talking, doors shutting, bells ringing and distant voices. Before the age of six months babies respond to music with active listening and body movements and later indulge in 'musical babbling', their first experiments in making melodic sounds. By the age of twelve months they show definite likes and dislikes, generally preferring musical to non-musical sounds. Between one and two years they begin to tap or clap in time to music and to sing spontaneous songs. Music is a life force within all children, which develops, like language, from their hearing of sounds.

As the child develops, so does musical intelligence—that is, the ability to understand pitch, tone, rhythm, melody and other aspects of music. This learning begins through listening and trying to make sense of sounds around him. Like all human capacities, your child's musical intelligence can be developed or neglected. If there is little interest in music at home, or little or no musical teaching at school, he may not get much chance to express his musical inclinations. His home or classroom may be one that has no music, where no songs are sung, no tunes hummed and there is no beating rhythm to listen to.

Over recent years there has been a decline in music teaching in schools. Where there is strong emphasis on the 'basics' of reading, writing and number there may be no realisation that music too is one of the basics. The trouble is that music can easily be seen as part of leisure, pleasure and entertainment, an 'extra' to be fitted in rather than a human capacity that is an important part of human learning. If education is about fulfilling your child's potential, then music should be an important part of his educational experience. If not at school then at home, and in a variety of ways, your child should be introduced to the world of sound and music. He can learn about his musical capabilities, about rhythm and sound, to use his voice and to play music, and to give joy to himself (and to those who live with him) by listening to and appreciating good music.

Every kind of musical intelligence is different, and this is a different kind of intelligence from any other. Some musicians are good mathematicians, but some are not. Some research suggests that learning music will help your child be better at maths and reading. If your child concentrates on music it may help with other kinds of concentration. Playing an instrument may help physical co-ordination of hand and eye. Playing music with others may develop social skills. So developing musical intelligence may help develop other kinds of intelligence. But the best reason for bringing music into the life of your child is to develop his unique musical gift, his ability to make music and appreciate music. Even if he does not enter a music-related career a love of music can enrich life and learning.

Here are some examples of music being used to solve human problems:

- Paul finds it difficult to learn his multiplication tables. His family helps him by singing his tables with him, and this helps him remember.

- Donna hates long journeys. Others in her family don't appreciate her taste in music. She plays what she likes and listens through earphones. She says this gives her mind something to do on the journey.

- Sandy likes to do his homework in silence, but when he is doing a creative craft like woodwork or painting he likes to listen to music. He says it helps him to relax and concentrate.

DEVELOPING YOUR CHILD'S MUSICAL INTELLIGENCE

Music begins with listening. If your child is exposed to a wide variety of music from an early age, including popular, classical and song from a variety of cultures she will have a good grounding for developing musical intelligence. Listening is an important part of learning, and both listening skill and musical ability help brain development. Later your child can move on to playing and to the learning of musical notation. All children have the capacity to develop their musical intelligence to some degree; not all will become musicians, but whatever the potential of your child there are ways you can help:

If your child	What you can do	What your child can learn
Believes she cannot sing	Invite her to sing along with you	Realises anyone can sing and enjoy it

Becomes aware of sounds around her	Play music of different kinds, discuss which she likes	Names and recognition of sounds around her, including music
Listens to others play and shows an interest in music	Find a musical instrument she may like to learn to play	To play music alone or with others, and learn what music symbols mean

HOW DOES MUSICAL INTELLIGENCE DEVELOP?

Musical intelligence is turned on by the resonance of music and rhythm in the brain. This response is stimulated by sounds such as the human voice, sounds from nature, musical instruments, rhythmic and other humanly produced sounds. It begins to develop from the time a baby first feels rhythms and hears sounds, probably in the womb with the mother's heartbeat. The beat of the heart is echoed in the rhythmic drumming of much popular music. This rhythmic/musical intelligence is strengthened by listening to a range of music and other sounds. Tones and rhythms are recognised and reproduced. Gradually the child comes to realise that feelings can be expressed through tones, beats and vibrations of sound, that songs and rhymes communicate thoughts, and that music, humming and rhythm can alter moods. She begins to create her own spontaneous tunes and rhythms. I once asked a young child who was staring and nodding what he was doing. 'I am humming a special tune,' he said, 'and if I stop I'll forget it.'

Later the child comes to realise that music is a system of sounds that can be 'read' and reproduced. Sounds become associated with different sources, such as individual musical instruments and groups of instruments. More complex songs and melodies are sung and the child learns to reproduce rhythms of greater complexity. A wider range of music is recognised and enjoyed.

Musical intelligence is further developed if a child learns to play a musical instrument and grasps the meaning of musical symbols. With a basic understanding of musical language the child can become a performer and composer. If musical understanding develops further the child may become a teacher of music to others, and write music that is performed by others.

What is essential to musical intelligence is pattern-recognition. We have already seen the major role a child's hearing plays in the development of language and reading skill. So it is not surprising that musical experiences can benefit language development. We also know there is a connection between musical skill and mathematical skill. This is because both involve the interpretation of patterns. Teaching a child to read music, that is to 'read' the abstract patterns of musical notation in even a simple tune, can help her to decode language in reading and to understand the logical patterning of number.

As the composer Debussy once said, 'Music is the arithmetic of sounds.'

INPUT:	what you do	You stimulate your child by encouraging her to hear, play and discuss music.
OUTPUT:	what your child does	Your child listens to a range of music and has experience of singing and music-making.
SELF-CONTROL:	what your child learns	Your child learns to listen to and respond to music, developing a life-long interest in music.

Did you know . . . ?
Reptiles and amphibians don't hear very well, but their hearing cells are constantly renewed. Humans have sensitive hearing, but the hearing cells in humans can never be replaced. We must make the most of what we've got.

WHAT YOU CAN DO TO HELP

As we have seen, every child has a musical sense waiting to be developed. What can you do to help your child make the most of this musical sense?

Did you know ... ?
A project in Swiss schools involving 1,200 children discovered that those given extra music lessons did better at reading and languages. They were also more sociable, better motivated and more relaxed than those who had no extra music. Researchers at California University have concluded that music modifies circuits in the brain, leading to improved thinking skills.

Learning to listen

A musical home is where the following activities can take place:

- sounds and music are listened to;
- music is made—songs are sung or musical instruments played;

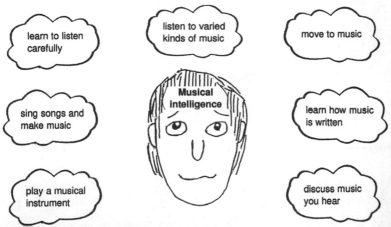

Some ways to develop musical intelligence

- music is valued and discussed.

Musical intelligence develops through listening, learning to control sound and sharing musical experience with others. Music begins with listening to sounds. You may not think that the sounds around you are very musical, but they alert the child's ear to rhythm, to pitch, tone and sometimes, as in the case of birdsong, to melody. Learning to be musical starts with learning to listen to the sounds that are around us.

Learning to listen will help improve your child's ability to distinguish between similar sounds, so important for many kinds of learning, particularly learning reading or a foreign language. A sound's loudness is measured in decibels. A whisper is about 30 decibels, a normal conversation is 60 decibels, a shout about 90 decibels. Encourage your child to listen carefully to soft sounds. What are the softest sounds your child can hear? With his eyes closed, can he hear a pin drop? Learning to listen takes practice. It is all too easy to hear without paying attention to what is heard.

One way of encouraging him to listen carefully to the sounds he hears is to have a sound quiz. Ask your child to close his eyes (no peeking!) and listen. You do a task and see if he can identify what you were doing. Ideas for tasks you can perform include:

- turning pages of a book
- drinking a glass of water
- counting coins
- combing your hair
- turning on a lamp
- tearing a page out of a magazine
- moving a piece of furniture

Encourage your child to tell you as much detail as he can, then reverse the roles. Ask your child to think up different tasks for you to identify with your eyes closed. Try putting something in a bag or box, shake it and see if your child can guess what it is from the sound it makes.

Another version of a sound quiz is to play taped sound effects and see if your child can identify the sounds. These can be domestic sounds around the house that you have recorded, or pre-recorded sounds from nature. Encourage your child to listen carefully to all the sounds he can hear. Can he hear the wind in the trees? Can he copy the song of a bird? Go on a 'sound walk' to collect sounds. Afterwards talk and try to recall the sounds you have heard. As Rosie, aged four, said after a 'sound walk', 'Now I know why we have two ears, there is so much to hear.'

KEY IDEA: TEACH YOUR CHILD TO LISTEN CAREFULLY TO DIFFERENT SOUNDS AROUND HIM

Introduce your child to a wide range of music. Start the stimulation soon after birth with soothing background music. Play what you like. Include classical as well as popular and ethnic music.

The essence of listening to music is the ability to distinguish between sounds and to hear the patterns they make. Even simple songs and rhymes have a pattern and an immediate rhythmic appeal. From a young age children can be helped to recognise and identify tunes, to move in time to music and to select their favourite music, for example as a background to some creative activity.

We learn to recognise music by its repeated themes. We learn to recognise things that are associated with particular kinds of music—music associated with danger, with comical cartoons, with death and with armies marching to war. These themes become 'musical frames' for hearing music. Film music tries to help us associate certain scenes with particular kinds of musical and rhythmic patterns. It becomes easy to ask older children what a piece of music reminds them of or makes them think about.

Did you know . . . ?

Researchers at the University of California have found that listening to the music of Mozart seems to boost students' scores in IQ tests. This may be because music has a calming and de-stressing effect, enabling better performance, or because the complexity of Mozart's music stimulates processing activity in the brain.

Even if you think you are not musical you can teach your child to hear music. The following are some musical activities to try:

Guess this tune
Hum or la-la the tune of a song or nursery rhyme your child knows to see if she can recall what it is. Ask your child to do the same for you or others to guess.

Replay the rhythm
Hum or tap out a rhythm. Start with one rhythmic beat, then add another in sequence, and then further patterns of sound. See if your child can hum (or tap) the rhythm just as you hummed it. Then reverse the roles and have your child hum a rhythm for you to replay.

Listen to silence
A famous modern piece of 'music' by the composer John Cage lasts for four minutes and thirty-three seconds. It is made up entirely of silence. Whether or not it is music, it certainly encourages the audience to listen. Sometimes, with

your child, simply stop and listen. Do you hear distant sounds
... or can you hear the sound of silence?

Relaxing sounds
Play soft, slow music to help your child feel quiet and relaxed.
This can be especially useful after an energetic or stressful
activity.

Aerobic sounds
Music can sometimes stir sluggish spirits and give energy.
Play Tchaikovsky's '1812 Overture', or sing along to a
favourite pop song. Add aerobic exercises to some strongly
rhythmic music.

Working sounds
When your child has a task to do, find out if background
music helps her to concentrate. Some people like relaxing
sounds to work to, some like energising sounds and some
prefer no sound at all. What works for you may not suit
your child.

Live music
Take your child to hear some live music, to meet some
real musicians and to look at their instruments. Remember, no instrument is too humble or too complex to inspire
her interest, from live drums, pianos and organs to guitars,
steel bands or penny whistles. Listening to real musicians
will add to your child's perceptions of people as music-
makers.

A child should hear music every day, so that from a young
age she finds it an enjoyable experience. Later she may 'con-
duct' the music with a wooden spoon, march in time or sing
in imitation of it. The job of the parent is solely one of
encouragement. Gradually the child absorbs what she hears
(if she hears nothing, of course she absorbs nothing). The
child is learning the language of music in much the same way
as she is learning spoken language, by hearing it at home
with a responsive adult. As the poet Shelley said, 'Music,
when soft voices die/Vibrates in the memory ...' or in the

words of Kelly, aged seven, 'Some tunes you just can't get out of your head.'

KEY IDEA: PROVIDE VARIED KINDS OF MUSIC FOR YOUR CHILD TO LISTEN TO

Musical intelligence develops through listening, making music and responding to music. The most natural way to respond to the sound of music is with the body.

Your child's body is her first musical instrument. As you sing or listen to music with your baby or young child, try tapping out the rhythm on her arm, leg or bottom. Move her arms in time to the music and introduce her to the fun of conducting. Try clapping, tapping finger-rhythms on the palm of the hand, stamping feet on the ground, slapping hands on thighs and patting on puffed cheeks. Teach how to click fingers, to beat out rhythms on tables, to make tongue noises, teeth-snapping and blowing or whistling sounds.

Moving to music is a natural activity for any child. Throughout the ages humans have moved to the sound of drumming, song, the call of the horn and the piping flute. Music and dance have developed together as people have celebrated their joy and mourned their loss, have danced for rain and to ward off evil spirits. Although today these rituals may have declined, people still march and dance or tap their toes to music. Your child too will respond to music with her whole body in dance. Encourage her to listen to the music first, before she begins. Show her how to clap, stamp and sing along to the music. You can ask about any music you hear: 'Does it sound like dancing music?' Try dancing to a wide variety of music, for example:

- classical music
- jazz and pop music
- military march and drum music
- ballet, waltz and tango music

KEY IDEA: ENCOURAGE YOUR CHILD TO MOVE AND DANCE TO MUSIC

Making music

Music-making is important not only for developing musical intelligence, but also for developing manipulative skills and the co-ordination of hand and eye, so important in writing and other creative activities. In learning a musical instrument your child is not only learning music; it also helps to train his memory, his ability to concentrate, his physical skills and, above all, when music teaching is successful, his self-confidence.

Music-making can begin simply with your child repeating songs he has heard, by clapping or beating in time to the music he hears before moving on to make music using a chosen instrument. Even if you cannot play a musical instrument you can help your child make music with the instrument with which he was born—his voice.

Sing some songs with your child. Start off with nursery rhymes, then move on to simple folk songs or pop songs, and special occasion songs like 'Happy Birthday', 'Auld Lang Syne' or hymns. Encourage him to sing along with you, or with singers on tape or TV.

Try creating your own song together. Choose a favourite poem or rhyme and try to turn it into a song by singing, chanting or reading it to a tune. Learning the alphabet, the spelling of a word or multiplication tables can be better remembered if sung to a tune. Make up your own work songs, like the slaves of old. Sing or hum as you engage in repetitive work—for example 'Hi ho, hi ho, it's off to . . . we go!' (fill in a suitable activity). If you feel bold, sing some comments to your child. Create your own home musical or opera: 'Sam, can you hear me? I'm coming!' (in a musical voice). This is a way of supporting your child's interest in song fragments, and encouraging him to sing back, too.

Here are some more ways to develop a young child's singing and musical skills:

Sound the waters

Fill a row of glasses with differing amounts of water. The amount of water in the glass will determine the sound tone (high to low pitch). Tap each glass with a pencil to check the sound. Try to get a good range of sounds from low to high, then make some water music by tapping the different glasses. Sing the sounds and make up some tunes.

Make some instruments
Whatever object that comes to hand, whether it be a spoon, bowl or jar, can become a musical instrument if played with care. Make home-made instruments from scrap materials. Try to create some interesting sounds and use them to accompany your songs.

Buy some instruments
Buy over time a range of instruments for your child to try— whistles, tambourines, flutes, xylophones and any musical toy that produces a good tone. Allow him time to explore and experiment with each one.

Make musical sound effects
Every word has its own rhythm. Sing your child's name, or beat out its rhythm on an instrument. Once he knows the rhythm of his name, try playing it on different notes on a xylophone, recorder or piano. Try making musical sound effects to go with stories or pictures.

KEY IDEA: SING SONGS WITH YOUR CHILD AND TEACH THE SONGS YOU KNOW AND LIKE

Write it down

Once your child can make a pattern of sounds, the next challenge is to write it down. You can begin by writing the sounds down for him using any notation of your own— numbers, colours, dots, lines, notes, any way you like so that you can play the rhythm or tune another time. Any child can be a composer provided he has someone to write his first music. Play it back, or record it, adding more sounds. Teach your child that real music, those clusters of black dots, are simply sounds written down in a particular way. Then why not introduce him to those dots and teach him to read simple music?

When music is written down it is called musical notation. Teachers often find that children who are taught to read musical notation from an early age, even in its simplest form, become better at reading as a result. It is as if the skill of following notes on a musical line helps the ability to read words on a page. Those good at music are often good at maths, for both rely on the recognition of symbolic patterns.

There are many ways to introduce your child to written music. Some child-sized instruments include simple musical tunes to play using letters, colours or numbers to correspond with the real notes. Tunes are transient and difficult to remember, so learning how to write music down is a useful way of recording what your child wishes to play. Once he can read music he will have an extra language at his fingertips. You may prefer to leave this aspect of musical education to a qualified teacher. If you have introduced your child to the fun of music-making you will have done much to prepare him for learning a musical instrument of his choice.

Computers provide wonderful opportunities for playing with sounds and will reproduce any rhythm or tune in musical notation. A computer with a music program allows any child to compose and write music. 'Music is in the air,' said the composer Elgar, 'you simply take as much of it as you want.' But Jude, aged ten, complains, 'Tunes are stuck in my head, I just can't write them down.' Composing is not easy, but if a computer can help with the hard part of writing notes down, this may be of help to your budding composer.

KEY IDEA: SHOW YOUR CHILD MUSICAL NOTATION, HOW MUSIC IS WRITTEN TO BE PLAYED

Which instrument to learn?

Do not try to force your child to play an instrument before she wants to do it. Let her watch others playing the instrument first, for example older brothers, sisters or friends. Let her become familiar with tunes played on the instrument. Musical talent is not only born, it is made. Begin young but begin slowly.

The three main groups of instruments are percussion, wind and string. Ideally your child should experience instruments of each kind. The most versatile percussive instrument is the piano. Let her see how a piano 'works' on the inside and experiment by 'playing' on the strings. Show by plucking them that vibration produces sound. A child can start learning the piano by the age of three (Mozart began the keyboard when he was two!) but it is more usual to begin lessons between five and twelve years old. If your child begins taking piano lessons bear in mind the words of Oscar Wilde: 'Please don't shoot the pianist. He is doing his best.'

The recorder is the most popular wind instrument for beginners, and children can begin learning when they are about six and have a sufficient handspan to play the notes. A wind player needs a good memory for learning music, good manipulative ability and skilful breath control. Wind instruments were not George Bernard Shaw's favourite. He once wrote, ironically: 'The chief objection to playing wind instruments is that it prolongs the life of the player.'

Finding a music teacher who suits your child, and with whom she is willing to learn, is essential. One of the pioneers of music teaching was a Japanese, Dr Suzuki. The Suzuki method has produced amazing results, enabling a child to start learning the violin from a very early age. The violin, as someone once said, is a better instrument than it sounds. A child can begin on a quarter-sized violin around the age of three. Suzuki described a very small girl whose mother, instead of buying her another doll, one day bought her a violin. She just let her play with it around the house, suggesting from time to time that she do this or that to help her 'playing'. The young girl's attention was easily distracted (the attention span for three- to four-year-old children is about three and a half to five minutes). But her ability to concentrate was built up over a long period of support and encouragement, and with the help of a professional teacher.

Not all parents would want to follow the Suzuki method, especially when it comes to paying for a professional teacher. The advantage of being young when starting to make music is that children are usually at their most open and relaxed. They have not yet learnt to be tense and tight like adults.

> **Did you know . . . ?**
> Studies of the neural circuits in the brains of violinists who began their training before the age of twelve are markedly more complex than those of violinists who began their training later.

For them music is a natural activity, like throwing a ball. Music is still in the head, not in the black dots you have to read on a musical score. Too many people are put off by the notes. Start by making some music, the notes can come later.

The guitar can be played from about the age of six on a 'student' size instrument. Like other stringed instruments it is best taught by a professional teacher.

Once your child has found a good teacher your job does not stop there. It is most important to sustain her interest, especially during practice. Remember a child rarely has the same attitude to performance as an adult—she will like to enjoy music in her own special way. Do not destroy her confidence by pushing her too far, or demanding that she demonstrate her ability or skill. Never judge her by your own standards or compare her unfavourably with others. As one frustrated child said to her over-anxious parent, 'I can't play music your way, I can only play it my way.'

KEY IDEA: OFFER YOUR CHILD THE CHANCE TO LEARN A MUSICAL INSTRUMENT OF HER CHOICE

Responding to music

The point of listening to music is to enjoy it. However, we don't always enjoy it the first time we hear it. There is good evidence to show that children (and adults) need to hear the same music several times before it becomes sufficiently familiar to be liked. The formula for success in familiarising your child with music is to keep it simple (clear melody and firm rhythm), keep it short, and play it often (a formula that commercials use for success, often pillaging great composers for theme tunes). In any piece of music there are things to listen out for, to think about and to share with others.

The following are some activities to encourage your child to think about the music he hears:

Questions to ask
Questions to invite your child to think about music include:

• Where does the sound come from? Near or far?	*Direction*
• Is it loud or soft? Louder or softer?	*Volume*
• How long did the sound last?	*Duration*
• Which instruments can you hear? How many?	*Instruments*
• Are the sounds high or low? Do they go up or down?	*Pitch*
• What rhythms or patterns of sound can you hear?	*Rhythm*
• What is the tune, or main tune? How many different tunes?	*Melody*
• What does the music make you feel?	*Feelings*
• What does the music make you think of?	*Images*
• What did you like, or not like, about the music?	*Response*

Sound stories
Play interesting sounds or music and ask your child, 'What does this make you think of—for example a scene, a story, a feeling, or an idea?' Closing his eyes may help your child to concentrate and to visualise things in his mind's eye.

Musical art
Listen to some music and give your child a number of pictures to look at (postcards, magazine pictures or reproductions). Which picture does he think best matches the music? Ask him to choose a picture and say why.

Music to work to
Discuss the choice of music that could be used as a background to creative activities or study. Research by the Bulgarian scientist Lozanov shows that music (especially the largos and adagios of baroque music) helps to produce the alpha levels of brain waves that provide the optimum conditions for a receptive state for learning such things as foreign languages or revision for exams. It can help the mind be relaxed and attentive.

What is music?
Discuss with your child what he thinks music is. Is birdsong a kind of music—why, or why not? Is the sound of a machine, like an engine, a kind of music? Is the sound of the sea a kind of music? Can silence be musical? What is a musical person?

Pictures in the mind
Play a piece of music and discuss what pictures or images came into your mind as you listened to it. What feelings? What thoughts, ideas or other associations (connections) did your child think of? When six-year-old Jane heard part of Mussorgsky's 'Night on a Bare Mountain' she said, 'It makes me think of a dark wood, with witches all around.'

Did you know . . . ?
Musical history can be traced back to 3000 BC when the yellow bell (*huang chung*) used in Chinese temple music was reported as having a recognised musical tone. Today those who believe in 'gong therapy' argue that musical vibrations from gongs can have a therapeutic effect on human bodies and minds. Some 'gong therapists' argue that each of us has a particular tone to which we respond and which will be of most benefit to us.

Listen to a range of tones. Talk about which tone you, or your child, most prefer. Can you or your child remember the tone and hum it later?

Music accompanies us through our lives, marking important occasions from birth to death. Music draws children into their culture and into the rituals of the community—birthdays, religious observance, weddings and festivals. Music conveys emotions, heightens experiences and marks personal and historic occasions. Music develops in a music-rich environment, where it is heard, sung, danced, played and where music and music-making are valued and discussed.

KEY IDEA: DISCUSS DIFFERENT KINDS OF MUSIC WITH YOUR CHILD

There are many ways to enjoy music, and your child will find his own way and make his own musical choices. He may reject what you like. As you probably found, his musical tastes will change. What he rejects today he may come back to later. Whatever his response, try to pass on your pleasure in music. As the great conductor Leopold Stokowski once said, 'It is not necessary to understand music, it is necessary that one enjoy it.'

SEVEN STEPS TO MUSICAL INTELLIGENCE

- Teach your child to listen carefully to different sounds around him.
- Provide varied kinds of music to listen to, including music your child chooses.
- Encourage your child to move and dance to music.
- Sing songs with your child and teach the songs you know and like.
- Show your child musical notation, how music can be written and played.
- Offer her the chance to play or learn a musical instrument of her choice.
- Discuss different kinds of music, including live music you take your child to hear.

7 Body Power

developing physical intelligence

To return an average serve, you have about a second to do this. To hit the ball at all is remarkable and yet not uncommon. The truth is that everyone who inhabits a human body possesses a remarkable creation. Tim Gallwey, author of *Inner Tennis*

I am so happy I could jump over myself! Child, aged 6, after a gym lesson

Pat is a physical child. She responds to the world through touch and movement. She enjoys sport and physical movement (sometimes she finds it hard to keep still). She has a good sense of direction and timing when she moves her body. She is a natural dancer, and seems full of energy. She likes to make things with her hands, and has the skill to take small objects apart and reassemble them. She learns best by handling things and likes things to be physically demonstrated, not just talked about. She likes drama and team games. She seems to have boundless energy, but her mother is worried. The question she asks is: If Pat spends all her time playing games and making things, will she have the time to make a success of her school work? Is all this physical activity of any value?

WHAT IS PHYSICAL INTELLIGENCE?

This is the intelligence that enables us to control body movements, to manipulate physical objects and to create a healthy balance between two elements that make us who we are—our mind and body. Being fit is part of our feeling of wholeness and wellness. Being confident in the use of our body is part of being confident in ourselves. Help your child understand how physical exercise, health and achievement in physical and sporting activities will help her take control of her body and develop positive attitudes for life.

The trouble with physical education in schools is that it may be seen as an 'extra' in the school curriculum for most children, and teachers may concentrate only on those who are going to be the stars and play for school teams. Sometimes only the best get special treatment. However, at home you can help your child maintain a healthy body and mind, and make up for opportunities she may not get at school.

The Spartans of ancient Greece built their whole culture around the importance of the body and how it performs. In modern days the Olympic Games and big sporting competitions continue this tradition. The mistake can easily be made of limiting this intelligence to the athletic or sporting world. A car mechanic, carpenter or plumber needs as much physical intelligence to perform his tasks well as does a prize athlete. They are different physical skills, of course, but all aspects of the same physical or bodily/kinaesthetic intelligence, which requires the co-ordination of eye, body and mind. Could brain surgeons or dressmakers perform their tasks successfully without finely tuned physical skills?

The sorts of career choice open to a child with well-developed physical intelligence include actor, dancer, mechanic, surgeon, car driver, manual worker, inventor, physiotherapist, trainer, or sports person. But whatever our way of life we can all benefit from developing our physical potential to control bodily movements and to handle objects skilfully—for example, in the use of our body to communicate (as in dance and body language), to play a game (as in sport), or to create something (as in crafting a product). Learning by doing is an important part of every person's education. As the Chinese proverb says, 'I hear and I forget, I see and I remember, I do and I understand'; or as Tim, aged nine, said, 'If you do it yourself you have to concentrate more.'

Physical intelligence helps us to solve the practical physical problems of life. Its positive aspect gives us physical confidence, its negative aspect can take the form of fighting and aggression towards others. We need to be able to control physical intelligence positively in ways that will help solve problems, for example:

- James has a problem understanding how to do sums; however, when he is given objects to use, and can be shown how to do it on an abacus, he can succeed. Using physical objects helps him to get a 'feel' for numbers.

- Peter is very keen on woodwork. He would like to design and make his own furniture. As a child he was encouraged to build with Lego, to make models and to draw whatever he liked. Later he was able to put his manipulative skills to good use.

- Paula was a naughty child who never did well at school. Her parents and teachers despaired of her. Paula liked to go to the local skating rink and her parents encouraged her. She took lessons, and later entered the local skating championships. Skating had given her a purpose in life, self-discipline and achievements she could be proud of.

DEVELOPING YOUR CHILD'S PHYSICAL INTELLIGENCE

We are all born with automatic physical reflexes. Gradually we learn how to control these and gain physical independence. Our physical gestures become expressive as we learn how to use our bodies to communicate what we want and what we do not want. We experience being able to create and solve problems with our hands, and learn the basic skills of sports and games. Later, if we are lucky, we develop complex physical skills of manipulation and co-ordination that enable us to be successful in challenging physical and creative activities.

Developing physical intelligence means developing control of bodily movement, and the use of the body to express oneself and to learn. This development does not happen by chance. It develops, or does not develop so well, through our experience at home, school and in the world.

If your child	What you can do	What your child can learn
Is very clumsy and unco-ordinated	Encourage physical activities in which he can do well, like riding a bike	He can succeed in physical activities if he practises
Enjoys one particular sport above all others	Encourage her to play this sport as often as possible, and join a club for training	How to play and enjoy a favourite leisure pastime in which she could achieve success and satisfaction
Likes to use his hands in making or mending things	Encourage him to learn craft skills like woodwork, dressmaking or modelmaking	How to use his manipulative skills to make things and solve problems, to be 'handy' in life

HOW DOES PHYSICAL INTELLIGENCE DEVELOP?

Physical intelligence begins developing in the womb. Your child had fingers after about seven weeks as a foetus, and could open and close his hands after about fifteen weeks. At birth he had a grasp reflex strong enough to support his own weight. From the first weeks of independent life your child could reach in the right direction for objects, and by the third week had learnt not to stretch for things that were out of reach. By five months he knew how to intercept a moving object, and by nine months could orientate his grasp to the size and shape of an object he wished to pick up.

As your child grows he learns to tighten his grip when

things are slipping out of his hand. He finds that physical tasks are so much easier when you can see what you are doing. This is because physical tasks, like handling things, rely on visual feedback, the information that the eye and brain give to the body to help it perform any conscious task. The most important fact about physical intelligence is that it relies on body-brain (for example hand-eye) co-ordination. We learn to grasp objects without conscious thinking, but not without the help of an experienced brain co-ordinating our movements.

Physical intelligence and body-brain co-ordination improve through practice. The brain also develops strategies that help it cope with complex physical demands—for example, by co-ordinating various joints so that they automatically combine their movements. That is why some unco-ordinated movements, like patting your head with one hand whilst simultaneously rubbing your tummy in a circular movement with the other, are so difficult (try it and see). Tapping different rhythms with your hands is also very difficult, unless one rhythmic pattern is the exact multiple of the other. The brain responds to rhythm—that is why physical practice is better when it has flow and rhythm.

Children who have poor co-ordination are described as clumsy. We are all clumsy from time to time, spilling things, missing our aim, knocking things over. Some children who are clumsy all the time are called dyspraxic. They are not less intelligent than their friends, it is just that their brains cannot properly co-ordinate their physical activity. The range of this disability, like all human disabilities, is wide. Some children are only occasionally clumsy, others are clumsy about everything. Sometimes it is called lack of 'motor' competence (that is brain-body co-ordination). This can lead to problems in learning (physical skills like writing become more difficult), in forming relationships (children don't like clumsy playmates) and in self-confidence (they come to accept themselves as physical losers). If you think your child is especially clumsy you should consult a health visitor or doctor. Any child can learn to improve his co-ordination and to overcome problems, given help and support.

INPUT:	what you do	You stimulate your child to undertake varied physical activity such as sports, dance and exercises, as well as expressive activities like handicrafts, dance and drama.
OUTPUT:	what your child does	Develops powers of physical co-ordination, more skilled games-playing and creative self-expression.
SELF-CONTROL:	what your child learns	Self-confidence and physical skill in control of his body and in the use of his body for play, pleasure and learning.

Did you know . . . ?

Like other primates a human baby is adapted for physical exercise from the first days of life. It is natural for babies to clutch, cling and climb both horizontally and vertically. A baby can hang on to mother's hair and support its own weight when it is a few weeks old. Babies are able to climb a ladder once they can crawl. They are adapted to ride on a parent's back and to climb trees. Giving babies, from one month old, physical exercises and apparatus to play with will help stimulate them to crawl and walk from an early age.

WHAT YOU CAN DO TO HELP

Why are some people so much better at physical activities than others? What makes a winner at sport, or a better cook or carpenter? Part of the answer is that those who succeed

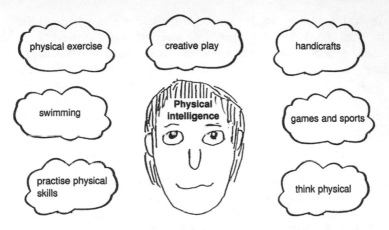

Some ways of developing physical intelligence

have found out what they are good at. They may have tried many things before they found the one or more physical activities in which they could achieve success, satisfaction and recognition from others.

One reason for introducing your child to a wide range of physical activities is that not only is she more likely to be physically healthy as a result, but she may well find an activity at which she can excel. The first principle for developing physical intelligence is to expand your child's opportunity to participate in physical activities. As well as helping her to develop physically, this will help her develop socially and she may discover lifelong interests. As Jayne said, 'I like to try different things because you never know what you might be good at.'

Another reason why some people succeed in any sphere of activity is that they have spent more hours practising it than others. Practice is a measure of motivation rather than innate skill. We could all become better at any physical activity if we practised more. Practice makes the difference between being good and being better than good, but it cannot guarantee you being an expert or champion. We need to encourage children to practise, for as Paul, aged six, said, 'I'm not much good now, but if I keep practising I will be.'

We need to work hard to improve, but we need to 'work

smart'. Only by applying our minds to what we do will we be sure of doing it better. We need to help children to be mindful about their activity, to think ahead so that effort is not wasted, and to review their progress so that they learn from experience. We want the mind-body to work in harmony to co-ordinate our best efforts. As one sporting champion reported, when asked the secret of his success, 'I don't think about it while I am competing, but I think before to prepare myself, and I think after to work out how to improve.'

So your child will need to experience a range of physical activities to find out what suits her best; to practise key techniques to make the most of her experience; and to increase her sense of well-being and confidence through such activity. These three principal ways of developing physical intelligence can be summed up as:

1 *Expand the physical*—broaden your child's experience of physical activity.
2 *Promote practice*—sustain her focus on a chosen physical activity.
3 *Improve confidence*—plan and review progress towards success in physical activity.

KEY IDEA: UNDERTAKE REGULAR PHYSICAL ACTIVITY AND EXERCISE

Expand the physical

Recent studies have shown that many children do not experience vigorous exercise either at home or in school. Many spend their spare time slouched in front of the TV or computer screen. At school physical education lessons are often cut in favour of more reading, writing and arithmetic. These factors all contribute to the low levels of fitness characteristic of many older children. Regular exercise is important for maintaining good health at any age. The body is like a machine that stays healthy with use; it needs to be cared for, and if a child becomes aware of the value of healthy exercise it can become a habit that will stay with him throughout life.

Healthy exercise is essential for physical *growth* and for

the healthy functioning of the various systems in the body. Regular exercise leads to greater physical and muscular *strength*. A varied range of physical movement will increase *suppleness*, and improve the ability of the body to respond to physical challenge. Exercise also improves the heart and cardiovascular system which helps develop *stamina* and the capacity to do more. Varied use of hands and other parts of the body will increase *dexterity* and the ability of your child to put his body to creative use.

Drama, playacting and mime are ways creative movement can be used for learning. Making things can also enhance physical intelligence. The great sculptor Henry Moore began as a child playing with clay, and continued to develop his hand-eye skills with clay throughout his life.

> *I really make the little idea from clay, and I hold it in my hand. I can turn it, look at it from underneath, see it from one view, hold it against the sky, imagine it any size I like, and really be in control almost like God creating something.* Henry Moore

There is probably more to be learnt through cookery than any other creative craft. Part of this can be scientific and other knowledge (p. 153) and part social skills (p. 254), as well as manipulative skills. As with other physical skills, let your child do it alongside you at first, helping where he can. Later let him try on his own, with your supervision. Other valuable hand-crafts include making puppets, needlework, knitting, woodwork, origami and other decorative crafts. Encourage him to use his hands at home, introduce him to any and as many crafts as you can, whether it is in making models such as Technic Lego, or decorating a cake. Indoor games like board, card or computer games can also help develop dexterity and hand-eye co-ordination.

A young child has a vast store of energy. He wants to move, to experience the world through his senses, and to express what he knows about the world through movement. When six-month-old Karen sees and hears her mum coming to pick her up she comes alive and wriggles, squirms and smiles. Her whole body says, 'Hi, mum, I'm here!' as well as any words could.

Did you know . . . ?
Research shows that regularly rocking a baby
promotes brain growth. It does this by stimulating
what is called the vestibular system, the nerve system
linked closely with a baby's inner-ear mechanism
which plays a vital part in balance and co-ordination.
Babies who are given vestibular stimulation by
rocking develop powers of perception, including
vision and hearing, earlier than others. Fifteen minutes
of rocking, rubbing, rolling and stroking a baby will
greatly help its co-ordination and ability to learn.

Babies can begin to learn to crawl from birth. Crawling is
good because it needs all four limbs, as well as eye and brain-
work (if not they soon bump into the sofa or chair). Crawling,
like other physical activities, is good for eye and brain development. The more a child crawls the sooner he will creep
and then walk. As children grow older they learn to move
with increasing skill. They run, climb, throw, dance, build,
cut, paint, draw, act out feelings, mime movements, bounce
balls, and play all sorts of games. In so doing they not only
learn about themselves and the world, they are learning skills
of co-ordination, timing, but also improved physical performance, pleasure and self-confidence through physical activity.
Whatever stage of development your child is at, try to think
of ways to offer fresh challenge (provided it is a safe challenge) to his physical performance.

The job of home and school is to expand the child's range
of physical experience, encouraging more complex activity
such as gymnastics or typing, so that this aspect of intelligence
is extended and challenged. Remember that all physical challenge risks failure. As a child learning to skateboard said: 'I
didn't know it was hard to stay on until I came off.' Encourage a 'think first' approach. Even creative play can benefit
from planning, with questions such as: 'What do you need?'
'What will you do?' 'How will you do it?' or the frequently
heard, 'And who's going to clear up afterwards?'

KEY IDEA: OFFER OPPORTUNITIES FOR CREATIVE, COMPLEX AND CHALLENGING PHYSICAL PLAY

What you can do to help your child is:

Provide space and time for physical play
From as early an age as possible, make sure your child has as much physical activity as she wants, with as much free body as practical. All exercise with a young baby is better done naked (the baby, that is), so that her movements are unrestricted—hands free, feet free, able to crawl and climb. Allow your growing child to make mistakes, but be there to catch her when she falls!

Children need open space both indoors and outdoors in which to move and play. They also need 'psychological' space—that is encouragement and support to move, play and explore. When John's father takes him for a walk he always brings a ball in his pocket to throw, catch or kick around.

There are many environments in which your child can experience physical challenge, movement and play—homes, parks, playgrounds, adventure areas, beaches, hills, riversides and forests. Try to give your child experience of as many different play-spaces as possible. Anywhere in the world can provide a space for physical learning, so long as it is safe, and your child is encouraged to use all her senses.

Physical play is an important means of self-expression,

211

through movement in dance and drama, model-making and creative crafts. A home should have spaces for physical play, where your child can make models, do jigsaws, play active games, as well as sometimes sharing your own activities such as DIY or other skilled handicrafts. One parent remembers: 'The kitchen was a favourite play-space at home. It began with my mother encouraging me to model strange beasts out of her bread dough.' Another recalls: 'The garage at home was the place where I first became fascinated with engines. I've been taking them apart and putting them together ever since.'

KEY IDEA: INVOLVE YOUR CHILD IN HOME DIY AND HANDICRAFT ACTIVITIES

Encourage varied physical exercise
By encouraging your child to experience a variety of physical activities, you will help to develop a wide range of physical skills. He needs games that promote running, dodging, jumping, skipping, hopping, walking, throwing, catching, rolling, balancing and other kinds of play activity. Introduce your child to unusual games, try balancing along a fallen tree trunk, playing hopscotch on a patio, throwing stones at tin can targets, jumping to see how high your child can touch.

The following is an activity that many parents find instinctively that young children love—holding the child firmly by his hands and spinning him round and round like a helicopter. Research suggests this spinning action can help to promote brain growth. Try the Helicopter Spin with any child from aged three and above, once he can walk and run:

Helicopter Spin
Say, 'We are going to be helicopters' and do the following:

1 Ask him to balance himself by extending his arms out as far as he can either side of his body, like the blades of a helicopter.
2 Ask him to spin as fast as possible for 15 seconds.
3 After 15 seconds say, 'STOP and close your eyes. Keep your balance and stay still.' Let him stand for about 30 seconds until he no longer feels dizzy.

4 Spin again, going round the same way. Spin 15 seconds, rest 15 seconds, spin 15 seconds and so on up to ten times. See how fast he can spin. This should take about 5 minutes.

Eventually he should spin with his eyes closed, opening them when he needs to check on safety. If your child has problems with this, stand by and help by grasping one hand and quickly pulling his arm round to create a spinning movement. It is important to spin one way only, and remember, the greater the intensity of the activity the more it stimulates brain growth.

Brachiation exercises can also encourage brain growth. These involve exercising the upper part of the body, particularly the arms—for example when climbing trees, swinging from a rope or clambering over climbing frames. Jane's mother was with her in the park and was pleased to see Jane set about trying to climb a tree. She did not know Jane was having brachiation exercise, but she did know that varied physical exercise was good for her growing girl. It is not just a throwback to our ape-like ancestry: many sports depend on brachiating abilities, including gymnastics, tennis, golf, cricket, rowing, rounders (baseball) and that most complete exercise of all—swimming.

Water is a natural element for your child. Before birth children are totally immersed in a membrane of warm fluid. Babies are born with a natural swimming reflex, which accounts for the fact that they can learn to swim before they can walk. So take the plunge and help your child to swim, at whatever age. You do not have to be able to swim yourself to teach your child. Confidence is the key. As soon as your child is prepared to splash, submerge and open his eyes under water, learning to swim will follow naturally through trial and error. Being in the water is more important than getting in—either slide, jump or dive (some children learn to dive before they learn to swim). To become a good swimmer your child will need a good technique taught at school or club, as well as a strong, healthy and flexible body, and the motivation to make the most of his swimming skills. Given these, who knows? He may end up swimming the English Channel. Markus Hooper was only 12 when he swam from Dover to the French coast in 1979. But whether your child is destined to be a champion swimmer or not, by introducing him to the joys of swimming you will have given him a life-preserving as well as a life-enhancing skill.

Remember that for many children swimming is a complex challenge that may not come easily. As Carla, aged six, said, 'I wish I was a fish—swimming would be so much easier!'

KEY IDEA: TEACH YOUR CHILD TO SWIM AND BE ACTIVE IN WATER

Play games of different kinds
From about the age of two or three onwards, children can be introduced to most sports and games, in an appropriately simplified form, including football, cricket, golf, bowls, volleyball, martial arts or tennis. Coby Orr of Colorado learned to play golf young, and at the age of five astounded everyone by holing a shot of 94 metres (102 yards) in one. Joy Foster won the Jamaican tennis singles championship aged eight. Sonja Henie was Norwegian skating champion at the age of twelve. A child is never too young to start a simplified version of any sport or game.

You can make up your own games with a young child with simple objects in any space. Can she roll or bounce a ball into an empty can? Can she catch or dodge a ball, or juggle with two balls? One reason why some families have been remarkably successful in producing sporting champions is that they have begun very young in introducing ball skills to their children, teaching them to 'love the ball' and playing daily ball games.

The child who cannot catch or throw is generally a child who is afraid of the ball. A child who is denied the experience of play is denied success. Once she can play with a ball, your child in a sense need never be alone. A young girl once told her teacher she was going to play with the angels. 'How do you play?' asked the teacher. 'I throw the ball in the air,' said the girl, 'and the angels throw it back.'

'When I dance I feel my whole body come alive,' said Nadine. Dance, or any other kind of controlled movement like T'ai Chi or martial arts, is good for developing physical intelligence. Encourage your child to use her body in controlled and co-ordinated ways through her chosen games or sporting activity.

KEY IDEA: PARTICIPATE IN A WIDE VARIETY OF GAMES AND SPORTS

Actions can speak louder than words. Even as children we learn that we can alter our mental states by rocking, dancing or other means. We can banish stress, physical or emotional pain by intense involvement in physical or mental exercise. So we have good reasons to play. And like most things in life, our ability to engage in any physical activity improves with practice.

Did you know ... ?
When rats are placed in a physically challenging environment, put with other rats and given access to toys, ladders, wheels and other playthings to use and explore, their brain cells increase in size far more than rats brought up in a safe but dull environment, in cages on their own and with no toys. The rats brought up in a physically enriched environment do better in tests of 'intelligence', such as being tested to see if they can find food hidden in a maze, than the lone, physically inactive rats.

Promote practice

'I like games because you don't have to learn anything— you just do it. But if you want to get better at games you have to practise.' Chris, aged six

Hand-eye co-ordination is essential in all human activity. Without this ability we would not be able to butter a piece of toast, or hit a ball with a bat. Our small muscles generally respond quicker to nerve signals than larger ones, so our eyes respond more quickly than our hands. This gives us a split second in which to steer the hand in doing the activity. One way in which individuals differ is in the speed of the eye. Another way is in the precise movement of the hand. These small variations go some way to explain the differences between the performance of individuals, whether they are chopping onions, threading a needle or playing a sport. What helps to improve hand-eye co-ordination?

Practice improves hand-eye co-ordination, and the ability to perform any physical skill. As in all learning, what practice does is to build on and expand connections of cells within the brain if physical experience is repeated. Practice in speaking will help us to speak better, practice in a sport will help to improve our game. We therefore need to encourage our children to practise what they want to get better at, and to reward them for their effort.

One reason why practice is so important is that it encourages kinetic or physical memory. An example of this is touch-typing. There are good reasons for teaching our child to type, for children tend to spell better on the computer than they do with a pen. This is not to do with the spellcheck facility but with your child's own software. It is through practice that the fingers 'remember' groups of letters typed into the computer which they get wrong in handwriting. They also get faster with practice, if they have a five-finger instead of a one-finger approach to typing. Children often get frustrated at the computer because their brain works far faster than their fingers can type. Knowing how to type means teaching their fingers to do the thinking needed to put words onto paper. Doubling their typing speed halves the time they need to spend on getting the words into the computer. If you cannot type yourself there are software programs that can teach you, or your child, to type.

Even with proper coaching and practice humans will develop different levels of physical skill, and no two human beings follow the same pattern. Don't expect your child to follow your pattern of physical development or to have your skills. Some movements, like walking, running, throwing, jumping, and so on are mastered by all normal children, though each activity can be improved through training. Other skills like dribbling with a ball, sawing a piece of wood or typing will develop only if your child has the opportunity to develop them.

It is perfectly normal for children of the same age to have very different physical skills. Your child's body is uniquely his own, with an inbuilt pattern of development. In any physical activity there are three stages in learning a skill:

1 First attempts
This is the trial-and-error stage when the child is finding out what is involved. Not all these early experiments will be successful, so help him to cope with the frustrations of failure. Remember that failing is part of learning, and coping with frustration is part of coping with life. Allow time for this first experimental phase.

2 Practice play
Through repeating the activity your child will try different ways of doing things, and will have the chance to process the activity with different parts of his brain. Gradually, through his own effort and with advice from others, he will come to a better understanding of what he needs to practise.

3 Automatic skill
Gradually the physical movements become automatic, so that your child's mind is free to do something else at the same time, to direct his action at a goal or to talk or respond to someone else whilst performing the action. Once the skill becomes automatic he is in a better position to enjoy the sport, game or practical craft. Then he will be ready for more specific training if he wishes to become more expert in the activity.

Did you know . . . ?
Athletes who keep themselves super-fit are not
necessarily healthier than ordinary mortals.
Over-training the body can reduce its immunity to
disease. If the human body is stretched beyond its
normal limits of endurance it becomes more
susceptible to illness.

A good way to ensure regular practice is to join a club. At home try to add interest to whatever your child is practising by timing or recording his efforts. Buy something to measure with, like a watch with a stopwatch timing facility. Help your child find success in some form of physical activity, even if that success involves competing against himself. As Patrick, a boy who hates physical exercise, said, 'The only person I can beat is myself, and I don't always win!'

KEY IDEA: HELP YOUR CHILD IN REGULAR PRACTICE OF PHYSICAL SKILLS

Think physical

> *The centipede was happy quite*
> *Until the frog in fun*
> *said, 'Pray, which leg comes after which?'*
> *This set his mind in such a pitch*
> *he lay distracted in a ditch*
> *Wondering how to run!*

'You have to think about it if you want to do it better . . .' Advice given by a child to his younger brother.

Thinking about things can lead to worry and confusion (as in the case of the centipede, or as many feel when facing a driving test). But the right kind of thinking can help you, and your child, to do things better. We know that the body produces its best effort when it is in a state of relaxed concentration. The benefits of having relaxed muscles before any exertion are easily explained—a relaxed muscle can be stretched to a greater extent than a tense muscle. The same is true of the mind.

The mind thinks in terms of whole movements, so concentrating (like the centipede) on isolated parts will only interfere with your child's co-ordination. Whenever your child is trying to learn something there is a risk that she will be trying too hard. In trying too hard, or making that 'extra effort', the body becomes tense, producing unnecessary effort. Children need to be motivated, encouraged and rewarded, but not pressurised.

A good lesson does not deal in errors, but concentrates on what a child does well. She must of course learn how to fail and to lose, but repeated failure saps confidence. Start with what the child can do, begin in easy stages so that some success is guaranteed. Avoid boredom by making each practice game or activity fairly short and simple. Ensure your child has a fair share of winning and losing. Discuss ways of doing better next time.

Your encouragement is important. Research shows that most children receive far more negative comments than positive encouragement. Confidence lies in the mind and can easily be killed through others scorning effort or emphasising failure (or, in the words of a child, 'no put-downs'). Physical activity occurs in the mind as well as in the body. Henry Ford once said, 'If you think you can or think you can't, you're right.' Success comes in 'cans' not 'can'ts'. If a child feels good about herself, if she feels she can, she will try. Feeling good is not enough, but it is an important start. Help your child to feel good about herself and her body—even if her body is far from perfect. The world of sport provides countless examples of athletes overcoming crippling physical problems to lead the world. They do it not only because of training, and the faith of others in them, but because they have self-confidence and a will to win.

In gaining any physical skill, whether it is in acting, cooking or making a model, it is helpful to mentally rehearse the physical actions. Teach your child to 'think it first', to run over in her mind what she plans to do before the activity. If your child knows clearly what must be done before she starts she will not have to think so much while doing it, and instead of being like the centipede can run for the joy of running.

KEY IDEA: HELP YOUR CHILD PLAN AND REVIEW PROGRESS IN PHYSICAL ACTIVITY

SEVEN STEPS TO PHYSICAL INTELLIGENCE

- Undertake regular physical activity and exercise with your child.
- Offer opportunities for creative, complex and challenging physical play.
- Involve your child in home DIY and handicrafts.
- Teach your child to swim and be active in water.
- Encourage your child to participate in a wide variety of games and sports.
- Support your child in regular practice of physical skills.
- Help your child plan and review progress in physical activity.

8   Self-control

developing personal intelligence

Nature has concealed at the bottom of our minds talents and abilities of which we are not aware. François de la Rochefoucauld

I don't like people telling me things all the time. I like to work some things out for myself ... and sometimes I can. Jo, aged 6

Four small girls were walking home one afternoon from their school when a car drew up beside them. The man inside the car said to them, 'Your father said you are to come with me at once. He sent me to fetch you.' The man held the door open and three of the girls got in. The fourth girl did not, she ran off. The car sped away, while the girl ran as fast as she could to the nearby police station. She told her story, describing the colour of the car and the direction in which it was going. Patrol cars were alerted and the car was later stopped. The girls were unharmed and were returned home safely. When the girl who raised the alarm was asked what made her run off instead of going too, she replied, 'I don't know, but Daddy and Mummy are always saying "Think!" They say, "You've got a mind of your own, use it." So I thinked. I thinked that if Daddy really wanted us he'd have come himself, and I thinked that the man only said one daddy and we've got three daddies, all of us I mean. So I ran.'*

---

* This story was reported by Penelope Leach in *Baby and Child*, published by Michael Joseph.

WHAT IS PERSONAL INTELLIGENCE?

Personal intelligence is your child's ability to know himself, to be in control of what he thinks and feels and to know why he does things. A child with a well-developed personal intelligence has an accurate picture of himself. He understands who he is and what he wants to do. When the ancient Greeks were looking for words of wisdom to carve in front of the shrine of the oracle at Delphi, they decided on the words 'Know thyself'. They went to consult the oracle in order to find out about themselves and about what to do. Personal intelligence means knowing oneself, and being able to take responsibility for what one does in one's life. It is having the resourcefulness to know what to do when no one is there to tell us.

Like the Greeks, we all need help in finding out about what we think and need to do. From your child's point of view you, his teacher and his friends are his 'oracles', but the danger is that children may come to rely on what other people think and say they should do. As one child said to me, 'I like Miss Smith' (his teacher). When I asked why he said, 'She does your thinking for you.' If children do what their parents, their teachers and their friends tell them, they will have a lot less thinking to do, but they may grow up without minds of their own. They make obedient children but this can be dangerous, for they can become easily swayed by what others want them to do, and this as we know can end in trouble— as in the case of the three girls who went into the car. We want our children to do as we say, but we also want them to think for themselves. To do this we need to give them time to think, and opportunities to make decisions and choices for themselves, to develop their own personal practical approach to the world.

Personal intelligence helps us to solve the practical problems of life. The Greeks had a word for it, they called it 'nous'. This involves the ability to make wise decisions about our lives, through an understanding of who we are, what the situation is and what we want. Personal intelligence helps in solving personal problems. For example:

- Debbie knows she is not very good at spelling. She has thought about this and developed a number of strategies to help her cope. She checks words she is unsure of in a dictionary or with the spellcheck on a computer. She tries hard to learn words she often spells wrong. She is getting better at spelling but knows she must work hard at it.

- Paul has a bad temper. He knows he 'flies off the handle' easily when in a bad mood, but is trying to control it. One thing he does is to count to ten when he feels angry feelings rising within him. He is also quick to say sorry now when, as he says, he 'goes over the top'. Recently he has tried meditation and this helps to calm him down.

- Kerry likes to plan things but finds it difficult to remember what to do. She uses a notebook or her memo pad to write down things she is planning or wants to remember. Her parents help her by asking whether she has made a list. She used to forget things when going away. Now that she keeps a list of things to remember she feels better organised.

Did you know . . . ?
An autistic child is an example of an individual with an impaired personal (and social) intelligence. He may be unable to refer to himself as a separate person. He seems to be unaware of his own mind or the minds of others. However, some autistic children have remarkable abilities in other areas of intelligence—such as music or in computing numbers.

DEVELOPING YOUR CHILD'S PERSONAL INTELLIGENCE

The personal intelligence of your child is awakened when she is in a situation where she must think about herself, about what she thinks and feels. Developing personal intelligence means helping your child to be more mindful. Children become easily focused on the outcomes of their actions: 'Can I do this?' 'Why can't I do that?' 'Is this right?' This can create an anxious preoccupation with getting things right. So a child may use other intelligences successfully—getting sums right, drawing a good design, making the right model, spelling a word correctly—but may do it in a mindless way. This is why children who have been brought up in a rigid educational system may find it difficult to cope with change. They must learn what to do when there is no one to tell them what to do. They must learn how to cope with uncertainty and with failure. Like Amy, aged 14, who said about a test she had taken, 'I had to answer a question I had never been asked before and my mind just went to pieces.'

How do we help prevent a child's mind 'going to pieces' when faced with the unexpected? One way is to direct the child's attention as often as possible to the *processes* involved in solving problems. For example, instead of just saying, 'Never go off with strangers', ask questions like, 'What would you do if a stranger in a car said he had been told by Dad to fetch you home?'

Asking a child, 'How did do you do it?' instead of 'Have you done it?' or 'Tell me what you think' rather than 'That's right' or 'That's wrong', exercises the child's capacity for personal response. It helps a child think about herself as well as about the outcome of the task.

The development of personal intelligence begins with your child describing what she is doing and what she is feeling, with becoming aware of her separate identity. One reason for the 'terrible twos' is the typical two-year-old discovery that he or she is an individual self with needs and wants but without the control to satisfy them. Hence temper and tantrums. Later they learn to define what they want, what they like and dislike. Questions that can help this process include: 'Tell me what you want', Tell me what you like (or dislike) about it?' 'What is the best way of getting what you want?'

As they grow older children also learn how their behaviour affects others. Again this is helped by developing awareness of how their feelings are influenced by the behaviour of others: 'How does what they did make you feel?' This sense of self in relation to others is also linked to social intelligence:

'How does your behaviour affect others?' (see Chapter 9) and to philosophical and moral intelligence: 'How should people behave?' (see Chapter 10).

As personal intelligence develops, so does conscious control over emotions and a sense of personal identity (who I am and who I want to be). It also helps us become better at solving practical personal problems through the processes of planning what to do ('What do I want or need to do?'), monitoring what we are doing ('Is what I am doing working?'), and reviewing what we have done ('Have I succeeded—why or why not?'). This chapter shows how to develop these capacities in your child. Developing personal intelligence is a gradual process but there is much you can do to help.

If your child	What you can do	What your child can learn
Does not do things without being told what to do or how to do it	Give her one task or job at a time that she can do and discuss how she did it	She can succeed if she tries and concentrates on one thing at a time
Thinks he is no good at learning or doing things	Build your child's self-esteem by praising what he does well	He is good at doing some things and can learn to do more
Never asks questions or takes much interest in things at home or school	Take an interest in and ask questions about what she thinks and does	That she can ask questions and think for herself

HOW DOES PERSONAL INTELLIGENCE DEVELOP?

Personal intelligence is awakened when your child is in a situation that causes him to think about himself and makes him aware of what he thinks, feels and values. A sense of who we are comes initially from others. The attitudes and behaviour of parents are major factors influencing the way a child thinks of himself and his sense of control over who he is.

INPUT:	what you do	You stimulate your child by asking questions and helping him make sense of life.
OUTPUT:	what your child does	Your child becomes more aware of himself, what he thinks and feels and what he can do to help himself (and you) in the future.
SELF-CONTROL:	what your child learns	Your child becomes able to take conscious control of his thinking and feeling, to plan ahead and think about what he has done.

Did you know ... ?
The frontal lobes of the brain play an important part in personal intelligence. Injury to these lobes can result in personality change. Injury to the lower area of the frontal lobes can produce irritability or euphoria, while injury to the higher lobes can result in depression and apathy.

WHAT YOU CAN DO TO HELP

Personal intelligence, the sense of self, is partly a human invention, something the mind constructs by integrating all other forms of intelligence. This ability we have to think about our thinking is called metacognition. This understanding of 'me' is what is lost if we lose our memory. Personal intelligence represents all that there is to know and understand about ourselves. But what is this 'self'? What is 'me'?

How a child thinks of himself is called his *self–concept*. It

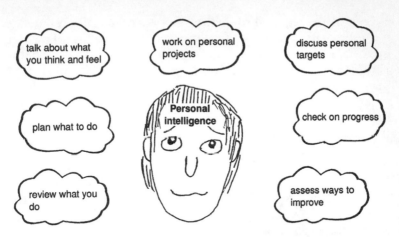

Ways to develop personal intelligence

is shown in the way he describes what he is good at, or not good at. Self-concept refers not only to what your child does but also to how he looks, his *self-image*. Self-image is what he thinks of his body and the way he looks, as well as what he thinks of his personality and talents. A person with a positive self-image believes the best about himself and so is often confident, able to tackle new things and not easily discouraged. Those with a negative self-image tend to think badly of themselves, often lack confidence and are easily discouraged. The trouble with a poor self-image is that it becomes a self-fulfilling prophecy. 'There, I knew I couldn't do it,' said James as he missed the target. 'I knew I could do it,' said Alice (who had as it happened also missed the target!). Getting children to draw themselves can sometimes reveal what they think about the way they look. What sort of picture does your child draw of himself?

The trouble with a positive self-image is that it may encourage a false idea of how good or successful you are, as with Alice. Napoleon was an example of the pitfalls of over-confidence. He won every battle and thought he was invincible as an army leader, then he marched to Moscow and was defeated. The ideal is to develop a positive but realistic self-image, so that you are confident of success but aware of how you might fail.

One of the signs of a well-developed personal intelligence is the capacity to cope with failure, the ability to 'pick yourself up, brush yourself down, and start all over again'. What helps here is to have an image of your *ideal self*. What sort of person would you like to become? Asking children about what they want to be when they grow up is one way of finding out about this ideal future self. Some children think they have few choices in life. As Ben, aged six, said, 'I guess when I grow up I'll be what my dad is.'

Self-esteem is low when there is a big gap between self-image (what we think we are like) and the ideal self (what we would like to be). A high self-esteem gives children the confidence to explore new environments, to learn new things, to develop a 'can do' approach to new tasks. High self-esteem is one of the keys to success in life. You build this by helping your child think positively about who he is and who he might become. Joey, aged six, expresses this self-esteem when he says, 'In the future I could be anything, anything I wanted.'

KEY IDEA: TALK WITH YOUR CHILD ABOUT WHAT HE THINKS AND FEELS

'Every person has two educations,' said the great writer Edward Gibbon, 'one which he receives from others, and one, more important, which he gives to himself.' The trouble with a poorly developed personal intelligence is that it blocks out ability to learn for ourselves. This helps to explain why some people find it hard to learn from their mistakes, and develop a false view of themselves. Some children think they cannot do or learn things that they are able to do quite easily, or think they are capable of doing things when they are not. What stops them getting a better understanding of themselves? What blocks the growth of their personal intelligence?

One defence against frustration and failure is regression—that is, going back to the immature behaviour of yourself when younger, usually the tears, sulks, tantrums and screams of the helpless infant. In extreme forms the child may wet the bed, return to sucking her thumb and using 'baby talk'. Sometimes this is an attention-seeking device (for example, if there is a new baby in the family and the older child is feeling left out).

What such a child needs is comfort and attention and fresh challenge, love and learning. Ways of combating this kind of 'learned helplessness' will be discussed below.

Another defence is blaming oneself, saying one cannot do it and therefore will not do it. 'I can't and won't!' said the child. 'You can and will!' said his mother.

A common defence is blaming others or the situation, or finding any excuse—for example, she is tired or has a pain rather than the real reason. She may blame her school or her teacher or other children. Her lack of success is therefore not her fault and there is nothing she can do about it.

Another defence is blaming the task. 'This is stupid!' or 'This is boring!' implying she could do it if she tried, but it is just not worth the bother. Other strategies for avoiding a task include spilling or dropping something, asking to go to the lavatory or feeling ill. At its worst she will 'lose' or destroy what she has done rather than face the risk of criticism or failure.

Another defence is that of escape. Sitting in front of the TV can be such a comfort in stressful or challenging times. Daydreaming is another form of escape from the problems we face, like the following poem by a child:

DAYDREAMS
My teacher thinks I am listening
but really I am flying across the sky
on my magic dream carpet
I am lying in the sun
on silver sand by the sea
I am finding pots of gold
at both ends of a rainbow
I am climbing the beanstalk
with Jack
I am at the ball
with Cinderella
I am painting my room
yellow
I am planning a party
and thinking who not to invite
My teacher thinks I am listening
but I am really not there

Another way is just to do the easy bits and leave the rest. 'Can I draw a picture first?' is a request familiar to teachers of young children (who hope there won't be enough time to do drawing *and* writing). Some children become impulsive, trying to get it over as quickly as possible, guessing the answer, saying the first thing that comes into their heads. A 'think first' approach is so important in trying to overcome the habit of not thinking about the question or guessing the answer. Not listening, or 'turning off, is another way to mini-mise failure. Some children become very adept at learning how to be helpless. By being helpless they come to rely on others, for example their teacher or parent, to give them clues, then perhaps more help or clues and then finally just to tell them the answer or do it for them.

Maria Montessori was in a park one day when she saw a young child trying to fill his bucket with stones. The child's nanny was with him and, thinking to help, filled his bucket for him. At once the child protested violently and burst into tears. Why was this? What the child wanted was to do it himself. Many nurseries and kindergartens today use Montessori's methods. The purpose of education, she said, was to help children become independent. This is summed up in her slogan: 'Never do for a child what the child can do for himself.'

If you encourage your child to work by herself on personal projects you not only foster the sort of independence Montessori would approve of, you can also strengthen her personal intelligence. Giving your child control and responsibility over some tasks encourages a sense of self-reliance and personal identity. It gives her the chance to see what she can do on her own, to know herself without someone else all the time defining what she should think and do.

Keeping a personal notebook, journal or diary and writing or drawing things to remember is a good way to help children reflect on themselves and express their personal thoughts and experiences. Younger children can make a 'My Book' of their lives, with pictures and personal captions. Older children can be given blank diaries or notebooks for their own use. Remember to honour the privacy of anything your child writes, or letters received that are 'personal'.

Teaching an older child to meditate has a similar effect of throwing the child back on her own inner resources. I once came across a child in school sitting staring into space. 'Haven't you got anything to do?' I asked. 'I'm not doing nothing, I'm meditating,' came the reply. Later I learned that this very self-possessed ten-year-old meditated with his parents for half an hour each day, and by himself whenever he felt the need. 'It helps me concentrate,' he explained, 'and sort out anything I need to think about.' Teaching children to meditate can help them become more calm and reflective. When I taught a tough inner-city class to meditate one of the children said it was the first time he had heard silence. It not only showed them how to find an inner space for thinking and reflection, but it also brought me peace, if only for a minute, while I was with them. Many years later, when I met one of these children, I asked if he could remember anything I taught him. He replied, 'I'll always remember the time when we sat there doing nothing.' He was, I hope, remembering the meditation.

KEY IDEA: ENCOURAGE YOUR CHILD TO WORK BY HERSELF ON PERSONAL PROJECTS

One way to help a child overcome problems in learning, and the sense of helplessness ('I can't do it, and I'll never be able to do it') that all children face from time to time, is the HEAD START approach of 'plan-check-review'. Help your child to think ahead, to think while he is doing, and to think afterwards about what he has done. Here are the stages in more detail:

1 Plan: teach your child to think ahead

One day nine-year-old Tom told his mother he was bored, so she found him something to do. Later she asked him to write down all the things he could think of to do when he was bored. She stuck this on a notice-board in the kitchen so that it was ready to hand in case her son complained again. Here is what Tom wrote:

WHAT TO DO WHEN I AM BORED

Learn a trick from my book *Almost everything there is
    to know* by Hunkin.
Draw a cartoon.
Try writing left-handed.
Make up a computer game.
Play a computer game.
Make a collage out of coloured paper.
Play Patience in cards.
Build a house out of cards.
Draw a map of a battle.
Draw graffiti on magazine pictures.
Write my latest dream in my diary.
Have a gossip with an imaginary friend.
Make a crossword out of Scrabble.
Act a sketch for a TV show.

For Tom this was not just an exercise in thinking about what
to do on a rainy day, but an exercise in personal intelligence,
in thinking for himself about how he could plan a solution
to a problem in his own way.

The greatest challenge the self has to face is that of frustra-

tion, either because we have failed to do what we wanted to, or because we have not had the opportunity to do what most satisfies us. Your child will face the possibility of failure in learning and in life, and he will face frustration like Tom who was bored and did not know what to do. So how can we help?

Showing your child how to plan is one way you can help him avoid possible frustration and failure. Showing your child how to plan means helping him to identify what he wants, and helping him to put his plan into words.

Did you know . . . ?

One reason why people succeed in what they are doing is that they spend time in planning, and preparing before they begin. Experts, whether they are good cooks, writers, painters, builders or athletes, spend more time planning than those who are novices or who are less successful. Research shows that good cooks do a lot of 'mental cookery', that is preparing menus and recipes beforehand in their minds. When they come to do the cooking they are well rehearsed.

Identifying what your child wants
Planning starts with your child thinking about what he wants, his aim or purpose. It is not enough that your child wants to do something: he should think about it first, and form some kind of plan of what he wants to do. Questions to encourage this kind of thinking include:

What do you want to do?
What do you want to achieve?
What do you want to happen?

Depending on your child's age, he will express his intentions in action (by getting something), by gestures (by pointing to something) or in words (by saying something). Always try to get your child to say what he wants. Encourage whole sentences. The ability to plan is linked with the ability to form mental pictures of things which are not actually there. We

233

don't want our children to live unthinking lives, but to think about purposes and reasons for doing things. So we need to help a young child to put things in words, like the following dialogue between a mother and child aged four:

> *Mother:* Where are you going?
> *Child:* Out.
> *Mother:* Why are you going out?
> *Child:* I don't know.
> *Mother:* Have you got a reason? . . . What do you want to do?
> *Child:* I'm going to see the guinea-pigs.
> *Mother:* Will you take them something?
> *Child:* Yes, I'll take them some carrot and find something in the garden for them to eat.

Encouraging your child to set targets or goals is important. Help him to work out what he wants to do or achieve. In particular, if you are getting him to do something that takes effort on his part, explain why it is important. Use his 'why' questions to help him make sense of life.

KEY IDEA: HELP YOUR CHILD THINK ABOUT WHAT HE WANTS AND WHY

Expressing a plan in words
As children plan they imagine something that has not yet happened. They have to think ahead. They think of different possible outcomes. They begin to understand that life involves making choices, that their decisions can make things happen. The child who wants to make a boat says, 'I will get some wood, and a hammer and nails.' The child who wants to buy a certain toy thinks about how she can ask, get or work for the money she needs. The child who wants to see a certain TV programme must think how to fit homework and supper into the schedule.

When a child plans she pauses between an impulse and an action to think how her purpose is best achieved. To do this she must stop and think, not only to make her ideas work, but to work in the best way possible. Learning to adapt plans that did not or may not work is an important skill. 'The last time I did it, it didn't work,' says Paul, aged six, 'so should I try it a different way?' Helping children to anticipate means asking questions like, 'Do you think it will work?' 'Is there anything else you need to think about?' and 'Can you do it another way?'

Any child who can solve problems, form mental images and think what she wants can make a plan. But planning is often not a habit, and is not done consciously. It is therefore a process that needs help and support. Putting their plans into their own words helps children to think about them and to be clear about what they want, need or do. Talking it through helps them to make clear mental pictures, gives them a chance to consider consequences and alternatives. 'I don't know what to do,' said William, aged five, 'so I'll have to go away and think of a plan.'

Turning ideas into action—the importance of making plans

STARTING POINT	IDEAS	ACTION	RESULT
No planning	vague ideas	aimless action	see what happens next
Planning	clear ideas	purposeful action	learning from experience

Planning helps to promote self-confidence and a sense of control, an 'I can think this through' attitude. Children who plan their play usually concentrate longer at it than children who do not plan. Older children will be able to work out more detailed plans for themselves. 'When I go to Grandma's, 'says Kim, aged eight, 'I am going to take my pastry-cutting set so I can make gingerbread men. We'd better take the ingredients too, just in case Gran hasn't got them.' Her mother then asks Kim what they need to take. Kim mentions these, and the bowls and spoons they may need, and says: 'I guess we've got the plan, now we've just got to cook and eat it!'

What planning can your child do?
Children learn from imitating others. If you want your child to plan, then share your own plans with her. Invite your child into discussions about family plans. Encourage her to make a variety of plans over time. For example:

- a weekly calendar of TV programmes she will watch;
- homework, or revision plan for a forthcoming test or exam;
- for a holiday—activities for a week or a fortnight, and a list of items to pack;
- ask: 'What plans have you for this morning/day/week/month/year?'
- an action plan for a specific task like making a model, cooking a recipe or decorating a room;
- planning a journey, saying what the best route would be;
- planning a shopping trip, with things listed to buy in order;
- plan a birthday or celebration party, the invitations to send, food and drink, games to play;
- plan a list of presents to buy or cards to send at Christmas, or for friends.

KEY IDEA: HELP YOUR CHILD TO PLAN WHAT SHE WANTS OR NEEDS TO DO

2 Check: teach your child to think about what he is doing

Making plans is just the beginning: children need to be just as mindful when they put their plans into action. They may need to modify or change their plans to find what works best. They may need to think about safety, or to correct mistakes. Help them to monitor or check what they are doing from time to time by asking them about what they are thinking and doing. This can be equally useful for a young child in a sandpit, or a fifteen-year-old struggling with his homework. Their needs in this respect are the same. They need to have someone occasionally there to take an interest in what they are doing and to challenge their thinking. Not that it is an easy role for a parent to get right. As one exasperated teenager said to his monitoring mother, 'You're like a guardian angel, except you're not there when I need you, and you come when I don't!' Better perhaps this than the thirteen-year-old who said of his parents. 'They're never there. They don't seem to care.' The child was wrong. The parents did care, they just thought their care was best shown by leaving the child alone.

Monitor progress by inviting your child to say what he thinks while you are working, reading or playing together. Invite your child to check what he is doing in a variety of situations. For example:

- while you are reading to or with your child;
- while he is working on personal projects, such as creating a dolls' house or model farm;
- while he is solving problems or puzzles, such as a jigsaw puzzle;
- while he is helping around the house, like clearing his room or washing the car;
- while he is playing games alone or with friends;
- while he is doing his homework.

Did you know . . . ?

At High Scope nurseries children spend time first thing every morning working out and discussing their plans for that day. While they work and play teachers will encourage them to think about what they are doing, and at the end of the day the children are asked to review and tell what they have done, how their plans worked out or had been changed.

Asking your child to explain what he is doing can help him to understand it better. The following is an excerpt from a 'think-and-do' discussion between an adult and a child who was busy building a model out of bricks:

Adult: What are you doing?
Child: I'm building something.
Adult: What are you building?

Child: I dunno.
Adult: Well, I think it looks like a castle ... a magic castle. Maybe there's a princess inside waiting for a prince to come. Perhaps he's out hunting for a dragon, and he'll be arriving back soon with the story of his adventures. Is it a magic castle, with towers and a drawbridge?
Child: No.
Adult: Oh, why not?
Child: 'Cos it's a garage.

Children will also learn from your own self-checking. Let your child hear you thinking aloud when you do things. Talk about your plans and problems while you are doing a task like cooking, or making something. Here a mother models the process of monitoring what she is doing whilst cooking with her six-year-old in the kitchen: 'Now, how far have we got? The chips are on, the peas are ready. Now we need to make the omelettes. Is everything ready? We've got the bowl, the flour, the milk, the frying-pan ... What have we forgotten?' Child: 'A hen to lay the eggs?'

KEY IDEA: ENCOURAGE YOUR CHILD TO BE AWARE OF WHAT HE IS DOING

3 Review: teach your child to think back

Planning is about what your child might do, *monitoring* is thinking while she is doing it and *review* is thinking back on what she has done. Take time each day to help your child remember, recall, report and review. Do this by encouraging her to remember and recall to mind what she has done. This helps her to think back and make sense of her actions. Recall means remembering and saying or showing what she has done. Review means exercising memory, reflecting on experience and learning her own lessons from it.

Reviewing is more than simply bringing things to mind from memory. It involves constructing the various fragments of remembered experience into a story. To do this a child must form a mental version of her experience based on her ability to understand and interpret what she has seen and done. When you ask your child each evening to tell you about her day you are asking her to select those experiences that have special meaning for her and frame them in some sort of reported story. This will help her to create the memory structure that will contain the story of that day for the rest of her life. It is through talk that memories take shape. It is therefore one of the most important things you can do as a parent—helping your child form meaningful memories.

Did you know . . . ?

Children develop the capacity to talk about the past from a very early age—between the ages of two and two-and-a-half. What two-year-olds find significant to recall are past events that went wrong or were harmful, causing some kind of pain or confusion. At any age people tend to find it easier to recall the 'bad times' in their lives than the good times. One role you can play with your child is to help him to remember the good times.

As a child tries to select events to talk about and interpret what happened, she will develop a better understanding of her experiences. She is helped by having an audience, such as parents, who draw out her memories, discuss relationships and explore connections. Sometimes this will mean helping children relate their experiences to their plans or hopes about what might happen. Help by asking a few thoughtful questions—for example, 'Did you plan it that way?' 'Did you expect it to happen?' 'Was it what you wanted?'

Young children rarely give a strictly chronological account of their time. Usually they pick out what was of special significance for them. As they get older they are able to recall more accurately, and to put things into a timed sequence. It can help them to remember shared experiences together, adding your own questions, memories and opinions as you tell the story together. Use questions to help your child remember:

- What happened?
- How do you know that?
- What else can you remember about it?

Once memories have been recalled they can be reviewed—
that is, carefully considered and thought about. Help your
child assess what was important about her experience, find
out what she feels about it, what she has learnt (if anything)
from it and how it might develop in the future.

Review what happened to you during the day. Discuss
what went well, or badly, and why. Share what you remember about experiences in your past. It is by recall and
review of the past that we strengthen self-awareness. Those
who do not learn from the past tend to repeat the mistakes
of the past. As James, aged eight, asked, 'Why do the
same things keep coming round and hitting you on the
head?'

KEY IDEA: REVIEW WITH YOUR CHILD AND HELP HER REFLECT ON WHAT SHE HAS DONE

Successful people do not live in the past, but use past experience to help inform the future. They do this by thinking not
only about what they have done but about what they need
to do next. The process of thinking back is most useful when
it helps to develop self-awareness. The following are some
questions to encourage review:

Assessing your child's learning:	Did you learn anything? Did you find it hard or easy? What do you think you need to learn/find out/do next?
Assessing your child's feelings:	How did you feel? What did you like/not like about it? What do you feel about it now?
Making plans or setting targets:	What will you/do you need to do next?

> What could you do to make it
> better next time?
> What do you think will/should
> happen next?

Your child will not learn from his mistakes or improve on his success unless he thinks back (learning from last time) and forward (planning for next time). Personal intelligence is the ability to be aware of our inner selves. You can strengthen your child's self-awareness through helping him to recall and review, for example by:

- having personal 'heart-to-heart' talks with your child, discussing what he thinks and feels;
- asking each day what your child has been doing, discussing what he remembers;
- talking about your child's personal targets and goals, what he wants to do and achieve;
- sharing your own memories with your child, recalling your thoughts and feelings;
- making scrapbooks, diaries and journals with your child of significant events in his life;
- encouraging him to keep a personal notebook and to write or draw things to remember;
- teaching your child to take a positive view about himself and his experiences.

One way is to ask your child to report on his progress at school. Here a seven-year-old is discussing a story he has written:

Adult: What is the best part of the story?
Child: I like the bit where the boy finds the bottle and wonders what is in it.
Adult: Yes, that was a good idea.
Child: I got the idea from the story of Aladdin, finding the magic lamp. I changed it into a bottle.
Adult: What is the hardest thing about writing a story like this?
Child: I know what I want to write but I don't always know how to spell it.
Adult: What do you do when you can't spell a word?

241

Child: I guess it, and if it looks right I leave it.
Adult: What is the best part of the story, the beginning, the middle or the end?
Child: The end, because then you can stop!

KEY IDEA: ENCOURAGE YOUR CHILD TO ASSESS PROGRESS, AND IDENTIFY WAYS TO IMPROVE

Personal intelligence is about developing self-knowledge and self-control. It is about helping your child understand the sort of person she is and wants to be. One characteristic of successful people is that they have self-awareness. They have come to know who they are and where they want to go. They are aware of their strengths and weaknesses, and know what they need to do to improve (even if they do not always do it). They know how they are similar to and different from other people. They are sensitive to their inner self. Tom, a bright child aged ten, showed some of this self-awareness when he said, 'I only do my best after I've given myself a really good talking to.'

In the next chapter we move from knowing me (personal intelligence) to knowing you and others (social intelligence). As Jane, aged six, explained tearfully one day, 'It's not me that's the trouble . . . it's the others!'

SEVEN STEPS TO PERSONAL INTELLIGENCE

- Talk with your child about what she thinks and feels about things.
- Encourage him to undertake personal projects, sometimes by himself.
- Discuss what she wants to do and why, encourage her to set targets and goals.
- Show him how to make plans about what to do, and share your plans.
- Encourage her to check on how she is doing, and adapt plans if necessary.

242

- Spend time reviewing with your child, helping him reflect on what he has done.
- Help her to assess her progress and identify ways to improve.

9   Knowing Others
developing social intelligence

I like my friends, it's just that I can't stand them for long. Karen aged 10

Gradually I learned to be indifferent to myself and my deficiencies; I came to centre my attention increasingly upon external objects: the state of the world, various branches of knowledge, individuals for whom I felt affection. Bertrand Russell, *Autobiography*

Simon has a well-developed social intelligence. He likes being with other people and they like him. He is friendly and sociable. He has a good sense of humour, and is good at making others laugh. He likes playing team games and learning through group activities. He doesn't much like being or working on his own. In his family he is the one who gets on best with his brothers and sisters. If his mother admitted to having a favourite (which she does not) it would probably be Simon. He has always got something to say, and most evenings he is on the telephone talking to friends (usually when he should be doing his homework). She knows his friendships are important, if only she did not have to pay the telephone bill, and that it is good to talk.

WHAT IS SOCIAL INTELLIGENCE?

What do a sales person, politician, army officer and market researcher have in common? They all need good social skills to do well in their work. Indeed, good social and communicative skills are needed in any job that involves working with other people. Social intelligence involves the ability to get on with, work with and motivate others towards a common goal. Every team needs a coach, and most groups need one or more members who help keep the group happy and together. The ability to make others help you to achieve what you (and they) want, involves many gifts, including the ability to understand other people, to get them on your side and to develop good relationships.

Social intelligence begins with the bonds made between child and parents. The baby learns quickly to imitate the sounds, words, and facial expressions of others. When you say words to a baby, pull faces and communicate with facial expressions, you are helping to develop his social understanding. This understanding expands beyond the family to include other adults and children. Gradually your child develops relationships with a widening range of people. Much of his happiness and success in life will depend on his ability to get on with other people and to benefit from what they have to offer.

According to the Greek philosopher Aristotle, those who are happy living entirely alone must be beasts or saints. We are social animals. We have survived as weak animals in a hostile world through our ability to co-operate with each other to overcome the problems, dangers and difficulties of life. This co-operation has been made possible by talk. We need to help our children to establish meaningful relationships with others, with family, with friends and sometimes with strangers.

Social intelligence helps us to solve the practical physical problems of life. Its positive aspect gives us the ability to relate well to others, and its negative aspect can be always relying on others for what we think and do. We need social intelligence to help solve problems, for example:

- John had to make a short presentation to a group of people as part of an interview. John was a sociable person, used to talking to groups of friends. When he came to make his presentation he was not as nervous as he thought he would be and was chosen as the best candidate at the interview. 'You seemed so confident,' they said after the interview. John replied, 'That sound of knocking you heard was my knees!'

- Lynne was walking one night in a lonely street when she was accosted by a strange man. She told him calmly and confidently that he had chosen the wrong person, and she would not go with him. The man swore at her, but went away. 'I knew my only hope was to face up to him, and show I was not a victim,' she said.

- Kim desperately wanted to be part of a musical show. When she went to audition for a part she was her usual friendly self with all she met and tried to reach the whole audience when she played her part. She was offered the part. The director told her, 'You really seemed to be able to project yourself.'

DEVELOPING YOUR CHILD'S SOCIAL INTELLIGENCE

Personal intelligence is about understanding yourself; social intelligence is about understanding others and acting wisely in human relations. Emotional intelligence is the way we combine personal and social intelligence. Personal intelligence includes the understanding of our own emotions, 'tuning in' to what we feel about ourselves and about life; social intelligence is about 'tuning in' to how other people feel and think. Because we are social animals and success in life (and in love) means being able to get on well with others, we need to help our children develop their social intelligence. For success and happiness in day-to-day living there is no intelligence that is more important.

Developing social intelligence means developing 'people skills'—that is the ability to form good social relationships with others. Some children find it easier than others, but you can help them to learn better social skills. In doing this you will be helping them to form better relationships with others, and perhaps even a better relationship with you.

If your child	What you can do	What your child can learn
Does not like to play, work, or be with others	Encourage your child to do things with one or two close friends	Sees the benefit of playing, working and being with others
Has a few friends but is rather shy of other people	Encourage her to join in club or team activities	Learns how to get along with different groups of people
Likes to be with others, sharing in their lives and problems	Encourage him to discuss his social life and ask him for advice about yours	Develops ability to listen, to give advice and to take an interest in others

HOW DOES SOCIAL INTELLIGENCE DEVELOP?

A child's capacity for forming social relationships begins in infancy with parents and carers. As infants grow into toddlers their social world expands to include brothers and sisters and familiar friends. As children grow they gain a widening experience of human contact. Their ability to talk and to form mental images enables them to develop social skills; they learn to distinguish their own needs from the needs of others ('me' and 'you'); they are able to describe their feelings and thoughts, recall past experiences with people and anticipate future social experiences. At a young age children begin to appreciate, understand and make judgements about themselves and other people in their world. As one four-year-old said, 'Oh no, not a visit to Aunt Mary again. I don't mind her cakes, it's her kissing I can't stand!'

Social intelligence develops through family life and friendships. Children are more likely to fight with their friends than with others in their group, and they also play their part in helping their friends to be friendly rather than aggressive. A friend becomes someone with whom you can share the ups and downs of everyday experience. They are both people you like and people you squabble with—for example, 'I want the car that Nick has' conflicts with the feeling 'I want to play with Nick'. Sorting out these conflicts is not easy at any age. It is by working through, and being helped to work through them that social abilities develop, alongside a growing awareness of the needs and feelings of others.

Did you know . . . ?

Diana, Princess of Wales, had a highly developed social intelligence, but when she was young her personal intelligence was not well developed. She found it hard to manage her inner needs, and this may have led to her eating disorder and to failed relationships. However, she learned to communicate well and charmed people into letting her have her way. She enjoyed an astonishing rapport with children, the sick and the dispossessed. She may not have managed her personal life well, but she learnt to manage her public life very successfully.

What helps develop social understanding is a supportive social climate. If your child's day-to-day experiences are positive, then she will see the world as a place of support and possibility. A sense of security and belonging will help her to grow in confidence, try out new ideas and rebound from setbacks. If her day-to-day experience is mainly negative, she will come to see the world as a place of danger and confrontation. She will not trust others for fear of being hurt or rejected.

INPUT: what you do   You stimulate your child
                              by engaging her in
                              co-operative activities and
                              games with others.

248

OUTPUT:	what your child does	Your child learns how to get on with others, and to take account of what others think and do.
SELF-CONTROL:	what your child learns	Your child is able to get on with other kinds of people and to learn from them.

WHAT YOU CAN DO TO HELP

'Other people are always a problem,' says Kate, aged six, and this is the hard part about living with other people—they pose problems. 'They want to do things you don't want to do,' explains Kate, 'and when you want to do something they don't.' The reason why social mammals like human beings are so much more intelligent than other more solitary animals is that they have had to face the constant challenge of living with others. When your child is explaining for the umpteenth time why his room is in such a mess, remember that he is exercising his social intelligence, which often means getting you to do something rather than doing it himself.

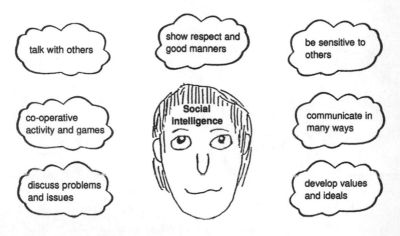

Some ways to develop social intelligence

What social life is good for is spreading ideas, what the experts call 'cultural transmission'. We learn from being with others, and seeing what they say and do. Being with others helps us to understand them. A child brought up in the wild, or with little contact with others, would find it hard to relate to his fellows or understand them. His capacity for social intelligence would not be developed. He would have no 'people skills'.

Did you know . . . ?
There are more arguments in families that are emotionally close. One sign of a family in trouble is if parents and children stop talking and avoid each other instead of arguing. It is often by arguing that we find out what others really think. Arguing can help a problem to be recognised and solved.

There are three main aspects of social intelligence. They are not easy to develop because they involve and depend on other people. The first of the 'people skills' is empathy, the ability to understand and to 'tune in' to other people, being aware of what they think and how they feel. The second is the ability to get on well with other people, to have the social skills that will enable your child to benefit from others through friendship, advice or practical help. The third aspect enables us to develop moral values and ideas about the kind of world we want to live in. Each of these aspects of your child's social intelligence is developed through talk.

KEY IDEA: ENCOURAGE YOUR CHILD TO TALK WITH FAMILY, FRIENDS AND OTHERS

1 Empathy: understanding others

When two-year-old Hannah saw her friend Lucy crying, she gave her own doll to her friend. When Lucy kept on crying, tears began to well up in Hannah's eyes. She was not just feeling sympathy for Lucy's unhappiness, she was sharing what Lucy was feeling. It is a capacity that develops around two-and-a-half when children realise that someone else's pain is different from their own. Some continue to be keenly aware of other's feelings, others are much less aware.

If your child is good at understanding her own feelings she is likely to be good at reading other people's. If she cannot do this her chances of success in life are limited. She will not do well in forming relationships. She will not make a good parent if she cannot imagine what other people might be feeling. She will not do well at work if she is unaware of the feelings of others, nor in forming any relationships that require mutual understanding. We can also see how important empathy is when we consider people who lack it to an extreme degree, such as psychopaths, rapists and child molesters. They simply do not understand the effects of their actions on others. They have no feelings of empathy.

Did you know . . . ?

Children who have impaired functioning of the frontal cortex of the brain tend to do poorly at primary school even though they may be intelligent and have high IQ scores. If there are poor connections between the lower centres of the emotional brain and the 'thinking abilities' of the cortex, then their emotional life will be impaired. They lack feeling for others, and run a high risk of becoming involved in criminal behaviour.

But what is empathy, and how is it developed?

Empathy means understanding other people and having an insight into what they think and feel. The trouble with young children is that they think the world revolves around them, they are very egocentric. As they discover the 'self' they become 'self-ish'. 'Me, me . . . I want!' It is hard for them to imagine what life is like for other people. Here is where you can help, by giving your child some 'empathy coaching'.

The aim of empathy coaching is to help your child see

and understand other points of view—that people may have thoughts, feelings, hopes and fears which may be like or very different from her own. Coaching can take place through discussing characters in a story, or when discussing situations in real life. The aim is to encourage your child to think about what life might be like for others.

When reading a story or seeing a play on television, talk about what the characters are thinking and feeling. For example, in the story of Cinderella ask why the sisters did not like Cinderella. Why were they jealous? How did Cinderella feel? What did she think? What did she (and they, and the prince) want? While reading the fable 'The ant and the grasshopper' by Aesop, ask questions like, 'What did the ant think?' 'What did the grasshopper think?' and afterwards, 'Which would you rather be, the ant or the grasshopper?' and 'What is the moral of this story?' While watching an episode of a soap like *Neighbours* on TV, ask about what the characters are thinking, feeling and hoping. As a child said about something he was finding rather dull, 'Whenever it is boring I try to make the characters come alive in my head.'

Try making the characters come alive in your child's head, and exercise her social intelligence at the same time by asking questions such as:

What are they thinking?
What do you think they are feeling?
What do you think they are hoping/fearing/wanting?
Why are they doing/saying/thinking/feeling that?

'I just don't understand other people!' yelled Kirsty, aged 15, as she stormed off to her room after a tiff with her parents. Understanding others is not easy, even if you have lived with them for many years. Living with others means facing dilemmas about what to say, and how to react to what others say and do. The following are some dilemmas parents have faced with children. Which of the responses do you think would best help coach a child for empathy and understanding?

Dilemma 1
Your child comes in from playing and says, 'I hate those kids. They won't let me play with them, they are so mean.' What is your response?
   Response 1: 'Don't be so silly. You have to learn to get on with others.'
   Response 2: 'That must have hurt your feelings. What happened? Why won't they let you play?'

Dilemma 2
While having a bath your child says, 'I hate my sister. I wish she were dead.'
   Response 1: 'That's a terrible thing to say. You don't hate your sister. You love your sister. I never want to hear you say that again.'
   Response 2: I know your sister can really drive you mad sometimes. What did she do?

Dilemma 3
Your child comes home from school and says, 'I am never going back. The teacher shouted at me. It wasn't fair!'
   Response 1: 'What did you do to make your teacher shout at you?'
   Response 2: 'It's not nice to be shouted at. There must have been a reason. What happened?'

Dilemma 4
Your child is playing at home with a friend. Your child says, 'You can't play with me. I am not going to share my toys with you.'
   Response 1: 'Don't be so selfish. You must play properly.'
   Response 2: 'I know it's not easy to share. What do you think your friend feels if you won't play? Can you find something you'd be happy to share?'

Dilemma 5
Your child says, 'I wish you weren't taking care of me. I wish so-and-so (naming your absent partner) was here.'
   Response 1: 'That's not a nice thing to say.'
   Response 2: 'I know you miss so-and-so. So do I.'

Dilemma 6
Your child disappears in a department store. You are very worried. After a while your child is found and brought back to you.

Response 1: 'You silly child. I told you not to go off without me. I'm not taking you shopping again.'

Response 2: 'I'm glad you are back. You must have been scared. I was scared too. What happened?'

NOTE: In each of the examples there is no right answer, but Response 2 is more typical of a parent who wants to help develop the child's social understanding and awareness.

KEY IDEA: TREAT YOUR CHILD WITH THE RESPECT YOU WISH HER TO SHOW OTHERS

What do other people feel? To have empathy your child must not only feel for other people, for example feeling sympathy for their suffering, she must also 'feel with' other people. This means being sensitive to the moods of other people, being able, for example, to read signs of joy and distress. Helping children to 'read' other people, to be sensitive to what they may be thinking and feeling, is an important skill to learn. One way of encouraging sensitivity to the range of emotions people have is to show your child photos of people from magazines and to discuss what you think they are feeling. Can she read emotions from the facial expressions in the picture? What words would she use to describe what the person is feeling? What other words describe feelings?

What helps in understanding is having a choice of words to use. We need to help children find words to describe a range of emotions. What words describe how you are feeling? What *other* words describe how you are feeling? What is another word for 'happy', 'sad' or 'angry'?

What we tell children they quickly forget. What they express in their own words is more easily remembered. It is not enough to lecture children about being good, we need to help develop those essential emotional and social skills through which they can practise a moral life, and encourage them to discuss the problems that inevitably arise when living with others. As Ricky, aged nine, said in a discussion of why there are 'goodies' and 'baddies' in the world, 'You cannot make people be good, they have to want to.' Penny, aged eight, summed up a problem for her as follows, 'What do you do to make people good, and like you, when they don't want to?'

KEY IDEA: HELP YOUR CHILD TO BE SENSITIVE TO WHAT OTHERS THINK AND FEEL

2 Social skills: getting on with others

Those with good social skills are popular with others. They have charisma, people are attracted to them, and they benefit from what others have to offer. Because they understand others they become good at defusing explosive situations. They often make good leaders. The value of such skills shows itself in your child's ability to make good relationships with others—and to talk himself out of difficult or dangerous situations.

But what are social skills and how are they developed? The key to social skills is communication. To get from others we need to be able to tell them what we want, and persuade them to help us If your child cannot communicate well, it will be difficult for others, including parents, to respond to his needs. 'If you could have told me what you wanted I might have been able to do something about it,' is a cry heard in many a failed relationship. Being able to communicate what you want in such a way that others will want to help you is not an easy skill to learn. The infant's cry 'I want! I want!' will be less effective as he grows older. Your child will need to learn how to control and marshal his emotions to best effect. This is the secret of human charm, and as someone once said, it doesn't come in bottles. One of the greatest challenges we face as parents is to help our child develop into the sort of person who is going to function successfully within a social system. Children want this too. As Nick, aged six, said after a quarrel, 'I want to be friends, but they don't tell you how.'

The way to develop social intelligence is not through blind

obedience to others, but through becoming good at communicating thoughts and feelings, being able to take responsibility for your actions and not being afraid to ask for help. Many children are not helped to do this. One child reported, 'I'd rather sit there not being able to do it than bother my teacher. She gets so cross if you can't do it.' Poor teacher, if there are children too afraid to ask in her class she is going to get cross very often, frustrated that they will not seek help when they need it. This was a teacher who always did most of the talking, and did not allow space to hear what the children might have to say. *Helping your child communicate means encouraging him to do half the talking*. It also means negotiating and discussing with your child rather than just telling him (unless of course it is a life-threatening situation).

Children's opportunities to talk at home can differ enormously.

Don was a child who was never encouraged to talk at home. He had two talkative and opinionated parents. A shy child, he hardly got a word in edgeways. He grew into a quiet adolescent, and later found it difficult to share his feelings with other adults. When he became a parent he said, 'I want to give my child what I never had . . . space to talk.'

Sally had a very different upbringing. She was the apple of her parents' eye, and always held the floor at home. A talkative girl, she liked to dominate every conversation. As an adolescent she had lots of friends but many were put off by what they saw as her bossiness. As an adult she got a well paid job in the city, but was later made redundant. 'They just wouldn't listen,' she complained of her former employers. The trouble with Sally, say her friends, is that very often *she* just doesn't listen.

Being a good communicator means being a good listener as well as a talker. It also means being able to communicate through a variety of means such as writing, drawing, using the telephone or computer (e-mail) to be in contact with others.

KEY IDEA: ENCOURAGE COMMUNICATION THROUGH WRITING, TELEPHONE, E-MAIL, ETC.

'A round man cannot be expected to fit into a square hole right away. He must have time to modify his shape,' said Mark Twain. Your child will need to learn to adapt to many different groups of people and social situations, including friends, family, strangers, foreigners, people at school and at work. In a changing world where new acquaintances are going to present fresh challenges, your child will need to be flexible and socially versatile, learning how to get on with a wide range of individuals. The way you treat your child can have a positive and lasting effect on the sort of person he will turn out to be.

Families that promote the most positive and happy relationships with their children (whether toddlers or teenagers) share the following common characteristics:

- *Clear talking,* which means that children feel they know exactly what their parents expect of them. Do your children really know what you think and feel about them? As one mother put it, 'It is never enough to say it once, particularly saying that you love them. I tell them as often as I can.'

- *Centring attention,* which means that children know their parents care about what they think or feel, not just in the grades they are getting, or the job they are doing. They do this by finding time to give them some full attention each day. As one busy father said, 'I try to give some quality time every day, which means a time when I give 100 per cent attention to what my child says.'

• *Giving choice* means that children are given opportunities to exercise choice, including sometimes choosing what their parents disapprove of. As one teacher put it, 'If you don't give them a choice, how are they going to learn to choose? One day when they control their own lives they will *have* to choose.'

• *Offering challenge* means children knowing that opportunities for action will be given that challenge them physically or mentally. It means expecting them to give reasons for what they say and do, and sometimes expecting them to achieve something difficult and worthwhile. As one parent put it, 'If you don't push them, no one else will.'

Children need security and stimulus. They get their sense of security from the love they receive at home; the stimulus they get from home is an added bonus. Friends provide the stimulus of novelty; if they are good friends they help us think, say and do new things. The trouble with the human world is that it is not always designed for comfort: friendship poses problems as well as opportunities for happiness. John has good friends at his play-school. One day they say to him, 'You can't play with us.' 'Yes, I can,' says John. 'No, you can't,' they reply. 'We don't like you today.'

We all have to learn how to manage our emotions, and being rejected by others can be traumatic. One of the most important lessons we learn in childhood is what to do when we feel upset. Parents can help by coaching their children socially and emotionally, encouraging them to talk about their feelings, not by being critical but by problem-solving, and discussing alternatives. 'Tell me about it', 'What did you feel?' 'I would have felt very hurt', 'Sometimes we all say things that hurt other people', 'This happened to me once . . .', 'What could you have done?', 'What would have made you feel better?' are 'door openers' that can encourage your child to talk through his problems. Children need to learn how to share their problems, how to discuss and negotiate with others, how to learn to control their emotions.

Today's parents have less time than ever to talk to their children. With increasing numbers of single-parent families, and parents often out working, with TV and computer screen absorbing hours of attention, children are deprived of the talk that nourishes their social intelligence. The cost of being deprived of talk is high, and contributes to the growing numbers of children who are aggressive or who withdraw into depression. The trouble is that children who act like this are not fun to be with, and this makes matters worse. They need help in making friends, for example by being encouraged to think of alternative viewpoints, to compromise with others rather than fight, to take an interest in others and ask questions, to listen to and look at them while talking, to say something nice when others do something well, to smile, help and encourage others. These are strategies we too need to use with our children.

Did you know . . . ?

Your child can be too upset to think straight. If he has problems to solve, the frontal lobes in the brain activate his working memory, including emotional memories. But if the incoming signals are too strong they flood the mind, blocking his capacity to solve problems. That is why a 'cooling off' period can be so useful in ridding the mind of emotional memories.

We need to show children that violence or withdrawal does not solve problems, and that there are other ways to control feelings and achieve the results you want. The following problem-solving steps encourage the use of social intelligence in finding more effective ways of relating to others:

- Stop, calm down, and think before you act.
- Say what the problem is and how you feel.
- Set a goal, say what you want to happen.
- Think of many possible solutions.
- Decide on the best plan and try it.

This basic strategy is a good one for helping children overcome their problems, and for dealing with the risks of adolescence and beyond. Find out what is going on before jumping to conclusions, think of other viewpoints, think of consequences. Children, like adults, easily fall into the trap of FOTSO—the Fallacy of the Single Option. They grow up to think there is only one way of doing things—the right way. We need to help them see and think about different options. The following is the sort of situation to discuss with a four- to six-year-old: *'Leo has been playing with Lego all morning. Now Claire wants a turn with it. What can Claire do to get a turn at playing with the Lego? Now tell me another thing she can do . . .'* Encourage your child to think of alternative solutions to problems.

Did you know . . . ?
The very first Girl Guide was Alison Cargill, a Glasgow schoolgirl, who in 1908 was told she could not enter the Boy Scouts because she was a girl. Alison was a girl with a highly developed social intelligence, a natural leader. She knew that if you were turned away from one group the best thing was to try to create another. So she created her own group of girl scouts which she called the 'Cuckoo Patrol'.

One of the best ways to learn about other people is to teach them. If your child has younger relatives or friends, encourage her to teach the younger child how to play a game, make something or do a job. Children teaching children benefits both the teaching child and the learning child. The teaching child learns that teaching is not easy. You need not only to know what to do, you need to be able to present it in such a way that the learner understands it. It is quite a challenge to a child's social intelligence to be patient, to try to understand the problems faced by a learner, and to be able to respond to his needs. No wonder children find teaching others very difficult (parents too!). If they have not got other children to help, get them to teach you. Whatever teaching your child does will help challenge and develop her social intelligence. As Paul, aged nine, said, after trying to help a younger friend to read, 'I didn't know it was such a hard thing to do until I tried to show someone how to do it.'

Joining a group or club will provide your child with opportunities for cooperative activity and games. Encourage role-play at home, to help your child understand what it is like to be someone else. When reading a story invite your child to take on the role of a character in a story. Swap roles. Ask questions like:

- What would you think if you were . . . (name a character)?
- What would you feel?
- What would you say?
- What would you do?

Organising parties and celebrations can also be a challenge to the social skills of all involved, as Kate, aged six, was beginning to realise when she said, 'Why are parties such hard work?' Organising a party is hard work because it takes many skills—planning, organising, coordinating—as well as the challenge of making others happy. No wonder they can be so exhausting!

KEY IDEA: PROVIDE OPPORTUNITIES FOR COOPERATIVE ACTIVITY, GAMES AND ROLE-PLAY

We cannot choose our emotions, but we can control how we respond to them. If you can use a 'think what it would be like for others' policy with your child, it will provide him with a model of social intelligence, and show ways in which the emotional mind can be controlled by reason.

3 Social ideals: developing values

'What sort of world do you want to live in when you grow up?' was a question put to a group of young children. Jamie, aged six, replied, 'I want to live in a world where there are no nasty people, where people are always kind and help each other. It only happens in story books, but I guess it could be real.' What Jamie was thinking about here was a possible world, an ideal world where people would be good. He was thinking not just about the people around him and how they should behave, but was exploring ideas about how all people should live. He was thinking about social ideals, the kind of person he wanted to be and the kind of world he wanted to live in.

One way of developing social intelligence is to encourage an understanding of different viewpoints and different values. Penny, aged eight, from a religious family, reported one day that she had been telling her friend in school all about God, about how Jesus was His son sent into the world to be friend and saviour of all who believed in Him, but, 'Unfortunately', she said of her friend, 'she's a Sikh.' What Penny was beginning to understand was that people have different religious and cultural values, but that this does not prevent you from being friends or sharing your ideas. Children learn what social ideals and values are by hearing about the cultural values of others. Talk with them about what you believe and about the beliefs of others; that way they will better understand different people and their viewpoints but see also what values and ideas are.

KEY IDEA: DISCUSS PERSONAL PROBLEMS, AND ISSUES IN THE NEWS

What we hope for our children is that they will become reasonable social beings, able to relate well to others (even those with views very different from their own), and committed to the creation of a better world. We do this by sharing our own values, and saying what we believe is right and wrong, but also by encouraging them to think about their own values—the kind of person they want to be and the sort of world they want to live in. We want them to think about themselves, but also to think about others and about the world, including their ideal world. This imagining of an ideal world and how it might come about has exercised and challenged the minds of the greatest thinkers. It is the exercise, among other things, of social intelligence at its highest functioning, and it is something we can begin to develop with children in discussions over the kitchen table.

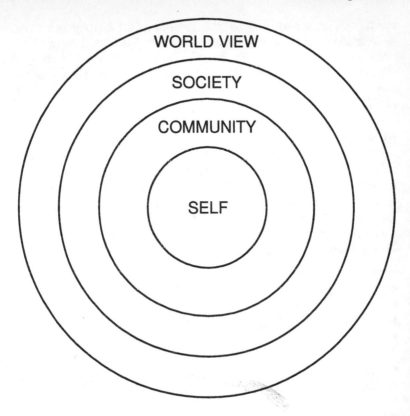

Different levels of social awareness

Kirsty and her mum were reading a book about princesses, castles and dragons:

Mum: Would you like to live in a world like that?
Kirsty: No. It's not fair having dragons frightening people. I don't think there should be any dragons.
Mum: Would there be any dragons in a perfect world?
Kirsty: Yes. But all the dragons would be pets. Everyone would have their own dragon to look after.

As your child grows older she will need to develop different levels of social awareness (see diagram). The first circle of awareness is oneself and self-awareness (see Chapter 8 on personal intelligence). Social awareness extends through friends and family. These are people who help your child understand who he is. They introduce him to new experiences, questions and problems. There are many ways to help develop your child's social thinking. The following are three key questions he will need to think about. The first question is: *What is a friend?*

Key question: WHAT IS A FRIEND?
One of the most important elements in any child's life is the friendships he forms. This can mean not only being able to make friends, but also understanding what it means to be a friend. What do you need to do to be a friend? What is an ideal friend? What kind of friend do you want to be? The following are some questions to encourage your child to think about being a friend and about his ideal of friendship.

- What is a friend? What is your definition of a friend?
- Can a friend be someone you do not like?
- Can people fight and still be friends?
- Can people be happy without friends?
- Can you talk and play a lot with someone and not be a friend?
- Can you be afraid of a friend?
- Can you be a friend of someone you have never met?
- Are friends of a friend always your friends?
- Could you be friends with everyone?
- How do you make friends?

As she learns more about her community and culture your child will be introduced to other role models and heroes. The next question to consider is: *Who are our heroes?*

Key question: WHO ARE OUR HEROES?
All children need role models and heroes. They cannot develop their ideas and ideals about how to live and how to behave unless they learn about the ways others have lived and behaved. If they see and live with selfish, rude and violent role models, this will be reflected in their own behaviour and expectations. Children learn what they live. If they experience, at least some of the time, the best kinds of human behaviour, through stories, TV or in real life, these will

become positive influences on their lives. The more they learn about good role models the more likely they will be to copy the model. But what are the best kinds of human behaviour? And who are the role models and heroes that live these kinds of lives?

Discuss with your child the various role models and heroes you come across in stories, on TV, in the news and in real life. Encourage her to collect pictures of her favourite cultural, sporting or religious heroes. Use the following as discussion starters:

- Who is your hero?
- Who would you most like to be? Why?
- What is your favourite character in the story? Why do you like him or her?
- If you could grow up like anybody else who would it be? Why?
- Do you think it is better for a hero to be honest or brave? Can a hero be both?

Discuss real-life heroes, for example friends or family members who have done something brave, honest or are heroes to you for some reason. Talk about why some people are given medals or prizes and how much work they have to do to merit their rewards.

Gradually your child will become more aware of the world, both its glories and its imperfections. The world of the future will be hers, so help her to start thinking about how she can contribute to its well-being. A question for her to think about is: *How can the world become a better place?*

Key question: HOW CAN THE WORLD BECOME A BETTER PLACE?
Many religious stories encourage us to see how we can help to make the world a better place by becoming better people or behaving in better ways. Many other stories also have as a theme ways in which the characters are trying to make a better world.

Make this a theme in your family discussions of news, events or stories—does it help to make the world a better place? Why, or why not? Be ready for disagreements. Encourage your child to think of her own ways to make the world a better place. The question to ask here is, How can we help? The answer of one family was to involve their children in a recycling programme in which as much household waste as possible was recycled, with each member of the family responsible for sorting and packing one kind of waste. The parents explained, 'We don't really do it for us, or for others. We do it to show our children that a small difference can make a big difference if you do it yourself. It helped them to think that the world is theirs, and that they can do something to make their world a better world.'

KEY IDEA: HELP THEM RECOGNISE DIFFERING VALUES, AND DEVELOP THEIR OWN VALUES

The following are some discussion starters in thinking about how to make a better world:

- How can we make our house, garden, street, neighbourhood a better place to live in?
- Who do we know who is unhappy? How can we help them?
- Who do we know who is lonely? How can we help them?
- Who in the world needs our help? How can we help them?
- How can we help people who are starving, or who are victims of a disaster?

There are no right or wrong answers to any of these questions, but by thinking and discussing them we become aware of our own feelings, motives and opinions and, if we discuss them with others, of what they think and feel too. Such a process is creative for it encourages children to think not only about themselves but others, and also to think about their view of the world. This is an exercise of social intelligence, but it is more for it helps develop the next amazing capacity of your child's brain—philosophical intelligence.

SEVEN STEPS TO DEVELOPING SOCIAL INTELLIGENCE

- Encourage your child to talk with family, friends and others who enter his life.
- Treat your child with the respect and good manners you wish her to show others.
- Help him to be sensitive to what others think and feel, and to what he feels.
- Provide opportunities to join in cooperative activities, team games, and work experience.
- Encourage communication with others, through letters, postcards, telephone and e-mail.
- Discuss personal problems, as well as current social and political issues in the news.
- Help her recognise differing values, and to develop her own values and ideals.

10   Your Philosophical Child

developing philosophical intelligence

Why is it that while children of four, five or six are full of curiosity, creativity and interest and never stop asking for further explanations, by the time they are 18 they are passive, uncritical and bored with learning? Matthew Lipman

There are so many questions in life. School can give you answers from books, but most of the hard questions like 'Should I steal?' or 'Should I tell a lie?' or 'Does God exist?' you have to work out for yourself. Tom, aged 13

We were reading a story about animals, when I asked my boys: 'Can animals think?'

'Yes,' said Tom, 'they can think because they can talk.'

'How do you know?' I asked.

'If they couldn't think they couldn't get away from their enemies. Like my guinea pigs hide under the cupboard to get away from us. If they didn't have brains they would die.'

'Rabbits can't talk,' said Jake.

'Yes they can . . . in fairy stories.'

'Foxes can think. They catch rabbits and eat them. They have to be pretty clever to do that.'

'All animals can think. They're just not as clever as we are.'

'If all animals can think,' I said, 'and rabbits are animals, then all rabbits can think.'

'I know some rabbits who can't think.'

'Which rabbits are they?' I asked.

'Stuffed rabbits!'

We carried on talking about the difference between a stuffed rabbit and a real rabbit. The children decided that the toy could speak, but it didn't think because it did not know what it was saying. Jake concluded by saying: 'A toy is not real . . . like us.'

What we had found in the story were some interesting questions—not questions just about the story (scc Chapter 2 on linguistic intelligence) but about the concept of thinking, whether animals can think, and what is real or fake, true or false, and whether any animal that did not know what it was saying was not a clever animal. What enabled us to do this was that important capacity of the human mind called philosophical intelligence.

WHAT IS PHILOSOPHICAL INTELLIGENCE?

'All people by nature desire to know,' said Aristotle, and anyone who has spent time with young children will be in no doubt that their way of finding out is to ask questions. Some of these questions, such as, 'Why doesn't the sky fall on our heads?' 'Why do cows eat grass?' 'How old is the cat?', are questions about the physical world, and are asked because children are puzzled by what they see and hear. When they ask these kinds of question children are being curious in a scientific way (see Chapter 4).

Other questions that children ask are not about the physical world, but about our ideas (or concepts) of the world, about what we think and believe. With some of these questions, such as, 'Why are people cruel to each other?' 'Does God exist?' 'What is love?', the right answer may not be known, or there may be several possible answers. These questions arise out of a child's natural curiosity, but they are not scientific. There is not one right answer, but many possible answers, and many different viewpoints. They are questions about what we think as human beings, and are about the way we make sense of life. These kinds of question are philosophical.

Philosophy differs from science, from mathematics and from other forms of understanding. Philosophy relies not on

269

things in the world but on our *thoughts about* the world, the universe and everything. Personal intelligence answers the question: 'What does it mean for *me*?' Social intelligence answers the question: 'What does it mean for *others*?' Philosophical intelligence answers the question: 'What does it *all* mean?' It works by asking questions, arguing a point of view, trying out ideas and wondering if they make sense. When Jenny, aged four, asked, 'What does "love" mean?' her question was philosophical if it was about our idea or concept of love. When Carl, aged six, asked, 'Why did God let grandad die?' his question was philosophical if it was asking about God and the reasons for death.

Most of the time we are not philosophical. What usually concerns us is 'What's next?' It is easy to be like that with children, forever hurrying them on to the next thing. As a mother said to her child in a supermarket, 'Don't ask clever questions, we've got shopping to do.' Philosophy begins when we stop to ask 'Why?' The more we allow children to stop and wonder why, the more chance there is for their philosophical intelligence to develop.

Young children are natural philosophers, if they are given the chance to ask question and have someone to discuss their ideas. They will not be philosophers in the sense of coming to know all the answers, but will begin to be philosophical when they wonder about the world and ask the sorts of questions which have puzzled philosophers for centuries. Like the five-year-old who asked, 'Where does time go when it's over?'

Children want to find out why things are as they are and what words mean. The trouble with adults is that we use many of our everyday ideas without thinking about them. For children these ideas may be new or strange. Children will use words in an unthinking way, not really understanding them, unless we take time to ask them what they mean and not just hurry them along to the next thing.

Child: How long will the world last?
Parent: I don't know, dear, we're late already.

Some questions have no easy answer. When a child asks, 'Where is grandma now she is dead?' there may be many possible answers. What kind of answer do we give? One kind of answer may be scientific, for example what happened to grandma's body after she died. But the question may also refer to more than a scientific explanation about the physical body, for example to all that 'grandma' means to those left behind. The question can be answered in different ways, and some of these answers will be philosophical—like the child whose answer to this question was, 'She doesn't live in the world now, but only in our hearts.'

Philosophical intelligence is what all the great thinkers and religious leaders have used in working out solutions to the human problems about how to live and what to believe. Science can tell us what things are, but we need philosophical intelligence to show us what to believe and how to behave. Philosophical intelligence is something we all use when we try to find meaning in life. If you have ever been floored by a real poser of a question, or by a thoughtful enquiry on a delicate topic by your child, then you will have seen philosophical intelligence at work.

We need philosophical intelligence to help solve problems about what to think and do—for example:

- Simon was walking to school when he found a £20 note on the pavement. He took it in and gave it to his teacher. 'That was very honest of you,' said his teacher. 'Well, I figured that if it was *me* who lost the money I'd like someone to find it and give it in. So I thought it was the right thing for someone to do.' Simon had thought of a moral reason for handing it in.

- Jane was out with some friends and they could not agree what to do. Some wanted to go shopping, some wanted a walk in the park, while others wanted to go back to Jane's house. Jane said the fairest way to decide was to have a vote. They voted and the majority was to go shopping. Later Jane explained, 'I didn't want them to come to my house but didn't want to say so. I got out of it by having a vote. I knew that a democratic vote is the fairest way to decide things.'

- Fiona had heard a scandalous piece of gossip. When she

told Laura she got a reply she had not expected. 'How do you know?' asked Laura. 'Gabby told me,' said Fiona. 'How does Gabby know?' asked Laura. 'Someone must have told her,' said Fiona. 'Then we don't know if it's true,' said Laura. 'I suppose we don't,' said Fiona, suddenly looking glum. 'Don't worry,' said Laura, 'I don't believe the things they say about you either, not without proof anyway.'

Like other forms of intelligence, a child's philosophical thinking can be developed or inhibited at home. A parent who says, 'Don't ask questions', 'You'll find out when you grow up', or 'I'm too busy to talk now' and never does talk about it, deprives her child of the opportunity to exercise this intelligence. What, then, can we do to help a child to develop this intelligence, and help him make the most of his mind?

DEVELOPING YOUR CHILD'S PHILOSOPHICAL INTELLIGENCE

Philosophical intelligence is about asking questions, and trying to work things out when you don't know the answer. Your child needs it to work out what to do when there is no one to tell him what to do. It will help him search for what is true, right and good in human life. It is the way he learns to apply what he knows to problems where there is no easy answer.

Developing philosophical intelligence means developing the ability to question and to think critically and creatively about the answers he is given. Some children are more naturally philosophical than others. They ask more questions, they take more interest in what goes on around them, they are more aware about the puzzles of life. All children, however, can be helped to think more deeply and widely about the world, and to have their attention focused on what is interesting, curious or puzzling in life.

If your child	What you can do	What your child can learn
Does not ask questions or show much interest in the world around him	Encourage your child to ask questions, and discuss what interests him	How to ask questions, think for yourself, and discuss your views with others
Asks questions, but accepts any answer that is given	Encourage her to suggest her own answers, ask her what she thinks and why	It is all right to speculate when you do not know, provided you have reasons or evidence
Likes to question, and to argue about and discuss things	Encourage him to question, argue and discuss with you and with others	Confidence to question, and to be critical, creative and imaginative in his thinking

HOW DOES PHILOSOPHICAL INTELLIGENCE DEVELOP?

What a child lacks is experience, not the capacity to think about and discuss things. Children need very little experience of the world to be able to discuss some of the important issues of life—for example, 'What is right?' 'What is real?' 'What is true?' 'What is beautiful?' 'What is puzzling?' and so on—all questions that thinking people have asked since the time of the ancient Greeks. This capacity to ask philosophical questions may not be recognised, or it may wither through lack of use, but any child, unless he or she is brain-damaged, has this capacity. So how does this intelligence develop?

Philosophical intelligence, like other forms of intelligence, develops slowly over time, through the use of reasoning in thinking, questioning and discussion. What we can do as parents is find time for discussion, and create a home where questioning is allowed, where views are listened to and sometimes challenged. 'In a good discussion,' says Michelle, aged ten, 'there are no put-downs.' Philosophical intelligence develops in an atmosphere where people can think things through, where others are interested in what they have to say and try to build on their ideas and where it is all right to change your mind.

INPUT:	what you do	You stimulate your child by encouraging questions and asking for reasons in her answers.
OUTPUT:	what your child does	Your child learns to think about and discuss matters of importance with others at home.
SELF-CONTROL:	what your child learns	Your child becomes aware of problems in life and is able to discuss them in critical and creative ways.

Did you know . . . ?

Research shows that if you give your child time to think after you have asked a question—say at least five seconds—rather than always expecting an immediate answer, your child will give better answers, longer answers and more interesting answers. You also are likely to give your child better answers if you pause and think before replying. So make your motto: 'Stop and think'—at least for five seconds!

WHAT YOU CAN DO TO HELP

Children bring with them into the world an elastic mind capable of being stretched in all sorts of directions, and an ability to ask not only important everyday questions like

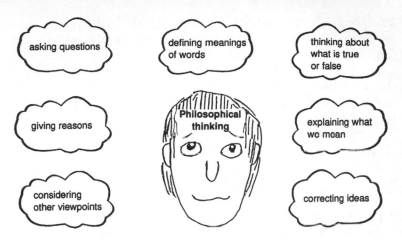

Ways to develop philosophical thinking

'Where's my food?', but also deep and challenging questions like the following from four-year-olds: 'Why do people die?' 'Why do chickens lay eggs?' and 'How does an oak tree fit into an acorn?' This curiosity is early evidence of philosophical intelligence. But a child's questioning spirit can wither. This may partly be to do with the effects of school and ageing, but it may also be the influence of home. As a child once said to me, 'I like school. You don't have to think. They tell you what to do.' When I asked what happened at home, the reply was, 'Oh, Mum does the thinking there.' Keeping your child's questioning spirit alive at home can be one of the keys to success in learning.

The philosophical home

We cannot force our children to be philosophical, but we can help provide the conditions at home where questioning, thinking and discussion can flourish. The situation is like the old story of 'The Tyrant's Nightmare'. The king wants all his subjects to love him, so he sends out an order that everyone must love him. The people pretend to love the king. Whenever they need to they say so, out of fear. The king knows this, but he cannot be sure they *really* love him. So

275

he despatches spies to find out the truth. The spies return and report that the people behave as if they love him. But the king can never be sure.

So how do you provide the conditions for your child to think philosophically at home?

A philosophical home is first and foremost a listening home. In some families people do not listen: children do not listen to adults, adults do not listen to children, and children and adults do not listen to each other. They may hear enough to get by, particularly if people shout at each other. In some homes children's questions go unnoticed, or are ignored. There may be many reasons why there is no time to stop and listen to your child, but try to find time to come back to a question later. Take time to ask, 'What do you think?' Look at your child while you listen, and expect your child to listen to you.

One of the great problems teachers report in schools is that children are finding it harder to sit and listen. Many are so used to having a TV screen as their constant spare time companion, with its endless images flickering by, that they are finding it hard to focus attention on one person, one face or one voice. The philosophical home is a place where people make time to listen to each other. This has become so rare and precious in some families that it is often described now as 'quality time'. Some children have very little quality time, and so find it hard to sustain a conversation or to focus on any one topic for long. Try to make yours a listening home, and have some 'quality time' each day with your child.

The philosophical home is also a questioning home, a place where people talk to each other about issues that puzzle and concern them. If questions are asked, people listen and try to work out an answer together. Times are set aside when news can be shared, when thoughts and feelings can be discussed. The prime time for this is a meal-time. In all human societies sharing a meal is more than simply satisfying hunger. It is a symbolic time where the family or group find time for each other and celebrate their relationship. It is where people show their care, both in the providing and preparation of a meal, but also in being there to share in talking with and listening to others.

KEY IDEA: SHARE AND DISCUSS QUESTIONS THAT PUZZLE YOU OR YOUR CHILD

In some homes meals are not a shared experience. People eat at different times, away from each other, or huddled around a TV set watching in silence, each in his or her own private world. They do not spend time together sharing food, as well as news and ideas. There may be no set times when the parents are with their children, helping them through talking and listening to develop their minds. In a philosophical home families try to ensure one meal a day when the family can come together, or guard special times like bedtime or story time when worries can be discussed.

For some families spiritual or religious beliefs play a vitally important role in giving meaning to life. Religious festivals and celebrations are a time for discussing what we think and believe, when we should be open to questions. When we explore the meaning in life or the possibility of life beyond the physical world, we are using philosophical intelligence. When we ask not 'What is it?' but 'Why . . . ?' and 'What if . . . ?' we are becoming philosophical.

Let's examine some ways of developing your child's philosophical intelligence at home:

- thinking through stories
- thinking about the everyday world
- thinking about other worlds, including spiritual and religious beliefs

Thinking through stories

'A philosophical story is a story with a secret meaning,' says Anna, aged eleven. A story is not only an enjoyable journey into an imagined world, but also a means of thinking and learning (see Chapter 2).

In a philosophical home story time, maybe when a child is safely tucked up in bed, or when cuddling together on a sofa, provides what can be a daily treat for both parent and child. It also provides a wonderful opportunity for developing philosophical thinking. Here is an example of how a mother became involved in exploring the meaning of a story, after reading a book about a talking robot to her two children, Karen and Graham:

> *Parent*: Is a robot the same as a person?
> *Karen*: It is a person, a kind of machine person.
> *Parent*: Why?
> *Karen*: 'Cos it talks and does things.
> *Graham*: It's not a real person . . . it's made of metal.
> *Parent*: But it walks and talks.
> *Graham*: How can something made of metal walk and talk?
> *Parent*: Suppose a robot who could walk and talk came into the room . . . ?
> *Karen*: It wouldn't be a person. It would be a robot.
> *Graham*: It would be a person if it was Dad dressed up . . .

What the children were engaged in here was not only talk about the story, but the beginnings of a philosophical discussion about what it means to be a person. Can a robot be a person? In what ways are people and robots different? In what ways are they the same? What can you do that a robot can't do? What can robots do that you cannot do? What is a robot?

KEY IDEA: ASK YOUR CHILD TO DEFINE THE MEANINGS OF WORDS SHE USES

The question that followed Karen's first answer was the most important question of all—'Why' If there is one characteristic of a thinking home it is the use of 'Why?' as a follow-up to a child's answer. It means 'Why do you think that?' and is a request for reasons, evidence or explanation. It invites your child to think and say more. It probes her reasoning. If she doesn't know or can't say why, then suggest a reason yourself. In other words, ask yourself why. But what happens if you, or your child, don't know the answer?

If you don't know the answer, say so and suggest a theory or possible idea. That is after all what intelligence is all about, making the most of what we know and trying to make sense of it. Make the most of story time by making them stories for thinking and make more of the story by asking questions and suggesting possible answers. While reading *Winnie-the-Pooh*, a family reached the part where Piglet's grandfather is said to have two names 'in case he lost one'. 'Could you lose a name?' asked the parent. 'You could if you forgot it,' said a child.

For young children picture books provide an endless source of ideas to discuss with your child. For example, picture stories like *Where the Wild Things Are* by Maurice Sendak, or *Would You Rather?* by John Burningham, provide good opportunities to discuss what is real and what is imaginary, to think about what characters are thinking and feeling, and suggest reasons for what they do. The following is an example of this kind of discussion while reading *Where the Wild Things Are*:

> *Parent*: Do you think it was all a dream?
> *Jane*: No, he came out of the bed. He wasn't dreaming. He got up.
> *Parent*: Sometimes when I dream things, I think it's really happening.
> *Jane*: I think he could have been dreaming, because he was hungry and wanted his supper. Then he dreamt about the Wild Things.
> *Parent*: How do you know when you are dreaming or not?
> *Jane*: Well, you don't know when you are dreaming or not. Only somebody else can tell you. So the Wild Things would know.
> *Parent*: Who are the Wild Things?
> *Jane*: I think they were things inside Max. I don't think they were real ... were they?

Fairy stories, folk tales and traditional stories provide much to think about. For example, Hans Andersen's story 'The Emperor's New Clothes' can lead to questions such as:

'Why did the Emperor want new clothes?'
'Why did he believe he was wearing clothes?'
'What kind of child would tell the Emperor he was naked? (Would you?)

Fables, such as *Aesop's Fables*, have for centuries been retold as thinking stories for children to learn from. Each is especially designed to teach a moral. When you read a fable, stop before the end and ask your child what she thinks the moral of the story is. All good fables contain issues that are philosophical—not only about the story but about dilemmas in real life. For example the famous fable, 'The Boy Who Cried Wolf', is about a boy who plays a trick on villagers by pretending there is a wolf attacking their sheep, but it is also about what truth is, and what lies, tricks and jokes are. So it is a story that can be read for pleasure, but it also exercises philosophical intelligence if it encourages children to think about when teasing and joking go too far and who should be blamed when things go wrong. Is it, for example, ever right to tell a lie? The following are some examples of questions that could be used to discuss Aesop's fable 'The Boy Who Cried Wolf':

- Did the shepherd boy tell a lie? What is a lie?
- Should he have told the truth? What is the truth?
- Why did the shepherd boy play a joke on the village? Was it a good joke? Why?
- Whose fault was it the wolf ate the sheep?
- Would the villagers trust him again? What should the boy do now?
- Do you think this is a true story? Why, or why not?

KEY IDEA: INVITE YOUR CHILD TO THINK WHETHER SOMETHING IS TRUE OR NOT AND WHY

It is not only story books that interest children. Non-fiction books and puzzle books can be just as fascinating, and a source of interesting discussion. The following is an excerpt from a discussion of a page from the picture book *Would You Rather?* by John Burningham. Each page illustrates a choice, for example: Would you rather live in a house surrounded by the sea, by snow or by jungle?

RF: Where would you choose to live?

Tom: I'd rather live in the jungle.

RF: Why?

Tom: I like animals, and you could swing from tree to tree like Tarzan. And no one would find you!

Jake: You wouldn't survive for long in the jungle.

RF: Why not?

Jake: Well, there's no electricity for a start, not in the middle of the jungle.

Tom: I'd have solar panels. There's plenty of sun . . .

Jake: Not in the jungle, under all those trees. The sun wouldn't get through

Tom: I'd build a house in a clearing of the jungle.

Jake: The trees would be too thick.

Tom: I'd cut gaps so the rays would get through.

RF: What else would be good and bad about living in the jungle?

Jake: There'd be poisonous snakes. Supposing you got bitten by a poisonous snake? You wouldn't live long then.

Tom: Oh yes I would . . . I'd use the jungle plants for medicines.

What philosophical intelligence enables you and your child to do is to explore the ideas you read about, and to think of new ideas for yourself. After reading the book *Would You Rather?* we had some fun thinking up different sorts of dilemmas ourselves—Would you rather be a horse, a dog, a pig or a spider? Would you rather be a giant or a dwarf? Would you rather have a million pounds and a short life, or be poor and live forever?

As children get older they need a wider range of stories and books to be read to them. One of the advantages of reading to your child at whatever age he may be is that you can read books that your child cannot (or will not) read for himself, and you can talk about what interests you and him in the book. The following are some of the questions I discussed with my children when reading the first chapter of Ted Hughes' book *The Iron Man*:

• Where do you think the Iron Man came from?

- What was the most important part of the Iron Man's body?
- Is the Iron Man's eye a real eye?
- Do you think the Iron Man could be killed?
- What was he thinking?

Whenever your child gives a simple answer like 'Yes' or 'No', follow it up by asking why he thinks that. Encourage him to be 'reasonable'—that is, to give reasons or some evidence if he can to support what he says. And of course we should try to do the same.

KEY IDEA: CHECK THAT WHAT YOUR CHILD SAYS IS BASED ON REASONS OR EVIDENCE

It is not always easy to make sense of the world, or of books. One of the most philosophical stories ever written for children is Lewis Carroll's *Alice's Adventures in Wonderland*. It is full of weird adventures and characters who say and do things that are strange, interesting or puzzling. The story is about a girl who dreams she chases a white rabbit down a hole. Is it a dream? How do we know we are dreaming? How do we know that all life is not a dream? There are questions of interest to discuss in every chapter. For example, in Chapter 5 the Caterpillar asks, 'Who are you?' Alice replies that she hardly knows. She knew who she was when she got up in the morning, but she had changed several times since. 'Explain yourself!' demands the Caterpillar. 'I can't explain *myself*. I'm afraid, sir,' said Alice, 'because I'm not myself, you see.' There are many stimulating ideas here you could discuss with your child, including the question that philosophers have asked for centuries: 'What makes you you?' Is it your name, your personality, your physical looks, your brain, your memories, your soul, or what?

A good book for teenagers, to awaken and exercise their philosophical intelligence, is *Sophie's World* by Jostein Gaarder, a bestseller across Europe when it was first published in 1995. The story is about Sophie, a 14-year-old who in the course of the story faces questions that have long puzzled philosophers, such as 'Who are you?' and 'Where do you come from?' The book looks at the different answers that philosophers have given through the centuries to the most puzzling questions about life. What has made the book so successful is that it has appealed to parents as much as it has to the teenagers it was written for. It can provide a stimulating read for any thinking teenager or parent.

Thinking about the everyday world

If we want children to feel responsible about what they think and do, if we want them sometime to take control of their own lives, then we must help them to take an interest in the world, in family issues, local news, as well as national and international affairs. Instead of crushing their questions with 'Shhh . . .', 'I don't know . . .' or 'I don't care', we should try to help them develop their thoughts. It is not always easy, but it is worth the effort.

Children are not always very logical. Sometimes they say the first thing that comes into their heads, and they do not always make sense. They can ask awkward questions, like 'Did you love anyone before you loved Dad?' Sometimes they find it hard to give sensible answers. One reason for this is that they lack experience of life. All that we have heard, seen and done helps us to make meaning out of life. We have thought a lot, explained things many times, tackled many problems—a young child has not. She needs a lot of practice in explaining things in order to become better at making sense of what they mean. Many adults also find explaining things difficult. They may not be very logical, and sometimes they might not make much sense. But because they are not very good at it this does not mean they cannot do it, any more than a child cannot do it. What they need is to be helped and shown how.

Any child can be encouraged through everyday experiences at home to:

- ask questions and raise topics for discussion
- develop her own ideas, views and theories
- give reasons for what she thinks
- explain and argue her point of view with others

- listen to and consider the views of others
- change her ideas in the light of good reasons and evidence

Every day we are faced with questions about what to do, what to say and what to think. As Paul, aged eight, once said, 'Every one of us lives in a kind of soap opera.' His daily world was not quite like his favourite TV soap, *Neighbours*, but he was aware that his family had problems to face, that unforeseen things can happen and that his older sister had a number of interesting relationships.

The sorts of question we can ask about any everyday event, whether it is our own news or stories from local or national news, include:

What is the problem?
What do you think about it?
What do you (or others) feel?
What actually happened? How do you know?
What should have happened?
What might happen now?
What could be done about it?

Life presents us with all sorts of moral problems. Moral reasoning is part of philosophical intelligence. We need to tell young children what is right and wrong, but they will also need to make difficult moral choices for themselves. At some stage there will be no one there to tell them what to do. They will have to decide for themselves. Therefore the more we can discuss *why* things are right or wrong, and give them a chance to think about choices and consequences, the more prepared they will be when difficult choices arise. As Kirsty, aged ten, says, 'It helps to work things out in your mind before they happen.'

The world is a puzzling place. Living with others poses problems that we all have to face. The following are some questions asked by young children about living in the world:

- Is it right to kill people?
- Why should we pick up other people's rubbish?
- Why can't I do what I like?
- What is wrong with using swear words?
- Is there a Father Christmas?

- Is it right to eat animals?
- What is wrong with cheating?

Newspapers and TV news carry stories each day that provide issues for possible discussion at home. Philosophical intelligence is exercised when children are asked, 'What do you think?' and, 'What do others think?' and then are invited to explain what they mean and share ideas.

KEY IDEA: ENCOURAGE YOUR CHILD TO EXPLAIN WHAT SHE MEANS AND SHARE IDEAS

The following is part of a family discussion about stealing, after a child had reported the story of a case of stealing at school. The children are Donna, aged nine, and Paul, aged eleven:

Parent: Why is it wrong to steal?
Donna: You might get caught.
Paul: Your friends might tell on you.
Parent: Are there any other reasons why it is wrong to steal?
Donna: You won't go to heaven.
Paul: Some people say you'll go to hell. I don't believe that.
Donna: Well, I think stealing things just gets you into trouble. So it's better not to.
Paul: If the police find out you get a record. If you're old enough they put you in jail.
Parent: What about the effect it has on other people, if things get stolen?
Donna: Well, it's not nice for someone to steal your things. I haven't had things taken, but I wouldn't like it.
Paul: If someone stole my things I'd set a trap.
Parent: So is stealing always wrong?
Paul: It is wrong—unless it's your mum . . .

The easy way to respond to a difficult question is a strategy that teachers often use, which is to ask: 'What do you think?' Invite your child to share what he already thinks and knows. Check that he understands the main word or idea of his

answer by asking, 'What do you mean by . . . ?' Often children will use words when they are only dimly aware of the meaning (of course they are not alone in this!) So find out what they think they mean. Do not assume they know what they are talking about. This technique was first used by Socrates over 2,000 years ago, when he went into the marketplace at Athens to ask people what they meant by 'justice' and 'truth'. He knew that most people used words without ever having thought about what they meant. One of the important elements of philosophical intelligence is thinking about the words we use and making sure we know what they mean.

When you are answering a question, try to answer only what your child has asked and do not overload him with too much information. Do not be afraid of using long words, provided you have explained what they mean. There is no long word that a child cannot understand if it is explained in ways appropriate to the child's age. The child of a brain surgeon could explain the workings, and give the Latin name, of each part of the brain by the age of four, simply because he had been shown and told by an interested parent. The child was so proud of his knowledge he would sometimes ask visitors, 'Is there anything wrong with your head?'

We should encourage our children to think about what is puzzling in the world, and about the mysteries of life. There are things that puzzle us which we can see, and mysteries that lie beyond the visible world which challenge our thinking no matter what our age.

Did you know . . . ?

The famous scientist Albert Einstein was frequently found in his office at Princeton University staring into space. His colleagues were worried about him. They weren't used to seeing people actually thinking!

Thinking about other worlds

'Can you tell me how the world began?
Who made the first woman and man?

Before I was born, where was I?
What will happen when I die?

Where is heaven and what is hell?
Is there a God? How can you tell?

I have so many questions in my head.'
'Not now, darling, it's time for bed.'

One of the great powers of your child's mind is to see beyond the everyday world and to call to mind imagined worlds that do not exist, or that may exist beyond the world that we can see. He responds to stories of magic and mystery, of monsters and myths. He imagines what may be hiding in the dark at night, and who might live above the sky. He hears of heroes long dead, and of things that happen in countries he has never seen and that exist only in the mind or on the television screen. Some of what he hears is real, some is fancy. No wonder children are confused about where reality ends and illusion begins. How do they separate fact from fiction, and truth from fantasy? For a young child his parents are the people who first help to navigate him through what is real and unreal, what is fact and what is imagination, what is to be believed and what is not true.

The capacity to believe is born within us. The world is physical but it is also symbolic and invested with meaning. An object becomes precious if it is a special gift. A place becomes special if some event has given it added value. Special people are valued. When we ask *why* some things have special value the question is philosophical. These are more than questions about what exists in the world, they are about what we think and believe about them. These questions that are about more than physical facts are what some philosophers call 'metaphysical'. They include spiritual and religious questions.

Did you know . . . ?

Scientists from the University of California claim to have found a 'God spot' in the brain, which may be responsible for the human instinct to believe in religion. They found that when those who are religious or who have spiritual experiences think about God or spiritual words, a circuit of nerves in the front of the brain becomes stimulated and electrically active. This may account for the capacity for religious belief found in all human societies.

Examples of religious questions asked by four- to eight-year-old children include:

Are gods real?
Who made God?
How old is God?
Where does God live?
What does God do all day?
Why does God let people do wicked things?
Why didn't God help me find my toy when I asked Him?
What does 'eternal' mean?
Are there holy spirits?
Are all religions true?
What does 'evil' mean?
If God gives life why do people die?

When you die do you become a ghost?

Why are some people lucky?

There are many ways to respond to such questions. 'Don't ask me, ask your father/mother' is one of them, but not necessarily the best one. 'I don't know. Get on with your supper/homework, etc.' is a response some children face. What such a question offers a thoughtful parent is an opportunity to talk about things that the child is interested in and finds puzzling at the time.

There is nothing wrong with saying you do not know. This, after all, is what we want our children to admit to sometimes. There is nothing wrong with telling them what we think. In doing that we show them the value of explaining things to others. But we should aim for *equal opportunities* to speak and listen, by encouraging the child to say as much as you do to express her ideas, inviting her to say what she thinks, and to explain her thinking, by asking her to define what she means and to give reasons for what she says. We should also open the child to other points of view. What other people think may be as important as what we think. Knowing what others think gives us more choices, and if we are aware of other views our choices are better informed. As Jamie, aged six, said, 'You should listen to other people because sometimes they have good ideas.'

KEY IDEA: HELP YOUR CHILD CONSIDER IDEAS FROM DIFFERENT POINTS OF VIEW

Asking the right questions

Don't give your child mental indigestion by asking too many questions. Better to ask a few questions that you are genuinely interested in than to 'grill' or interrogate her for the sake of it. Here are some kinds of questions to try with your child:

Focusing:	What do you think? What is it that puzzles you? What is the problem?
Asking for reasons:	Why do you say that? Can you give a reason?

Explaining meaning: What do you mean by that? Can you explain it?

Testing for truth: How do you know? Can you prove it? Do you have any evidence?

Thinking new ideas: What else . . . ? What if . . . ? What more . . . ?

Some things to think about

  Child: What's a question?
  Adult: What's the answer?

The best questions may be those that your child comes up with. They are good to discuss because they are the ones that are of immediate interest to your child. Sometimes it is good to be given something to think about. Here are some philosophical questions to think about with your child:

1 How do you know you are not dreaming at this moment?
2 How do you know when something is true or not true?
3 Is an apple dead or alive?
4 Is it right to eat animals?
5 What is the difference between pretending and lying?
6 What is the difference between a real person and a robot?
7 Is there a difference between your mind and your brain?
8 Can animals think?
9 Is it ever right to tell lies?
10 What are the most valuable things in your life?

KEY IDEA: GOOD THINKING MEANS BEING WILLING TO CHALLENGE AND CHANGE ONE'S IDEAS

The world is full of interesting questions. Your child can help you rediscover your curiosity about the world. Were there any questions to which you have never found the answer? Are there any questions you were afraid to ask? It need not be so for your child. Your philosophical child needs a questioning home, a place where it is all right to ask and where people are interested in what you think and feel. A place where it is all right to ask 'Why?' A place where it is all right to argue for your point of view, provided you listen to what others have to say. A place where what people think is taken seriously, where words are thoughtfully used, and where it is all right to change one's mind when there are good reasons for doing so. A place where philosophical thinking can flourish. As Beth, aged ten, said, such a place is where 'people let you take out your mind and share it with others'.

SEVEN STEPS TO PHILOSOPHICAL INTELLIGENCE

- Share and discuss any questions that puzzle you or your child.
- Ask your child to try to define the meanings of words he uses.
- Invite your child to think about whether something is true or not.
- Check that what your child says is based on reasons and evidence.
- Encourage your child to explain what she means and share ideas with others.
- Help your child to consider ideas from different viewpoints.
- Good thinking means being prepared to challenge and change one's ideas.

Appendix A

Helping a child learn to read

The following are different stages in sharing a book with a child that will help him learn to read and to think about what is being read:

1 Share the book

- Start with the front cover. Read the title and point out the names of author and illustrator. *What book is this?*
- Talk about what you can see on the front cover, and how the title might help us know what the book is about. *What does the cover say?*
- Read the book to your child, pointing at the words you are reading. Read at a normal speed, with expression in your voice. *What does the book say?*
- Ask your child questions about the pictures, events and characters in the book. *What does the story mean?*
- Before you turn each page, encourage your child to predict what will happen on the next page. *What might happen next?*

2 Match sounds to words

- Read the title while pointing at the words, and encourage your child to say the title. *What does the title say?*

- From time to time read a sentence, and encourage your child to repeat the sentence while you point at the words. *What does this sentence say?*
- Ask your child to read what one of the characters says, in the voice of the character. *What does this character say?*
- Ask your child to see when you have reached the end of the page, and to turn the pages for you. *Do you know when to turn the page?*
- Talk about the book and ask if your child has any questions she wants to ask. *Do you have a question you want to ask?*

3 Read together

- Read the title together with your child while he points at the words. Let your child read the title on the inside cover alone. *Can you read the title?*
- As you read the book, sometimes miss out a word—for example, a word that is repeated or the last word of a sentence. *Can you read a missing word?*
  (If your child cannot do this, allow a few seconds of thinking time, tell the child and read on.)
- When you have finished a page or part of the book, see if your child can spot any words that have been repeated. *Can you see this word again?*
- Encourage your child to read some of the book together with you, if she can. *Can you read together?*
- Encourage your child to talk about his favourite part of the book, saying what he liked and why. *What did you like best? Why?*

4 Listen to your child read

- Teach your child to recognise the sound of each letter. *What sound does the letter make?*
- Read through the book with your child, encouraging her to read a page with you or on her own if she can. *Can you read a page on your own?*

- Ask your child to read the whole book to you, if he can. *Can you read a book?*
  (If your child does not know a word, allow a few seconds of thinking time, then say the word.)
- Encourage your child to read the book on her own. *Can you read it by yourself?*
- Encourage your child to ask questions about the book. *What is strange, interesting or puzzling about the story?*

For questions you can ask to help your child think about the story see p. 75.

Appendix B

Maths vocabulary

The following is a checklist of important mathematical words
to use with your child:

Age	Number	Measurement words	Shape
4–7 years	number zero, 1, 2, 3 ... 100 nought count on/back in 1s, 2s more, less odd, even count in tens, units equal, equally more than/less than difference between first ... twentieth halfway between	calculate answer/right/ wrong money, more/ less, pence/ pound measure length, width, height, depth longer, longest, etc. high/low, wide/ narrow deep/shallow, thick/thin weigh, balances heavy/light, heavier/lighter, etc.	flat, solid shape square, cube pyramid, triangle circle, sphere rectangle corner, line, point star curved, round edge, sides pattern symmetrical reflection, turn positions ... top, bottom, side opposite

Age	Number	Measurement words	Shape
	too many/too few	capacity, full/ empty	in front/ behind
	whole/half/ quarter	time/date/ calendar	beside, between
	fraction	days/months/ seasons	direction
	add/sum/total	always/never/ often/sometimes	left/right, up/ down
	subtract/take away	morning/ afternoon/ evening/night	forward/ backward
	sign/plus/ minus	times of day/ hours/minutes	
	once/twice/ three times	how long ago/ will it be	
	share, halve, left over	order, match, set	
		graph, chart, list	
		diagram	

7–10 years *All the above, and the following:*

	Number	Measurement words	Shape
	hundreds, thousands	more/most, less/ least expensive	spherical
	count on in 3s, 4s, 5s . . .	value, amount	hemisphere
	multiple of	unit of measurement	centre
	sequence/ continue	distance apart/ between/to/ from	oval
	prediction/ calculation	metre/ centimetre/ kilometre	cylinder
	rule/method	mile, kilometre/ miles per hour	cone
	numeral/digit	height measure	pentagon
	place/place value		hexagon
	equivalent to		circular/ semicircle
			triangular/ rectangular
			octagon/ octagonal

Age	Number	Measurement words	Shape
	estimate/ estimation	breadth/half way	clockwise/ anti . . .
	round to the nearest ten	ruler, tape measure	compass point diagonal
	whole number	kilo, half kilo, gram	north/south/ east/west
	times/multiply, times table	height, weight	angle, right-angle
	divide, divided by	litre, half litre, millilitre	column, grid
	remainder	measuring jug, scales	whole/half turn
	halves, quarters, thirds	digital clock, watch	horizontal/ vertical
	decimal/ decimal point/ tenth	seconds/ stopwatch a.m./p.m.	symmetrical pattern
	above zero/ below zero	leap year	
	positive/ negative number	diary, date of birth	
	problem/solve/ solution	earlier/later century/ millennium	

Further Reading

The following books by Robert Fisher provide further reading on ways of developing children's thinking, learning and intelligence:

BOOK TITLE	AREA OF INTELLIGENCE
Together Today (Evans, 1981)	*Linguistic and social intelligence*
The Assembly Year (Collins, 1985)	*Linguistic and social intelligence*
Investigating Maths (with A. Vince, Blackwell, 1989)	*Mathematical intelligence*
Teaching Juniors (Stanley Thornes, 1991)	*All aspects of intelligence*
Recording Achievement in Primary Schools (Blackwell, 1991)	*Personal intelligence*
Investigating Technology (with J. Garvey, Simon & Schuster, 1992)	*Scientific intelligence*
Active Art books and picture pack (Simon & Schuster, 1994)	*Visual intelligence*
Active PE (with D. Alldridge. Simon & Schuster, 1994)	*Physical intelligence*
Teaching Children to Think (Stanley Thornes, 1995)	*All aspects of intelligence*
Teaching Children to Learn (Stanley Thornes, 1995)	*All aspects of intelligence*
Stories for Thinking (Nash Pollock, 1996)	*Linguistic and philosophical intelligence*

Games for Thinking (Nash Pollock, 1997)

Poems for Thinking (Nash Pollock, 1997)

Teaching Thinking (Cassell, 1998)

Poetry anthologies for children:
  Amazing Monsters (Faber, 1982)
  Ghosts Galore (Faber, 1983)
  Funny Folk (Faber, 1985)
  Witch Words (Faber, 1987)
  Pet Poems (Faber, 1989)
  Minibeasts (Faber, 1992)

Linguistic, mathematical and visual intelligence

Linguistic and philosophical intelligence

Philosophical and other aspects of intelligence

Linguistic intelligence

For further information contact: Dr. Robert Fisher, Centre for Research in Teaching Thinking, Brunel University, 300 St Margarets Road, Twickenham TW1 1PT, or visit the Robert Fisher website: http://www.brunel.ac.uk/faculty/ed/Robert__Fisher/

Index

acalculia 87
accidents, *see* safety
ADD (Attention Deficit Disorder) 60
adult, encouraging and inhibiting
    21, 43
Aesop's Fables 280
Aitchison, Janet 84
Alfred, King of Wessex 71
alphabet 79–80 193
arguments 250
Aristotle 245, 269
art galleries 173–5
art 34, 198
attention 173, 276
autism 223

babies 28, 35, 45, 46, 48, 50, 63,
    87, 157, 163, 185, 204, 206,
    209–10, 213
bored, what to do when 231–2
Blake, William 134, 146
brachiation 213
brain
    alpha waves 199
    brain cells 215
    capacity 18
    connections 14–15, 16, 216
    control centres 30, 45, 48
    damage 10, 21, 33–4, 38, 155
    development 21–2, 49
    left/right hemisphere 32, 33, 45

    frontal cortex 226, 251, 259
    motor cortex 34
    neural circuits 197
    number sense 87
    oxygen intake 23
    research 27, 31
    responds to rhythm 205
    stimulated by sounds 185, 190
    visual area 31, 161
Burningham, John 279, 280
    Would You Rather? 279–80

Cage, John 190
calculators 92, 99, 108. 109
calendrology 25
California, University of 187, 190,
    288
Cargill, Alison 260
Carlyle, Thomas 57
Carroll, Lewis 44, 51, 65, 282
childhood 38
Churchill, Lord Randolph 105
classifying 139
comics 72, 73
communication 26, 257, 266
computer 60, 70, 73, 79, 83, 88,
    92, 94–5, 115, 116, 130,
    138, 153, 172, 195, 209,
    216, 257
concentration 193, 218
concepts 45

confidence *see* self-confidence
Congreve, William 31
Constable, John 175
connections 25
conversation 53–6
cooking 143–5, 238
coordination 34, 205
counting 103–4
crafts 148, 171–3, 209, 212
curiosity 28–9, 128, 136, 150

Dahl, Roald 65
Dali Salvador 153
dance 191 214
Darwin, Charles 134
daydreaming 229
Debussy, Claude 186
decimals 106
Delphi, oracle of 222
Diana, Princess of Wales 248
dictionary 66, 83, 122
dilemmas 252–4
drama 209
drawing 133, 153, 158, 164–7,
    177–80
dyspraxia, 205

Einstein, Albert 125, 269
Elgar, Edward 195
Eliot, T.S. 44
emotions 10, 34, 37–9, 200,
    224–6, 251–4, 259
    emotional intelligence *see* social
        intelligence
    negative emotions 39
experiments 134, 140–4, 151
empathy 250–4
exams 118
exercise 208–14
eyes 30–1

Fallacy of the Single Option 260
Fisher, Jayne 85
Fisher, Robert 297–8
    Teaching Children to Think 43,
        298
Ford, Henry 219
French 62, 120

friends 264
Freud, Sigmund 13

Gaarder, Jostein 282
    Sophie's World 282–3
Gallwey, Tim 201
games
    blindfolding games 131
    board games 95–6
    calculator games 99
    card games 100–1
    dice games 99–100
    mathematical games 93–100
    number games 98–101, 149
    outdoor games 96
    pencil and paper games 97–8
    Snakes and Ladders 123
    sport and games 214–15
    visual games 94–8, 134–5,
        176–7
    word games 25, 62–6, 67
geometry 27, 89, 95, 114–16
Gibbon, Edward 228
'God spot' 288
Goldman, Sylvan 149
gong therapy 199
Goethe, J.W. von 164
grammar 63
Grandma Moses 29
Guinness Book of Records, The
    107

hand-eye coordination 205,
    215–16
handwriting 79–80
Hazlitt, William 77
hearing 29, 30, 50, 57, 59, 74,
    186
helicopter spin 212–13
heroes 264–5
High Scope 237
history 29, 83
homework 105, 117–20,
    236
Hughes, Ted 281
    The Iron Man 281
Hutchins, Pat 115
Huygens, Christiaan 132

Head Start

idiots savants 26
imitation 48, 256
impulsivity 24–5
information processing 35
input 4, 23, 43, 50, 91, 129, 157,
    186, 206, 226, 248, 274
intelligence 10, 11, 16–43, 49
intelligences
    dimensions of intelligence 21–2
    emotional *see* social, 246
    kinaesthetic *see* physical
    linguistic 11, 16, 25–6, 44–85
    mathematical 11, 17, 26–7,
        86–124, 186
    musical 13, 17, 31–3, 181–200
    personal 13, 18, 35–7, 221–43
    philosophical 13, 18, 39–40,
        268–291
    physical 13, 17, 34–6, 117,
        201–20
    scientific 12, 17, 28–9, 125–52
    social 13, 18, 37–9, 244–67
    spatial *see* visual
    verbal *see* linguistic
    visual 13, 17, 29–31, 117,
        153–80
IQ (intelligence quotient) 18, 26,
    253

jokes 15, 25, 64–5

Kant Immanuel 40
Kepler, Johannes 129
Kipling, Rudyard 74
Klee, Paul 165
Knight, Margaret 149
knowledge
    'know-how' 34
Kubrick, Stanley 135

language 11, 14, 45
    language learning 50, 52, 66–7
late developers 49
Leach, Penelope 221
'learned helplessness' 229–30
learning styles 35
left-handedness 33
Lipman, Matthew 268

listening, 56–60, 187–92, 197–8,
    256–7, 276, 289
    sound quiz 188–9
    sound walk. 189
logic 27, 94, 98
Lozanov, Georgi 199
Lyons, Lewis 170

manipulative skill 77–8, 168, 193
marshmallow experiment 24
maths *see* mathematical
    intelligence
    maths phobia 87
    maths vocabulary 295–7
    multiplication tables 105, 117,
        193
    natural mathematicians 89
    pure and applied maths 93
Matisse, Henri 169
mazes 95, 96
McKee, David 53
    Not Now, Bernard 53
measurement 112–14
meditation 223, 231
memory 33, 66, 81–2, 119, 121,
    193, 216, 223, 238–9
    visual memory 154, 175–8
Menuhin, Yehudi 32
Milligan, Spike 120
mindmapping 159, 178–180
'mind's eye' 175–8, 180
mnemonics 82–3
Moore, Henry 209
Montessori, Maria 77, 78, 230
moral problems 284–6
motivation. 117, 187, 207, 219
Mozart, W.A. 32, 190, 196
multiplication tables 98, 105, 117,
    193
music *see* musical intelligence
    musical instruments 195–7
    music-making 193–4
    musical notation 194–5
    responding to music 197–200
museums 138

Napoleon 83, 227
neurons 14–15

Newton Sir Isaac, 28–9
number *see* mathematical
    intelligence
The Number Sense 27
nursery 77
nursery rhymes 51, 58, 64, 193

optical illusions 132, 160–1
Orff, Carl 181
origami 95, 172
output 23, 41, 43, 50, 91, 129,
    158, 186, 206, 226, 248,
    274
oxygen 23

painting 168–71
parents 19–20
patience 43
patterns 78, 186
Pepys, Samuel 117
personal intelligence *see*
    intelligences
perseverence 77
philosophical intelligence *see*
    intelligences
phonemes (basic sounds) 68
physical intelligence *see*
    intelligences
photographs 164, 254
Picasso, Pablo 159, 163, 164, 168,
    174
planning 210, 231–6
Pliny the Elder 131
poetry 70, 85, 193
practice 207, 215–18
praise 71–2, 225
predictions 150
privacy 230
probability 118
problem posing 108
problem solving 45–6, 90–3
    problem-solving steps 259
puzzles 77

questions
    experiment 24–5
    investigating me 113–14
    linguistic questions 66, 74–7

mathematical questions 107,
    108, 118–19, 121–2, 124
memory questions 239–40
musical questions 198
personal questions 224–5,
    233–4, 270
philosophical questions 40,
    268–91
planning questions 210
religious questions 288–9
review questions 240–1
scientific questions 40, 129,
    136–43
social questions 263–6, 270
story questions 74–7, 262,
    292–4
visual questions 94, 174–5

Rabi, Isidor 136
Ransome, Arthur 115
reading 47, 49, 67–77, 195,
    292–4
reasoning 40, 60, 61–2, 92, 234,
    282, 283
    moral reasoning 284–5
review 82, 117, 238–43
rewards 48, 118
riddles 64–5
rhythm 194, 205
Rochefoucauld, Francois de la 221
role models 264
role play 260
Rossetti, Christina 69
Russell, Bertrand 89, 224

safety 10, 139, 144, 150–1
Saroyan, William 67
science *see* scientific intelligence
school 9–10, 40, 140, 183, 241,
    285
security 258
seeing 28, 30, 74, 125–6, 131–5,
    146, 153–5
Sendak, Maurice 279
    Where the Wild Things Are 279
self 35–7, 228
    self-awareness 240–2
    self-concept 226–7

self – *cont.*
  self-confidence 23, 90, 193,
    202, 205, 219, 227, 235,
    273
  self-control 23, 37, 41–2, 43,
    50, 91, 129, 158, 186, 206,
    226, 248, 274
  self-esteem 228
  self-image 227
senses 29–30, 77
Seuss, Dr 115
Shakespeare, William 65, 81, 93
shape 94, 95, 114–17
Shaw, G.B.S. 83, 196
Shelley, Percy Bysshe 191
social ideals 261–6
social intelligence *see* intelligences
social skills 38, 246–50, 255–7
societies 29, 149–50
spatial awareness 94
speaking 48–57, 120–4
  inner speech 47
spelling 80–3, 223
songs 32, 193
sport 34
Stokowski, Leopold 200
stories 51, 64–74, 198, 238–9.
  252, 261, 277–83
Straight, Dorothy 84
Suzuki method 196
swimming 213–14

Tangram 95, 115
talking *see* speaking
talking to yourself 37, 55
tape-recorder 59, 189
teaching 260
television 59–62, 140, 153, 193,
    236, 252, 264, 284
'terrible twos' 224
tests *see* exams
thinking skills 187
thinking time 54
Thomas, Dylan 85
touch 29, 142
Twain, Mark 257
typing 216

Valentine C.W., 53
values 265–6, 266
visual intelligence *see* intelligences
visual environment 162–4
vocabulary 49, 62
Volta, Allessandro 142

Waugh, Evelyn 77
weather 135
Wild Boy of Aveyron 52
Wilde, Oscar 67, 196
Winnie-the-Pooh 279
word games *see* games
writing 47, 49, 77–85, 194–5
  speedwriting 79